Also by Dennis Whitehead

The Day Before the War:
The Events of August 31, 1939
That Ignited World War II

Love and Sacrifice:
A World War Brings Double Tragedy to an American Family

Shell Shock: Twin Sisters Born Into the Gilded Age
Struck Down By the Horrors of War

The Cincinnati Strangler

*Murder, Mayhem, and Racial Injustice
in the Queen City*

by Dennis Whitehead

MMImedia LLC
© 2025

The Cincinnati Strangler
Murder, Mayhem, and Racial Injustice in the Queen City

Copyright © 2025 by Dennis Whitehead

All rights reserved. No part of this book may be reproduced or transmitted in any form or by any means, electronic or mechanical, including photocopying, recording, or by any information storage and retrieval system, without written permission from the publisher. Contact copyright@mmimedia.com

Library of Congress copyright Dennis Whitehead Registration Number: TXu 2-412-178,

ISBN: 979-8-9992298-0-9 Print
ISBN: 979-8-9992298-1-6 Ebook

Dedicated to the history of Cincinnati, a city central to our nation's story and a place with a rich legacy. Fortunately, Cincinnati has a great tradition of civic commitment to local history and keeping Cincinnati's story alive.

Table of Contents

Part I: Fear

- Chapter 1: Beginning of the End — 1
- Chapter 2: Murder in an Oasis — 7
- Chapter 3: Multiple Crimes – One Man? — 17
- Chapter 4: Murder Comes to the West Side — 25
- Chapter 5: A Deadly Walk in the Park — 41
- Chapter 6: Murder by Gaslight — 47
- Chapter 7: Death Looms Over Vine Street Hill — 63

Part II: Investigation

- Chapter 8: Help in the Stars — 75
- Chapter 9: Dragnet — 79
- Chapter 10: Pursuit — 93
- Chapter 11: "There's a dead lady in your elevator" — 95
- Chapter 12: Apprehension — 105
- Chapter 13: Probable Cause — 117

Part III: Death and Justice

- Chapter 14: Taxi Into Darkness — 123
- Chapter 15: A Killer's Trail — 139
- Chapter 16: Charges Mount — 155
- Chapter 17: Setting the Stage for Trial — 185
- Chapter 18: Is a Fair Trial Possible? — 215
- Chapter 19: Voir Dire — 223
- Chapter 20: Presumption of Innocence — 234
- Chapter 21: Witnesses for the Defense — 277
- Chapter 22: Closing Arguments — 291
- Chapter 23: Life or Death — 301

Part IV: Aftermath

- Chapter 24: Welcome to the Big House — 311
- Chapter 25: The Long Hot Summer of 1967 — 319
- Chapter 26: Life and Death in Prison — 335

Postscript / Acknowledgments — 353

Preface

The new year, 2026, marks a grim milestone in the history of Cincinnati, Ohio -- sixty years since the Cincinnati Strangler gripped the city in fear and suspicion.

Between December 1965 and December 1966, six older women across Cincinnati were strangled to death, with most sexually assaulted post-mortem.

The December 1966 arrest of Posteal Laskey, Jr. and his conviction the following year brought an immediate sense of relief and then closure. The city was confident Laskey was the Strangler as the murders stopped with his arrest.

But, was Posteal Laskey the Cincinnati Strangler? Six women were strangled to death over the year but Laskey was not tried for any of those murders.

You are about to embark upon a journey back to the 1960s when the country was coming apart at the seams. Civil rights workers in the struggle for voting rights were being killed across the South. President Johnson relied upon the military draft to fuel America's involvement in Vietnam. Hundreds of thousands of young men being drafted gave rise to an anti-war movement spreading across the country.

At the same time, American cities were burning as younger, more militant civil rights leaders were coming to the fore rejecting the tactics of peaceful civil disobedience advanced by the old guard.

Frustrations from unceasing racial discrimination were coming to a boil in the mid-1960s. The spirit of Jim Crow endured in the barriers African-Americans faced in finding decent housing, good-paying jobs, getting a meaningful education, and finding justice in the American legal system. Excessive force by police officers against Black citizens was decried, but the shooting death of a fifteen-year-old by police ignited the 1964 Harlem Riot and a simple traffic stop in August 1965 was at the root of the Watts Riots in Los Angeles. Despite passage of civil rights legislation, many felt that the pace of change was too slow and the progress was not reflected in their daily lives, giving way to a rise in militancy.

All of these ingredients played parts in the time you are about to enter.

It was a time when I was the only child of a widowed mother whose fear made an impression on me. She'd grown up in the Price Hill neighborhood where Lois Dant was murdered and went to school across Glenway from the Dant apartment, and I was born just down Grand Avenue from the intersection where Barbara Bowman died.

This book is the product of deep research into police investigation files on the murders, some 1,500 pages of trial transcripts, and multiple court fights over 5,000+ pages of Laskey's prison records that mysteriously appeared in the mail after I'd lost the second case, wrapped in such a way that I took the package outside to open it at a distance.

I've benefited from conversations and correspondence with knowledgeable people who've all been tremendous help. Sadly, few principals from these events in the 1960s remain with us today. Most of those around today either do not wish to return to those days or discuss the particulars.

Forward by Greg Hand

The 1960s were stressful for Cincinnati, Ohio. Once a vibrant industrial powerhouse with a mushrooming population, known as the "Paris of America" and the "Queen City of the West" when the United States pretty much stopped at the Mississippi River, the city had grown somewhat stale and even dowdy. Between 1960 and 1970, Cincinnati lost 10 percent of its population as residents abandoned the inner city for suburban tract homes usurping former farms out in the hinterlands. Those who departed were mostly white. Those who remained were mostly Black. The word "urban" was gradually becoming synonymous with African American.

The evolving demographics of Cincinnati exposed a racial rift that had long been suppressed among the people described in Alvin F. Harlow's 1950 book as "The Serene Cincinnatians." That serenity and its accompanying deference to traditional modes of behavior resulted in a racial divide as deep as could be found in any American city at the time. In 1950, just over 15 percent of the city's population was Black. By 1970, that proportion had nearly doubled. In 1950, those non-white residents were strictly confined to segregated neighborhoods. Red-lining was accepted practice in every real estate office. Most Cincinnati deeds still contain codicils prohibiting the sale of property to anyone not of the Caucasian race. Throughout the 1960s, as Black residents moved into formerly all-white neighborhoods, white flight to the suburbs accelerated. Many suburban communities were known as "Sundown Towns" where any Black person found after sunset would be escorted past the city limits.

Cincinnati's population decline coincided with a growing awareness among the city's Black residents that the old ways had to change. The call for civil rights disturbed the white neighborhoods. When the city's largest amusement park, Coney Island, was integrated by court order in 1955, many whites stayed away. The city's schools remained segregated until another contentious court case in the 1970s.

It is in this environment that Cincinnati's first violent serial killer emerged, his crimes portrayed as all the more horrific because of his race, and it is this highly charged environment that Dennis Whitehead brings to vivid exposition in this book. With persistent attention to detail, the author dives beneath the headlines to craft fully fleshed portraits of the killer, his victims, and the police struggling to solve the growing number of murders.

With deft insight based on countless hours researching archival materials, Whitehead takes us into a city in transition, in crisis and in fear. This is a complex story, laid out in endlessly fascinating episodes, a certain delight for fans of the true crime genre. Turn the page. You are in for a treat.

"And the Lord said to him, 'Therefore, whoever kills Cain, vengeance shall be taken on him sevenfold.' And the Lord set a mark on Cain, lest anyone finding him should kill him."

- Genesis, 4:15, New King James Bible

Part I: Fear

Chapter 1
Beginning of the End

Friday, December 9, 1966, 6:20 a.m.

Dark blue police cars filled West Ninth Street in downtown Cincinnati, Ohio, their flashing lights casting bursts of red on the rain-soaked pavement and buildings lining the narrow street. Gray and overcast painted a flat, dull picture. A steady rain alternated between drizzle and downpour, faint sunlight trying to penetrate the thick cloud cover. A still-life in black-and-white, the flashing red lights punctuating the monochrome.

Four young patrolmen stood at the entrance of The Brittany apartments; their faces shadowed beneath the stiff black patent-leather brims of their distinct white vinyl hats. Reporters gathered to one side of the entrance, detectives huddled across the way. Reporters used excuses to cross the entryway to eavesdrop on police chatter. The detectives wore London Fog raincoats, ranging in shades from beige to black. Their faces, damp from rain and perspiration, showed the strains of long hours on the job.

Despite it being December, the day was unseasonably warm and humid. Occasional downpours caused patrolmen to pull the drape of their coats over their hats. Across Ninth Street, a crowd of onlookers packed the sidewalk. Detectives circulated among them, asking if anyone had seen anything unusual.

Traffic in downtown Cincinnati was a mess. West Ninth Street was closed at Race Street, forcing frustrated drivers to find a different route. Horns blared, echoing in the compact urban canyons, the sound held low by the low-hanging clouds. Rush hour drivers were aware of the cause, The Strangler had struck again. Many of those in cars were tuned to WSAI and Jim Scott's morning show bringing the news to morning commuters. The station's Newsmobile, a Ford station wagon emblazoned with "WSAI" along its sides, was parked behind two patrol cars at the entrance to The Brittany.

At 8:20 a.m. that morning, the Cincinnati Police Department's central call center, Station X, received two calls in quick succession, both reporting a dead woman on the floor of an elevator in a downtown apartment building.

Inside City Hall, George Lecky, a police reporter for The Cincinnati *Post* and *Times-Star*, sat in the pressroom with Bob Weston, the local correspondent for United Press International. A detective ducked in, barely breaking stride, saying, "There's been another murder."

Lecky and Weston bolted for the exits. Another strangulation, the sixth in one year, would further push the city to the precipice of panic. Lecky was in such a rush that he forgot his hat. Weston grabbed his umbrella but left without his coat.

At The Brittany, Sergeant Eugene Moore, assistant commander of the homicide squad, conferred with detectives. All knew The Strangler had struck again and that they were no closer to catching the perp. Nearly a year had passed since the strangulation murder of Emogene Harrington on December 2, 1965. Since then, this series

The Cincinnati Strangler

of brutal slaying gripped Cincinnati in fear. Older White women were targeted, each victim strangled with a ligature. Many were sexually assaulted after the deed was done.

Little evidence was left behind at the crime scenes, but the presence of human hair led police to conclude a Black man was responsible for the crimes. The media, fueled by police leaks, fanned the flames of fear with near-daily headlines. Racial tensions in the city escalated. Citizen reports of simple encounters with Black men flooded Station X. Black men—innocent job seekers, laborers, and those simply going through the day—were caught up in the dragnet, questioned. In many cases, hair and blood samples were taken for analysis. Factors combined to deepen the divide between White Cincinnati and the city's Black community.

Fourteen Homicide detectives were supplemented by twelve uniformed officers on staff. Their numbers doubled as investigations into the growing number of crimes dragged on without an arrest. The entire police department was placed on twelve-hour shifts, and one hundred new officers were rushed through training; some employed even during their academy time. Five thousand men were deputized into an auxiliary force to assist in the search for the killer. The October 14, 1966 headline across the front of The Cincinnati *Enquirer* pronounced, "5000-Man Posse Beefs Up Hunt for Sex Maniac."

Despite the massive efforts, the target eluded capture as the killer, or killers, left no clues. Forensic technology of the time was limited to hair, fibers, fingerprints, and blood type. There was no testing for DNA.

In the course of the investigations, witnesses offered merely vague descriptions: a Black man from his early twenties to forties, weighing between 140 and 190 pounds, and 5'4 to 6'2 in height. As the pressure on the police mounted, sex offenders, cab drivers, and Black former police officers were brought in for questioning. Calls to Station X with sightings and suspicions led to a visit from detectives. The city's Black community leaders, clergy, and civil rights advocates condemned the indiscriminate roundup of Black men.

The atmosphere in the city was charged, and the fear of a lurking killer only compounded the existing racial divides of Jim Crow. Nationally, high-profile murders like the Boston Strangler killings and the gruesome murders of eight student nurses in Chicago fanned the flames of fear. Locally, the September stabbing deaths of the three Bricca family members in suburban Bridgetown added an additional layer of dread.

Now, another woman—an elderly resident of The Brittany—was dead, lying on the floor of the building's tiny elevator. As before, there were no immediate clues, no clear evidence pointing to the killer. Detectives carefully inspected walls and floors for the slightest clue but none were found, other than a small spot of blood. This sixth strangulation murder meant the search for the elusive killer would intensify.

Something was different this morning. Word spread through the press gaggle outside The Brittany that detectives were closing in on a suspect. They eagerly tried prying any details from officers at the scene, leaving them with mere hints that police had their eyes on a suspect.

The Cincinnati Strangler

Lieutenant John McLaughlin cautioned the journalists, "The individual is not a prime suspect at this time," but the growing confidence among the officers suggested otherwise.

Margaret Josten, a reporter for The *Enquirer*, captured the mood in the next day's paper. "The victim was killed by a strangler, maybe THE strangler," she wrote.

The body of Emogene Harrington lay in the basement bathroom of The Clermont apartments. (Cincinnati Police Department)

Chapter 2
Murder in an Oasis

Thursday, December 2, 1965

Fifteen-year-old Julie walked at a quick pace from Saint Ursula Academy, crossing East McMillan Street at the New Thought Unity Center in East Walnut Hills to her home in The Clermont apartments. She was picking up homework papers she'd earlier forgotten. Julie's wool knee socks were pulled as high as they could go, the breeze lifting her navy-blue woolen uniform skirt, worn shorter than academy regulations. Her monogrammed blue blazer offered little warmth but it was only a short distance.

Passing under a concrete colonnade separating the sidewalk from a small courtyard, Julie approached the five white marble steps at the building's entrance and was startled when a Black man ran from beside the building, seeming to emerge from the janitor's office. There was nothing unusual about a Black man in the integrated neighborhood, so Julie didn't think much of it, other than his hurry.

Climbing the interior marble staircase to the second-floor apartment she shared with her parents, Julie politely greeted the building's sixty-five-year-old custodian, William Eugene Waugh. "Hello, Mr. Waugh," Julie said as he slowly walked down the stairs toward her. Waugh routinely assisted tenants, toting groceries and deliveries up the staircases as The Clermont had no elevators.

Nestled in the eastern hills of Cincinnati, The Clermont was home to an amalgam of artists, intellectuals, inherited wealth, and inherent skills. A mature Bohemian enclave where Julie was the only resident under the age of twenty. The only residents under the age of fifty in the apartment complex were a graduate Pharmacy student at the University of Cincinnati, and his new wife.

The residents of The Clermont were neither Beatniks nor Hippies; rather, women and men who rose above the societal norms of their day with creativity and innovation, some with the assistance of inherited wealth. It was a magical world for a teenager who, at times, dismissed the eclectic assortment of tenants as oddballs.

Two sides of The Clermont jutted toward McMillan in a U-shape, appearing as a jigsaw puzzle piece when viewed from above. Inside, thirty-six apartments, numbers one through thirty-seven, no apartment thirteen, comprised the two halves of the single structure.

Beginning in the nineteenth century, the eastern hills were a fresh-air escape from the foul air and crowded conditions in the city's basin. The area was, and remains, home to Cincinnati's bankers, merchants, industrialists, lawyers, and doctors who built elegant cottages, tasteful villas, and grand mansions, surrounded by gardens, lawns and trees-shaded roads in hilltop communities rising from Mount Auburn to Hyde Park and East Walnut Hills. Successful Jewish entrepreneurs established Avondale as the "New Jerusalem," also known as the "Golden Ghetto."

The eastern hills were also home to established Black neighborhoods developed in the nineteenth century by the Lane Seminary and local philanthropists. Kennedy Heights and Walnut Hills were home to many of Cincinnati's wealthiest Black residents. O'Bryonville was a place where many Black servants and service workers of the adjacent homes of the wealthy lived. Lincoln Heights was an independent Black village established in the 1920s for African-American workers at industries lining the Mill Creek Valley. People of color were prohibited from living in most Cincinnati neighborhoods. Acceptable areas were designated by red lines drawn on official maps.

The nineteenth-century mansions and apartment buildings, like The Clermont, remained but demographics in the area were changing. The political machinations of urban renewal cleared the tenements, and residents, of the West End, forcing many toward Avondale and Walnut Hills. The West End is situated in the urban basin lying between the eastern and western hills, and it was being cleared to make way for interstate highways and low-rise industrial development. Black residents were herded in areas designated by the red lines, with Avondale taking the brunt of the relocation.

On the floor above Julie's apartment was number nineteen, the home of Russell Paul and Emogene Dyson Harrington. Russell, known by his middle name Paul, was chairman of the Department of Aerospace Engineering at the University of Cincinnati. Paul and Emogene had been married thirty-five years; their three daughters grown and no longer living at home. The couple contentedly settled into their two-bedroom apartment, Paul spending long hours at the university, while Emogene was active at the Knox Presbyterian Church in nearby

Hyde Park. Paul could easily have made his fortune in the aeronautics industry at the booming time of jet travel and the Space Race, but he dedicated his career to education.

They lived quiet lives in The Clermont enjoying the camaraderie and conversations with their fellow residents, occasionally hosting gatherings for Paul's engineering students. Being shy and introverted by nature, Paul was happy to defer to outgoing Emogene to organize gatherings while he comfortably and quietly mingled with his students.

Following breakfast, Emogene drove Paul to his UC office in Clifton and returned to their apartment to clean the morning dishes before going grocery shopping. At 11:30 a.m., she walked down the marble stairs to the basket-weave marble floor in the lobby of The Clermont. From there, Emogene walked out the front door to her 1955 Ford Country Sedan station wagon parked in front of the building. Thursdays were grocery days taking her to the Kroger store on nearby Hyde Park Square.

On warmer days, Emogene enjoyed strolling along Erie Avenue, window shopping at the stores lining the square, or meeting with friends for coffee and pastries, but on this damp December day, she was determined to do her shopping and get home.

Emogene perused the aisles, picking the items she needed for the days ahead. The young man bagging groceries filled three paper bags with her staples for the coming week. Emogene first handed the cashier a check for $30.00 but the total was $33.48, so she wrote another check for $25.00, putting $21.52 cash in her wallet.

Returning home, Emogene parked her car about two-hundred feet east of the entrance to her building in a space marked with a hand-lettered reserved sign. Leaving her groceries on the front seat, Emogene entered the side door to the basement in search of the custodian for help carrying the groceries to her third-floor apartment.

But, Waugh was not in his office. Emogene assumed he was helping someone else and would momentarily return, so she waited downstairs.

Suddenly, a man appeared and asked her where he could find the janitor. As Emogene began to answer, the man struck her on the head, knocking her to the floor. He continued hitting her face and head until Harrington's face was swollen beyond recognition. Emogene was unconscious as the man dragged her lifeless body into the grimy basement bathroom, throwing her head into a wall, knocking paint chips to the ground. He wrapped a length of yellow plastic clothesline, knotted at both ends in Poacher's Knots, also known as a "Strangle Snare," around her neck. Gripping the knotted ends, he squeezed the final breath from Emogene's already still body. The cardboard wrapping of the Royal Maid clothesline lying on the floor guaranteed, "ties easily, holds firmly."

Ripping open her grey wool suit top and blouse, he lifted her skirt and tore away her underwear. Spreading her legs wide, the man brutally desecrated the lifeless body of fifty-six-year-old Emogene Harrington.

The killer remained composed enough to open Harrington's purse, remove her billfold and quickly exit by the side door he'd entered, disappearing into the afternoon; unseen, except for the schoolgirl who caught only a fleeting glimpse. There is no sign police ever spoke with Julie.

Waugh returned to the basement around 1:20 p.m. and noticed the open bathroom door. As he approached, the custodian saw a shoeless leg extended across the doorway with a nylon stocking attached by clips. Peering around the corner, Waugh saw the woman's hat lying mashed and upside down in front of the body. Her other leg still bore its shoe. He saw a set of car keys between the woman's legs tangled in white underwear. The woman's brutalized face made it impossible for Waugh to immediately identify her. Blood ran from her nose, touching her grotesquely swollen lips. The victim's tan raincoat clung to her right arm and shoulder, having been pulled from the left. A purse lay open to one side, a small ring-bound booklet was open on the floor to her right. The yellow rope around her neck told him the woman on the bathroom floor was not alive. Waugh immediately called police.

Squad cars crowded East McMillan Street and Woodburn Avenue surrounding The Clermont. Waugh pointed detectives to the Harringtons's Ford wagon parked in the reserved spot, the grocery bags remained untouched on the front bench seat. Officers swarmed the building and grounds looking for clues. In the basement, detectives searched for evidence and dusted for prints.

The grim task of bringing news of Emogene's death to her husband fell to Detective William Rutledge. The dean of the college, Dr. Cornelius Wandmacher, quietly called Harrington from an afternoon seminar to break the news. Detective Rutledge accompanied Professor Harrington home, joined by the Harrington's family physician, Dr. Richard Bath.

As police combed The Clermont, Mrs. Proxie Justice, a seventy-year-old resident of the Over the Rhine neighborhood in the downtown basin, found a billfold on the ground at Elm and Findlay Streets near the Findlay Market, about three miles from The Clermont. The billfold held no money, but a driver's license and other cards were still inside. As she was doing her Thursday grocery shopping, Mrs. Justice asked Charles Weinley, owner of Weinley's Market, if he would call the owner of the billfold to tell her it had been found.

Weinley looked up the name on the driver's license in the telephone book, calling the Harrington number several times without answer. Finally, according to the next day's *Enquirer*, Dr. Bath picked up the Harrington's phone around three o'clock, responding curtly, "Call the police!" Detective William Rathman was dispatched to retrieve the billfold while officers canvassed the area around the wallet's discovery in the hope of finding the person who dropped it, without success.

Detective Chief Henry Sandman dispatched Homicide detectives to thoroughly search The Clermont and join the canvass covering a four-block area around apartment building. Officers and detectives trained their eyes to the ground as they searched for evidence discarded along sidewalks or in gutters. Clermont residents and nearby neighbors were questioned about any unusual sightings or sounds, without success.

Homicide Sergeant Russell Jackson noted distinct similarities between Emogene Harrington's strangulation murder and recent sexual assaults in the East Walnut Hills area.

A truck driver told police he was passing The Clermont the day of the killing when he saw a Black man leaving the building—about thirty-five, five-foot-four, weighing about 155 pounds, with a heavy mustache, wearing dark clothes and a cloth zippered jacket. Police combined this description with those from victims of recent assaults in the area to develop a notion of the killer's appearance, centering on his being a "male Negro." Police inquiries centered on known sex offenders who were rounded up for questioning.

"We've never received any complaints about a prowler here," Ira D. Falkenstein, The Clermont owner, told police. "The tenants have been in and out of this basement for years and they've never worried." Afterwards, Falkenstein installed large mirrors in the lobbies and hallways enabling tenants to make certain no one was following them.

Detectives asked Clermont residents if anyone had trouble with Mrs. Harrington, possibly a student, one who may have been upset with Professor Harrington? No one knew of any such ill feelings toward the popular professor.

Suspicions about William Eugene Waugh, who was Black, were quickly dispelled by residents. Police did find that Waugh's wife's cousin, a Black male, about five-feet to five-foot-three, weighing about 170 pounds, was a

The Cincinnati Strangler

patient at Longview State Hospital, a local mental health facility. Typical of Longview patients, he was accorded off-campus privileges, but he was at the hospital the day Emogene Harrington was murdered.

The yellow clothesline, fibers, and hair found at the scene could yield only slight clues about the killer, but the general state of the basement made discernment difficult. Police suspected the killer used a blunt object to beat Emogene unconscious, but no such object was found in the basement or surrounding area.

Harrington's clothing, the clothesline, along with fibers and hairs from the scene, described as "Negroid," were sent to the FBI in Washington, DC for analysis. Blood found at the scene was Type B, matching Harrington's. That was the extent of analysis and specificity available to investigators at that time.

Hamilton County Coroner Frank Cleveland said the cause of death was strangulation by ligature, adding, "It is our further opinion the deceased had been raped."

In the days following the murder, an *Enquirer* headline told the tale: "Police Still No Closer to Trail of Strangler."

"The fourth day of round-the-clock checking failed to bring Cincinnati police any closer to the rapist-killer of Mrs. Emogene D. Harrington."

One week after Emogene Harrington's murder, a memorial service was held in her honor at the Knox Presbyterian Church. Cincinnati Police Chief Stanley Schrotel, a member of the Knox congregation, attended the service, quietly sitting in the back row.

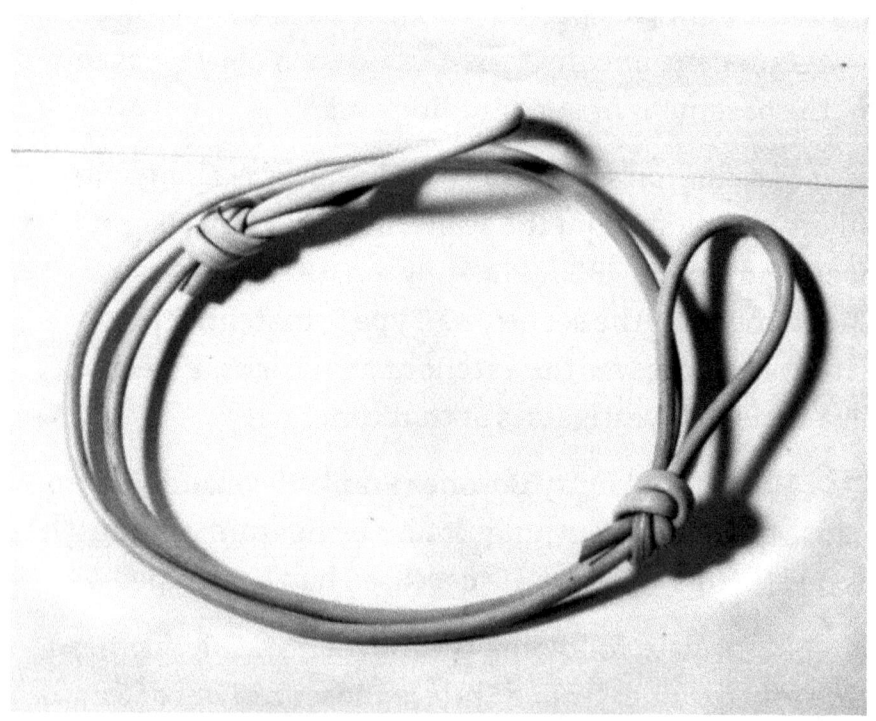

The clothesline used to strangle Emogene Harrington tied at its ends with "strangler's knots." (Cincinnati Police Department)

Chapter 3
Multiple Crimes – One Man?

"The oldest and strongest emotion of mankind is fear, and the oldest and strongest kind of fear is fear of the unknown," H. P. Lovecraft.

Sergeant Russ Jackson's sense of a connection between the murder of Emogene Harrington and recent violent assaults of women in the Avondale, Walnut Hills, and East Walnut Hills neighborhoods gained currency among investigators.

Could this series of assaults and rapes in the vicinity of The Clermont be the work of one man?

Shortly before noon on Tuesday, October 12, 1965, Elizabeth Kreco, a sixty-five-year-old widow, was approached by a man in the basement of The Verona apartments on Park Avenue, about four blocks from The Clermont, asking for the caretaker. Without warning, he suddenly struck Lizzie Kreco several times about her face and head, slamming her head into a wall, knocking her unconscious. He then dragged Kreco into the basement bathroom where he attempted to strangle her with a knotted piece of clothesline. Thinking she was dead, the assailant then raped Kreco. Hours passed before she was found by fellow residents, dazed but alive. She was taken to General Hospital where Lizzie was treated for shock, head injuries, and rope burns around her neck. Her clothes and purse were found near The Verona. The attacker made off with thirteen dollars. Kreco described the man as a Black male, between thirty-five and forty, standing about 5'4 with a medium build, wearing dark clothes, and sunglasses.

Elizabeth Kreco never fully recovered from the trauma of that attack, passing away in 1978 at the age of seventy-seven.

The police canvass of the neighborhood around The Verona revealed that on the Tuesday before Emogene Harrington's murder, November 30, a man entered the building elevator with a laundry deliveryman asking him if he knew where to find the caretaker. When he directed the man to the basement, the visitor curtly responded, "forget it," and left the building. The driver described the man as Black, in his forties, about 6'2, and 170 pounds; medium complexion, thick mustache, wearing a small-brimmed dark hat, grey gabardine topcoat or raincoat, dark trousers, light yellow sweater with holes at the waist, and dark shoes.

On October 15, a twenty-eight-year-old woman was awakened from her sleep and raped in her Avondale bedroom, the attacker choking her with his hands while demanding money. She described her assailant as a Black man, twenty to thirty years-old, five-foot-ten to six feet tall, 160 to 180 pounds.

On October 21, a 16-year-old Walnut Hills High School student was attacked on Windsor Street on a drizzly early autumn evening outside a friend's house. She described the assailant as a Black man, about forty-years-old, who struck her with a gun, knocking her to the ground, but he fled when she screamed.

That same evening, Digna Canales, wife of Dr. Louis Canales, a pediatric resident at Children's Hospital, was attacked while doing laundry in her Avondale basement by a Black male. She struggled with the man, described as about thirty-two, five-ten, and 155 pounds with a pockmarked face. The man fled when Canales screamed.

Four days later, on October 25, 1965, at seven o'clock on a beautiful autumn evening, petite, thirty-nine-year-old Margie Helton was leaving her job at the Baldwin Piano and Organ Company on Gilbert Avenue in Walnut Hills when a young man approached her, politely asking for directions to Dorchester Street. In a flash, he slammed Helton against her car's rear door. Opening the front door, the man threw Margie on the front seat. He then climbed into the back and, reaching over the seatback, slipped a rope around her neck, saying: "This is a robbery. Give me your money and you won't get hurt."

Margie's blue eyes bulged wide as she held up a ten-dollar bill, remaining composed enough to lay into the car's horn when the assailant relaxed his grip to take the money. Reacting quickly, he slammed Margie's head into the steering wheel and bolted away.

Helton described her attacker as a Black man, about twenty, weighing 150 pounds, with a small goatee on his chin.

A Cincinnati *Enquirer* story by Margaret Josten expressed the fears of a seeming crime wave, "Sex Crimes in Area Prove Nightmarish Problem To Citizens;" opening, "Cincinnati bears little resemblance to the asphalt jungles of fact and fiction, but it experiences enough sex-inspired crime to give some citizens nightmares."

The murder of Emogene Harrington faded from

headlines as 1965 came to a close. A year-end review devoted a single paragraph to her strangulation, but citizens remained on high alert.

On January 5, 1966, two women, one fifty-three, the other eighteen, reported separate attacks by a knife-wielding man in Riverview Park on the Mt. Adams hillside overlooking the Ohio River. The older woman was grabbed around the neck from behind with a knife pointed at her right side, threatening her life while demanding money. She successfully appealed to the man's better angels, begging him not to commit any further violence. This shamed the man into an apology as he escorted her to a park shelter, while warning her, "I'll kill you if you tell anybody," before walking away.

The younger woman was returning home from work as a nursery assistant when she was accosted by a Black man with a mustache and goatee, wearing a hat, matching the description from the previous assault. He also held a knife on her at the same park entrance. "Don't hurt me, I'm pregnant!" she screamed at the top of the steps. Managing to break the man's grasp, the woman ran away as the assailant fled down the staircase to Martin Street where he disappeared.

Soon after the second incident, a man was found sleeping in the rear lobby of a Mount Adams apartment building above Riverview Park. Speaking incoherently, he was taken into police custody. He was identified as a twenty-seven-year-old environmental analysis laboratory aide who, police learned, had been under psychiatric observation at the Veterans Administration Hospital. His hospitalization stemming from the December rape of a twenty-year-old Mount Adams woman who identified her assailant as a Black male with a mustache and goatee. Police held him in connection to both assaults.

Days later, Patrolman Raymond J. Herzog stopped James Purcell, a Black man with a mustache and goatee, matching the description from the two assaults, possibly three. Herzog's interest in Purcell was further piqued by the six-inch hunting knife he was carrying. A Cossack-style hat was found at the restaurant where he worked. With that, Purcell confessed to the two assaults and, later, the earlier rape of the Mt. Adams woman.

This was a case of mistaken identity between two men who simply shared the same skin color and facial hair. The man found sleeping in the Mount Adams apartment building was immediately cleared of the charges and released.

On January 16, 1966, an Avondale woman was setting out trash from the basement of her apartment building when she felt a cord tighten around her neck. Digna Canales, who'd been attacked in October 1965 while doing laundry in her Avondale basement, felt lightning strike twice. The man pulled her back, but she managed to reach over her shoulders to grab her attacker's gloved hands, loosening the ligature enough to let out a scream. Hearing his wife's cries, Dr. Louis Canales ran downstairs from their first-floor apartment, arriving just as the assailant fled. No one was found in the vicinity, but police recovered a frayed black shoelace, broken in the middle and retied. An overhand knot was used to tie one end of the twenty-three-inch strand. Digna Canales suffered a welt around her neck but otherwise was alright after escaping an attacker for the second time.

Two days later, at 10:00 a.m., forty-five-year-old Helen Smith, an apartment building caretaker, was working in the basement of a three-story Walnut Hills apartment building at the corner of Victory Parkway and William Howard Taft Road. She was startled by the sudden appearance of a Black man behind her, lunging at her as she fled, yelling, "Hey, wait a minute…" She ran to the apartment house next door and called police.

Twenty police cars responded to the scene in the vicinity of Elizabeth Kreco and Emogene Harrington's apartment buildings. The front door of the building had been forced open, the lock torn off, broken pieces of wood and plaster on the floor. Mrs. Smith told police she had seen the man before, describing him being in his thirties, about five-foot-ten, and weighing about 190 pounds. He had a mustache and possibly a goatee, wearing black gloves, a three-quarter tan car coat, and black hat.

By noon, police rounded up ten men in a sweep of the area, based upon the scant description of the perpetrator, but Mrs. Smith could not identify any as the assailant.

"Police have been seeking a stockily built Negro with a mustache in connection with recent strangler attacks," The Cincinnati *Post* reported.

The *Enquirer* called him, "the phantom attacker."

On January 24th, thirty-seven-year-old Bonnie Catoe called police when a Black man wearing a ski mask entered her apartment building at 2234 Park Avenue, near Elizabeth Kreco's Verona apartment, and started up the stairs after her. Catoe began banging on the door of an adjoining apartment, causing the man to turn, and run in the direction of Victory Parkway. Police were unable to find anyone matching the description of a Black man wearing a dark coat and "black head mask hat," though they did question ice skaters in nearby Eden Park wearing ski masks.

This attempted assault brought on the first use of what would become the standard description of the amorphous man, "Strangler Hunt Set in Motion," read The Cincinnati *Enquirer* headline. "The beefed-up strangler-hunting police detail in the Walnut Hills area was set in motion again on Monday…"

On February 16, a sixteen-year-old girl was assaulted while entering the north driveway entrance to Walnut Hills High School on Victory Parkway. She described the man as Black and wearing a beige raincoat. He grabbed her from behind, placing his hand over her mouth, saying in a deep voice, "Don't scream or I'll hit you."

The assailant fled upon hearing an automobile coming up the driveway.

On March 19, a nineteen-year-old nurse's aide at Christ Hospital accused twenty-eight-year-old, Joe Barksdale, a Black Yellow Cab driver, of raping her at knifepoint. Taking a cab from work that evening, she asked her driver to take her to Boudinot Avenue in the western suburb of Cheviot, but the driver suddenly stopped the cab, climbed into the backseat, and raped her at knifepoint.

Her story later changed, saying the driver forced her

into his cab at the corner of Clifton and Wolper in Clifton, near Burnet Woods, driving her toward her Boudinot Avenue home, but stopping where he forced her onto the sidewalk, and raped her. She said he released her near McFarlan Woods. Barksdale had been driving for Yellow Cab for only a week at the time of the incident.

He was charged with rape and bond was set at $10,000. The case was presented to the grand jury but, given the conflicting accounts by the victim, the grand jury decided not to indict and the charge against Barksdale was set aside in April. Six years later, Barksdale was accused of the abduction and rape of a nineteen-year-old University of Cincinnati student. He was sentenced to thirty years in prison.

Rose Winstel's door and locks with fingerprint dust spread across. (Cincinnati Police)

Chapter 4
Murder Comes to the West Side

Monday, April 4, 1966

In the western hills of Cincinnati, the assaults and strangulations on the east side of town were distant concerns. Yes, violent crime was at the fore of many minds, east and west, but these crimes might as well have been hundreds of miles away.

Attention was more attuned to the growing U.S. involvement in Vietnam and Civil Rights at home. The prevailing west side feeling about Vietnam was "Support the Troops," while sentiment about protesting against the war was hostile. Gene Kolodzik, a postal worker who grew up in the Cumminsville neighborhood, authored the popular bumper sticker, "America Love It or Leave it," printing a million placards at his own expense.

Teachers and clergy might speak about civil rights and loving thy neighbor, the overwhelming sentiment was not in my neighborhood. A catchphrase captured the underlying sentiment, "love the individual, hate the race."

For "colored" residents, the Cincinnati of 1966 did not differ much from earlier times in the city's history. Jim Crow still prevailed. Job opportunities were few beyond simple laborer for men and domestic employment for women. The Federal government was a local rung on the opportunity ladder as postal workers were among the most prosperous members of the Black community, while others struggled to find work as labor unions closed their apprentice ranks to people of color.

Cincinnati was a divided city. Hills to the east and west, with a wide basin between, kept people apart, as did the color of one's skin.

The early spring morning was chilled when sixty-six-year-old Frank Dant walked out the rear door of his Rutledge Avenue apartment building in Price Hill. Frank and his wife, Lois, lived in apartment #1 at 1210 Rutledge Avenue, a right-angled U-shaped, twenty-one-unit apartment building, 1210 being the righthand wing.

The Dants had lived in their four-room, first-floor apartment on the west side since they were married in 1937. Frank recently retired from his job as a purchasing agent for Cincinnati Union Terminal, the city's rail center, and Lois worked part-time as a saleslady in Jean's Gift Shop.

It was six-twenty in the morning as Frank walked to his car behind the building, exiting the gravel lot and driveway to Mckeone Avenue where Frank turned right, then a quick left on the main drag, Glenway Avenue. He drove east for two blocks on Glenway to a right, just past Carson School at the corner of Sunset Avenue. A short drive along the narrow residential street led to West Eighth and St. William Church for the 6:30 a.m. Mass.

Frank and Lois attended early Mass every morning, except Mondays when Lois stayed home to do laundry while Frank remained after Mass to help count the Sunday collection.

Mass ended at 7:10 a.m. and Frank stayed with nine other men to count Sunday's collection money in the downstairs library. Palm Sunday was a time when a large number of parishioners attended morning Mass when the pastor of St. William, Reverend Monsignor Robert J. Sherry, dressed in his bright red chasuble, blessed an array of palm outside the grand Romanesque church

Lois was already braiding the palm they received the day before into the shape of a cross for display on the wall next to the front door.

Fifty-nine-year-old Lois was excited as her daughter, Sue Ann, would be coming home for the first time in six years since she'd entered the convent. Sue Ann was returning home as Sister Francis Michel, having taken her vows as a Sister of Charity.

Lois spent the first part of the morning in the basement handwashing items in laundry tubs and then hanging them on clotheslines. Philis Swegman, the Dants's next door neighbor, heard Lois walk down the creaky wooden stairs in the narrow stairway to the basement around 7:30 a.m. She saw her again downstairs around nine when Philis was leaving to catch a bus downtown. Lois was chatting with twenty-nine-year-old Ruth Penno about Easter hats, grandchildren, and Ruth's health when Philis interrupted their conversation to ask Lois to keep an ear on her apartment for stirrings of her bedridden husband, William, a Cincinnati firefighter forced into retirement by serious illness. He passed away three months later.

At 9:10 a.m., the mailman arrived with Frank's pension check, depositing it into the mailbox for apartment #1, at the same time a priest arrived to visit ailing George

Bronstrop on the third floor. The bedridden Bronstrop was a retired Cincinnati Police detective with the Burglary and Larceny Squad who stepped down in 1962 after twenty-seven years. He passed away the next month, his funeral held at St. William.

After visiting Bronstrop, the priest came downstairs and left the building with the mailman.

Ruth Penno last saw Lois in the basement around 9:30, Penno returning to her apartment in the center building she shared with her husband Ed.

Twenty-nine-year-old Regina Albers, wife of the building caretaker, Ben Albers, picked up the garbage can from the stoop behind the Dant apartment around 9:45 a.m. She didn't see anyone but did notice the Dants's rear screen door was unhooked.

Around this same time, the collection counting at St. William was wrapping up. Frank Dant and Charles Miller drove to the Central Trust Bank at Glenway and Warsaw to deposit the collection. After a few more errands, the pair returned to St. William where Miller's car was parked. Frank then headed home by the same route he drove earlier.

Sometime between 10:10 and 10:15, Ruth Penno returned to the basement to pick up empty bottles from a storage area, neither seeing nor hearing anything unusual. She returned to her apartment to call a cab around 10:50 a.m.

Lois returned to her apartment to prepare breakfast for her returning husband. Between ten and ten-thirty, Lois's cousin, Mildred Geier, called Lois to talk about a sewing pattern Lois was cutting for her when, after a minute into their conversation, Lois was interrupted by a knock at the door.

Neighbors teased Lois about the four locks on her front door and her constant fumbling with the array as she sought to see who was there through the diamond-shaped peephole.

Lois returned to tell her cousin it was a man looking for the building manager, noting it being common for their ground floor apartment to be mistaken as the caretaker's apartment. The women returned to their chat when there was another knock at the door. "Someone's at the door again. Maybe he's back. I'll call you back," and, with that, their conversation ended.

Lois had not bothered to reset the locks, leaving the door secured only by the doorknob spring bolt. When she opened the door a second time, the previously courteous man violently pushed the door open, knocking Lois backward.

Closing the door behind him, the man unleashed an attack, stunning five-foot-six, fifty-eight-year-old Lois with a fist blow to her left cheek, knocking her to the floor, unconscious. The man went into the bathroom where he found a pair of stockings hanging to dry. Taking one, he returned to the prone woman, looping the stocking around her neck, using it to pull the dead weight of the 172-pound woman away from the doorway and toward the dining room. As he tightened the loop around the neck of the fifty-eight-year-old woman, she uttered a sound. With this, the man delivered another sharp blow to the left side of her head, using what police suspected was a heavy object. Then, with all his strength, he drew the final breath from Lois Dant.

The killer pulled off Lois's red, yellow, and blue polka dot apron containing a pack of Lucky Strike cigarettes, matches, and a set of three keys. He ripped her black cloth dress with white polka dots violently enough to pop its three white buttons and pulled the dress up above her left breast. He then ripped off her undergarments and violated the corpse.

Frank returned sometime after 10:30, entering the basement to see if Lois was still doing laundry. He r3ecognized the hanging items, but no Lois.

From the basement, Frank went up the back stairs to the apartment's rear entrance where the screen door was unlocked, but the back door was locked. He rang the rear doorbell but there was no answer, so Frank walked around the building to the front door.

By now, it was at least 10:40 when Frank entered the apartment to find the naked, lifeless body of his wife lying supine on the floor between the living and dining rooms. Lois's short, curly grey hair was saturated with blood from a wound behind her left ear. Deeply disturbed by this horrible vision, Frank staggered into the bathroom to retrieve a towel to place over her body and maintain some sense of modesty.

Five minutes passed before Frank called St. William Church for a priest and then District Three police station, speaking with Patrolman Harold Blackburn, the desk officer.

The Cincinnati Strangler

Blackburn reported the call from a man by the name of Dant and radioed a Signal 22 call – a sick person, sirens not required.

Patrolmen Albert Webb, Herman Distasi, Edwin Adams, and Donald Wells arrived at the Dant apartment from District Three within six minutes. Sergeant Raymond Schroth, District Three supervisor, joined them, as did two firemen from the Life Squad responding to the call for a sick person.

When they arrived, Frank Dant was sitting in a living room chair, head in hands, sobbing. His wife was lying on the threshold between the living and dining rooms, a stocking wrapped around her neck, a towel partially covering her body.

Homicide was notified. Detective Charles Rutledge, Specialist Kenneth Davis, Specialist Paul Morgan, and Detective John Huber arrived at the Dant apartment around 11:00. Sergeant Russ Jackson, a tenacious homicide investigator and veteran of the department from before his service in World War Two, known as Sarge, arrived a half-hour later.

A second strangulation murder and sexual assault drew the attention of headquarters brass. The arrival of Assistant Chief Jake Schott straightened backbones. Schott had been with the department since pounding the beat as a patrolman in 1937 and was beloved among the rank and file. Scott was regarded above Chief Stanley Schrotel who was great at promoting the department, and himself, but not regarded as particularly supportive of cops on the beat.

Patrolmen and specialists were assigned to keep the curious away from the scene, while other officers surveyed the overall crime scene. A fingerprint specialist arrived at eleven-thirty as detectives combed through the details of a life interrupted. Specialist Davis photographed the scenes while Specialist Morgan made sketches.

Police found the apartment's front door peephole open and the spring lock engaged. The three other locks were unsecured.

No unusual fingerprints were found and the suspected object used to violently strike Lois was not recovered. Otherwise, nothing appeared to have been disturbed in the apartment.

Police found the check delivered by the mailman that morning on the living room desk and the mailbox key hanging by the front door.

Patrolmen Urban "Sonny" Ebert and Webb canvassed the neighborhood, finding no one who saw anything unusual that morning.

Across the street from The Rutledge apartments, John Cox told police his wife, Alma, heard someone ring the bell around 9:00 a.m. but didn't answer as she was getting ready for work.

That afternoon, a prowler was reported in the vicinity – a White male, late forties, medium height, light or grey hair, and dressed in a suit. Two boys later found a stocking and wine bottle in the rear yard of a house across the street from the Dant apartment, but neither matched anything tied to the murder.

The Cincinnati Strangler

Detective John Huber interviewed Frank Dant in the presence of Father Robert Strassell from St. William who responded to Frank's call and performed Last Rites over Lois.

Afterwards, Huber interviewed Lois's cousin, Mildred Geier, and her husband, Jack. Mildred recounted her conversation with Lois about sewing patterns, but she could not recall if her cousin mentioned any details about the man at the door. Mildred did tell Huber she thought Lois said it was a colored man at the door, but was uncertain. The only sound she heard was Lois setting the phone down on the telephone stand to answer the door. Mildred could hear Lois talking with the visitor, but could not discern any details of the conversation or voices.

Amid the swirl of investigators lay the lifeless body of Lois Dant, on her back. Her arms were outstretched and feet spread wide apart, dragged between two chairs – a brown leather chair and a white plastic seat.

Her black cloth dress, decorated with white polka dots, was torn, the buttons popped, and pulled above one breast. A pair of white underwear peeked from beneath her right buttock. Her white bra had been ripped off and was lying on the floor to the left, between her left arm and torso. Beneath Lois's left arm was her red, yellow, and blue polka dot apron, cigarettes, matches, and keys still in the pocket. A pair of low-cut women's black leather shoes were on the floor to the right of her left leg. Three white bone buttons ripped from Lois's dress were scattered across the floor. A pair of plastic Cat Eye glasses lay some thirty-five inches from the top of Lois's head A pool of blood pointed to a laceration near her left ear. She also had a one-inch laceration on her left cheek under the left eye. The carpet beneath her head was soaked with blood, splatters fanning across the two chairs by the body. Lois bore no jewelry, other than a thin gold-colored ring on her left ring finger, her wedding ring. The stocking was embedded deep into Lois's neck, leaving a purplish ring around her throat and her face an unnaturally dark color. The killer completed his violence by sexually violating the deceased woman.

At 11:15, the coroner, Dr. Frank Cleveland, reported rigor mortis had not fully set in. Lividity remained in both arms and lower portions of the body.

After Lois's body had been removed, Detective Rutledge led the collection of evidence. Blood samples were taken from the floor and both chairs, along with a dark substance found in the bathroom sink. The lone nylon stocking hanging in the bathroom and a stained towel were placed in evidence bags.

After Detectives Huber and Robert Groppe concluded their interview with Frank Dant, they gathered the evidence and drove it to the Crime Lab. Huber personally delivered the evidence to the FBI Lab in Washington, DC for analysis the next day.

At the morgue, Dr. Cleveland performed an autopsy, noting the severe blow to the left side of the head slightly behind the victim's left ear was inflicted with a large object, not a fist. This render Lois unconscious, causing hemorrhaging of the brain.

He estimated the time of death between 10:00 and 10:30 a.m. Cleveland noted the cause of death was asphyxiation by ligature, with injuries inflicted by a silk stocking, and unknown weapon. A homicide.

Colonel Schott told reporters there was a possibility the killer may have been frightened off by the ringing rear doorbell when Frank Dant was unable to enter the locked rear door.

Reporters asked Sergeant Jackson if anyone had been seen leaving the building? The homicide veteran declined to answer, other than saying, "the killer can also read."

Detectives Huber and Groppe returned to the Dant home where Frank told them nothing was missing or misplaced. The detectives took head and pubic hair samples from Frank, and drove him to St. Mary's Hospital for blood typing, revealing he had Type A or AB blood. Blood found at the scene was, again, Type O.

Ed Penno, an employee of the Hamilton County Probate Court whose wife, Ruth, had been speaking with Lois that morning, told police about a telephone call he received at 7:50 a.m. that morning from an unfamiliar voice, "Ed, this is Charlie. What time are you going to work this morning?" The caller immediately hung up.

Third floor resident Mae Bronstrop recalled hearing a deep-throated exclamation of either surprise or fright, followed by the slamming of a door, presumably an interior door as the front entry door did not slam. Neither she nor her retired-detective husband looked out their door or window.

Police spoke with fifty-four-year-old Aelred C. Birkemeir, manager of nearby Rapid Run Park who lived on Rutledge, about suspicious persons and activities in the park. Nothing.

In 1966 Price Hill, a practically all-White part of Cincinnati, the sight of a Black man would have been noticed and noted.

Calls flooded Station X from terrified women and vigilant citizens, few reports containing actionable information. Most of the calls were made from vague fears or suspicions, but police did not want to dissuade citizens from calling. Colonel Schott urged women to report anything suspicious to police, "Don't put it off until tomorrow. It's no problem to dispatch a police officer."

A list of men convicted of sex offenses in Hamilton County and released from prison during April through November of 1965. All of the men shared one characteristic - Type O blood, same as that found at the Harrington and Dant scenes.

Bulletins from the Cincinnati Police Department were distributed across the country highlighting similarities among three cases of Elizabeth Kreco, Lois Dant, and Emogene Harrington, including the description, "Police believe the killer raped his victims after he strangled them…All victims were large women in good health."

Robbery appeared as a motive in the Kreco and Harrington cases, but nothing was disturbed in the Dant apartment. All three occurred in apartment buildings, during daytime hours, two of them in basements.

Absent a solid description and identifying evidence, the investigation sought a shadowy Black man no one could clearly describe. Police were convinced the same man committed all three of the heinous crimes.

The Cincinnati Strangler

Police visited nearby Carson School to inquire about all past and present janitors. They also examined records at the Reidy Janitor Service, less than a block away from the Dant apartment on Rutledge Avenue.

Former employees of contractors working at the three apartment buildings over the previous ten years were contacted and names were cross-checked across the locations.

By the end of the week, police had questioned seven men as possible suspects, three were immediately cleared, while one was held on a morals charge.

As the month wore on without progress, *Enquirer* columnist Frank Weikel blithely noted how April seemed to be the month of unsolved murders in Cincinnati, pairing Lois Dant's murder with the April 11, 1956, stabbing death of local socialite Audrey Evers Pugh in her Hyde Park home. A city meter reader, Robert Lyon, was charged with her murder but found not guilty by a jury, convinced the high-pressure tactics of assistant prosecutor, Donald Roney, negated Lyon's confession. The Pugh case remains unsolved today. Weikel's column triggered old suspicions of meter readers as potential killers.

Police questioned a Black former mental patient known to be in Price Hill at the time of the Dant murder. The man was committed to Longview Hospital in 1948, where he reportedly expressed desires to have intercourse with White women and then kill them. He visited Hamilton County Probate Court on the morning of the Dant murder, around 11:00 a.m., telling the clerk he wanted to see his records, repeating "all wrong."

After questioning, he was released since his blood was not Type O.

Around the metropolitan area, people were buying guns at a rapid clip.

"There is nothing to prevent a person from having a gun in his own home," Colonel Schott told the *Enquirer*, "but we would prefer that people rely on the police."

In the wake of Lois Dant's murder, an unnamed Rutledge resident spoke to an *Enquirer* reporter from behind her locked door, "Sure you hear about these things happening, but who would think this kind of thing could happen in Price Hill. They're always downtown or over on the other side of town."

Loren Biddle, a neighbor who'd teased Lois about her array of locks, told the reporter, "those things started happening out in Walnut Hills and I got worried, too. Now I keep everything locked. I'm even scared to go out and get my paper in the morning."

The Biddles and Dants were from Indiana and both couples moved into the building as newlyweds twenty-nine years earlier. "We've known each other for 29 years; it was such a terrible shock."

"They were good neighbors to everybody," Robert Scheck, a Rutledge Avenue resident, told the *Enquirer*, "and very involved with the church. I can't understand why anyone would want to do such a thing like that. We'd all like to get our hands on him."

Returning to Cincinnati from delivering evidence to the FBI, Detective Huber reported that initial tests performed by the federal lab yielded no clues. Hairs found matted on the back of Lois's hand were nylon rug fibers and fingernail scrapings were too minute to compare. Hairs found in Lois's other hand were either from an arm or leg, but unsuitable for analysis. Forensic tests on the clothing were still underway as Huber departed but the lab was slowed by the death of the technician in charge of the analysis, requiring another FBI laboratory agent to start from the beginning.

Two-hundred family, friends, and neighbors of the Dants attended a Solemn Last Blessing on April 7 at St. William. A funeral Mass could not be held as it was Holy Thursday. A Solemn High Mass followed the next Monday, the day after Easter. Lois's body was taken to Washington, Indiana by train for burial in the family plot.

The day after Lois Dant's murder, it snowed, but springtime would bring warmth and a respite from the strangulation murders.

Knotted stocking used to kill Lois Dant

Chapter 5
A Deadly Walk in the Park

Friday, June 10, 1966

A misty fog clung to the cool early morning air, the ground shimmering from the rain brought by the previous night's storm. As the city began to awaken, Burnet Woods stood as a tranquil oasis amid the growing cacophony of morning traffic, situated adjacent to the University of Cincinnati campus and Good Samaritan Hospital complex. Birds in the treetops regaled the rising sun, a faint light dappling the park's winding pathways.

Fred Scheuerle, a 65-year-old jeweler, and his Austrian-born wife, Theresa, lived on Nixon Street, across from Burnet Woods, where they'd resided for more than forty years. Scheuerle embarked on his usual early morning walk in the park with his dog, Jeff. A concrete path led down the hill from Bishop Street to Burnet Woods Lake where Fred let Jeff off his leash. The dog, full of energy, raced around the lake, ignoring Fred's calls to come.

As Fred neared a ravine known as Chipmunk Hollow, he heard Jeff barking frantically. Unlike Jeff's usual bark—this carried more urgency. Walking toward the barking dog, Fred spotted a figure in the brush appearing to be someone sleeping. With Jeff now leashed, Fred made his way up the stairs toward the park's bandstand, where he flagged down a passing police cruiser.

"I saw a bum sleeping in his underwear," Fred told the officer, pointing toward Chipmunk Hollow. The patrolman followed Fred's directions down the stairs toward the ravine, but when he reached the figure, he quickly realized this wasn't a drunk sleeping it off on the hillside. Rather, it was the nude body of a woman lying motionless in the brush. He immediately called police.

Sergeant Charles Killinger, District Five shift supervisor, took the call and arrived at the scene at 6:28 a.m. As he approached, he heard a small dog barking. Tied to a sapling near the woman's body was a black and white Toy Fox Terrier. The dog's yapping echoed in the stillness as Killinger approached.

The woman was sprawled among the brush, her body pale and lifeless. Torn clothing was scattered about, and her purse had been rifled through, the contents strewn nearby. Her wallet was missing, leaving police without the victim's name. A paisley necktie was wrapped tightly around the woman's neck, frayed and ragged, its grey lining exposed. The woman had been brutally beaten; her face swollen from the force of multiple blows. Both cheekbones were fractured, and the position of her body suggested she had been dragged through the brush from the stairs.

Scheuerle, retracing his steps, returned to find several police officers at the scene. One of them asked, "Are you the man who found the body?" Fred nodded, and the officer informed him that it wasn't a bum he had seen—it was a woman who had been murdered. Fred recognized her as someone he had often seen walking her dog in the early morning, though he didn't know her name.

The victim's body told a horrific tale. Bloodstains marked the path where she had been dragged, and her dress—a blue and green Tartan plaid—lay ripped open.

The Cincinnati Strangler

Her slip had been torn away, and her panties dangled from one leg. A single moccasin was near her body, the other shoe near the stairs. Dragging her body through the brush left small cuts and lacerations on her legs and back. Her face and chest were horribly bruised.

The coroner determined the cause of death to have been strangulation by ligature, but the autopsy revealed more. The victim had suffered multiple fractures, including ribs three through nine on her left side and three through six on her right. One of her broken ribs had punctured her lung, and her spleen was lacerated. The attack was savage, and there was evidence of sexual assault. The presence of sperm and Type B blood pointed to the killer. The blows to her face and body led police to suspect the killer used a two-by-four to beat the woman but no such weapon was found at the scene.

Judy (Cincinnati *Enquirer*)

As police continued their investigation, Judy, the little dog tied to a tree near the victim revealed the woman's identity. The dog tag she wore led investigators to the address of a woman living across Jefferson Avenue from the park.

By noon, the woman's son-in-law, Lonnie Kerr, arrived at the coroner's office to confirm the identity of the victim as fifty-five-year-old Mathilda Jeannet Messer, the fourth victim of the phantom killer.

News quickly spread. That afternoon's *Post* fronted with the headline, "Third Woman Raped, Slain; Body Found in Burnet Woods."

The next day's *Enquirer* story by Margaret Josten was headlined, "A Dog, A Walk, No Fear – The Death," quoting Mathilda's landlady, Bessie Jones, cautiously speaking to the reporter through a locked screen door, saying Mathilda took her dog for a walk every morning.

"Mrs. Messer always said, 'I'm not afraid,' when I'd warn her how women have to be careful these days. Why, she'd even go out with her dog and never lock the door of her apartment. She just didn't have no fears about nothing."

Mrs. Jones had two dogs inside with her, "Twenty years ago I used to take my dogs down to Burnet Woods early in the morning, but things didn't happen then like they do now."

Other neighbors shared their shock. Mrs. Josie Chambers, who lived next door, recalled that Mathilda walked her dog every morning around five. "I told her I wouldn't go into those woods for anything, but she said she didn't go too far," Josie recounted.

Mathilda always stopped by her neighbor's apartment on her return, "but she didn't stop today, and I was about to go to her apartment at seven a.m. to see if anything was wrong when I saw policemen coming to her door."

Another neighbor, Dora Johnson, was shocked by the news of Mathilda Messer's death, "she was such a nice little thing."

"I often had her in her for a cup of coffee and she'd tell me about her daughter and her son in the service. Just a little bit of a woman, she was. I liked her. I guess you'd call her a nice lady."

Meanwhile, life in the park went on. Children played on the swings, while a group of fifth graders picnicked near the stone stairs leading to the bandstand—unaware of the violence that had occurred just hours earlier. But for many women in Cincinnati, the terror was real. The city was on edge, and hardware stores reported an overwhelming increase in sales of chain locks, while tear gas sprayers disguised as fountain pens flew off the shelves.

Police remained convinced the same man was responsible for the three rapes and murders over the past six months.

"This man is a maniac," declared Colonel Schott. "He is definitely the same man who raped and strangled two other women here. There cannot be three of them."

Despite a thorough search of the area and the involvement of the FBI, no solid leads emerged. Investigators learned this killer's blood type was B. Altogether, the scant evidence was not enough to identify any one man.

A June 25 Cincinnati *Enquirer* headline: "Negro Killed Three Women, Police Say," revealed the only clue police had to the killer drawn from hair samples found at the scene of Mathilda Messer's slaying, that of a Black man.

Chief of Detectives Lieutenant Colonel Jacob Scott and Homicide Sergeant Russell Jackson and let their belief be known that one man was responsible for all three crimes.

With this, police launched a widespread roundup of men across the city based upon one dominant profile - the color of their skin; questioned, fingerprinted, sampled, and photographed, with little, if any, connection to the crimes.

The manhunt inflamed racial tensions across the city, worsening as White citizens became automatically suspicious of any Black man they saw, often times calling police to report they'd seen the killer.

As the investigations dragged on, the *Enquirer* expressed the public's frustration: "Unless the killer is spotted, all three murders will end up in the unsolved-case files—and those files are getting bigger all the time."

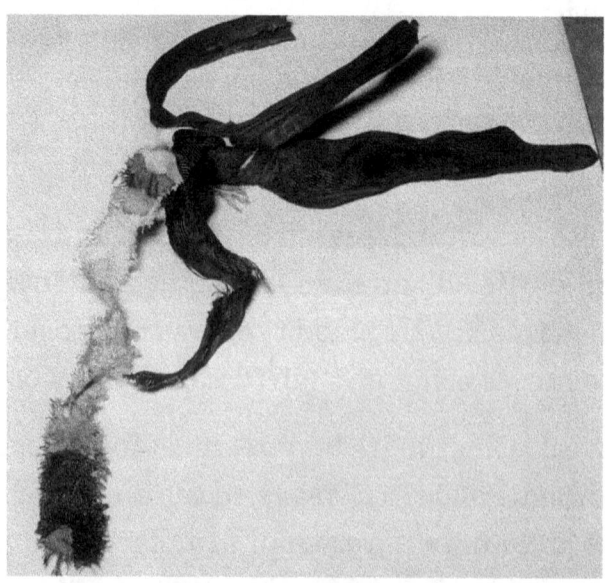

Tattered necktie used to strangle Mathilda Messer.
(Cincinnati Police Department)

Chapter 6
Murder By Gaslight

Tuesday, October 11, 1966

The summer of 1966 passed without another strangulation murder, offering the city a hint of calm.

The calm was interrupted in August with the stabbing death of thirty-one-year-old Barbara Bowman in Price Hill but police did not believe Bowman's murder was connected with the others.

Any sense of relief turned to dread in the darkness of an October night.

This was the day housewives across Cincinnati, and the region, eagerly awaited the return of Ruth Lyons, the beloved doyenne of her noontime television chat and variety show, The 50-50 Club. Lyons had been absent for a year-and-a-half due to personal health issues and lingering grief from the death of her daughter, Candy Newman. The afternoon Cincinnati *Post* featured a detailed report about her return broadcast.

That evening, the PTA of Annunciation Catholic School in Clifton was holding its bi-monthly meeting. With the new school year underway, mothers rushed to feed their families before hurrying out the door. The meeting was expected to cover school activities and holiday preparations, but the city's grim reality overshadowed the proceedings. As a murderer stalked Cincinnati, fears about Halloween trick-or-treating consumed the conversation, extending the meeting well into the night.

Alice Hochhausler

Among the attendees was fifty-one-year-old Alice Hochhausler, mother of nine, and a seasoned participant in school meetings. She'd been attending PTA meetings at Annunciation for years, since her eldest son, Carl Joseph Jr., now twenty-four, attended the school. Alice and her husband, Carl, chief of surgery at Good Samaritan Hospital, lived in the upscale Gaslight District near Good Sam and UC with their younger children, including her two youngest boys, Joe, twelve, and Tom, nine.

Alice returned from the PTA meeting at 10:45 p.m. She changed into her nightclothes and checked on her children to make certain were either in or preparing for bed. Then, as was their routine, she sat with Carl to watch the eleven o'clock news. Watching Al Schottelkotte deliver the news on Channel Nine was a weeknight ritual before switching to The Tonight Show. That evening, however, Johnny Carson was off, and singer Steve Lawrence was guest hosting. Alice had to leave the house again—this time to pick up their daughter Beth from Good Sam where she worked as a nurse.

The Cincinnati Strangler

Alice, wearing a light coat over her robe and slip, and tennis shoes on her feet, left the house around 11:40 to fetch Beth. Since Mathilda Messer's murder in nearby Burnet Woods, Alice had been especially cautious, refusing to let Beth walk home alone. Carl had fallen asleep in his chair and made his way to bed around 11:45 p.m.

Beth was already waiting on the hospital steps when Alice arrived, and the two began their short drive Beth's apartment on Ludlow Avenue, near her parents's home on Cornell Place. Stopping across from the apartment building just shy of Cornell Place on the right. As she and her mother talked, Beth noticed a car stopping behind them.

"I wonder if he wants to pass me or what?" Alice asked her daughter.

Beth thought the driver wanted to turn but was blocked by their car, so she would get out, then her mother could move. As soon as Beth opened the car door, the other vehicle, driven by a Black man, pulled around and continued west on Ludlow. After waving goodbye to her mother, Beth walked into her apartment building.

Seeing her daughter safely enter the front door, Alice turned right on Cornell Place to reach her home, only two blocks away. Arriving, she parked her white 1964 Mercury station wagon next to the family's 1957 Chevy Bel Air in the driveway beside the detached garage. As Alice walked down the driveway toward the house in darkness, she was suddenly struck on the side of her head by a heavy blow. The force knocked her unconscious, sending her keys flying into a nearby shrub and dislodging a denture. The assailant used the sash from Alice's robe to drag her body up the driveway to the threshold of the garage where he squeezed the life from his helpless victim. After violating her corpse, the attacker left her body next to a Triumph TR3 parked in the garage.

The following morning, Dr. Hochhausler awoke at 7:15 a.m. and noticed his wife wasn't in bed. Assuming she had fallen asleep elsewhere in the house, he checked, but Alice was nowhere to be found. Stepping outside, he saw her shoe in the driveway, followed by her dentures, and then his worst fear lay before his eyes—Alice's body, lying partially clothed at the garage entrance.

Horrified, Carl immediately called the police and then Annunciation Church asking for a priest to administer Last Rites. The call to Station X came in at 7:30 a.m. and was put out as a Signal 22, the call for a sick or injured person, a code used to avoid prying citizen ears on police radio bandwidths.

Specialist Bob Thoss and Patrolman Bart Mellon were dispatched to the scene. Upon arriving, Thoss found Alice's body and quickly realized this was no mere injury. The scene bore the hallmarks of another brutal strangulation. By 7:44 a.m., Sergeant Russ Jackson and Detective Robert Bluhm arrived from Homicide. They were pointed to Alice's lifeless body in the garage, her bathrobe sash knotted tightly around her neck.

The large family was devastated, and police quickly began searching the area for evidence. As they canvassed the neighborhood, Alice's daughter Beth provided a crucial detail. The car she'd seen after work, driven by a Black man, was a cream-and-tan 1959 Chevrolet Bel Air. This lead became central to the investigation, with Colonel Schott calling it "the most solid lead we've received yet." Officers were tasked with tracking down every registered 1959 Chevrolet in Hamilton County, leading to a massive manhunt for the two-tone sedan.

The murder of Alice Hochhausler shocked the entire city. People were deeply upset over the grisly murder of this mother of nine, a vibrant person who lived for her family and community.

Police doubled their efforts, extending shifts and reassigning officers to work exclusively on The Strangler cases. Station X was flooded with more tips than ever. Panic was spreading across the city.

The once-quiet Gaslight District was now at the center of police investigations, with officers combing the area and interviewing everyone in the hope one saw something on that dark October night. Despite heightened vigilance, the killer remained elusive, and Cincinnati remained paralyzed by fear.

In the days following the murder, acting police chief, Colonel Guy York, was quoted across the front page of the *Enquirer*, "York Certain Someone Knows the Strangler of Five."

Outside their ranks, police sought professional help in the search for the elusive killer. Convinced the murderer must be mentally disturbed, Safety Director Henry Sandman, Detective Chief Schott, Sergeant Jackson, and several detectives met with Dr. John Ordway and five other psychiatrists at Cincinnati General Hospital. For two hours, they discussed the personality and behavior of the man terrorizing the city. The psychiatrists told the assembled police that profiling such a killer before capture was far more difficult than analyzing him afterward. The meeting ended without any official report or public comment.

With little progress, the police escalated their efforts, enlisting retired officers, security guards, firemen, mail carriers, and meter readers to join the search. Taxi drivers were already involved. The *Enquirer* headline trumpeted, "5000-Man Posse Beefs Up Hunt for Sex Maniac." At the same time, the city's Crime Study Committee urged residents to remain calm and leave the investigations to the police.

"This is no time for self-elected vigilantes to take the law into their own hands," said committee chair Councilman Jake Held.

Former Police Chief Stanley Schrotel, who had retired in September, testified before the Crime Study Committee, calling for increased support and funding for the police department. "We want more authority. We want more power. We want more money," Schrotel declared. "The crisis is here. Now we need some help."

City Manager William Wichman also met with local business leaders, encouraging them to heighten their vigilance and instruct their employees to be alert for suspicious activity. Cincinnati Gas & Electric committed its 2,000 field employees, assisting police by distributing photographs of a 1959 Chevrolet Bel Air to their meter readers.

The Cincinnati Strangler

The city's Fire Safety Week took on new task as fire department personnel went door-to-door distributing flyers about personal safety as a murderer prowled the city, advising women to lock their doors, avoid walking alone at night, and refrain from giving the impression of being alone in their homes. Wichman's message reassured residents that city officials were committed to solving the case, urging them to report anything suspicious to the police without delay.

Delivery drivers established a system of passwords to ensure the safety of their customers. "Some of these women are terrified, afraid to open their doors, and I don't blame them," John Almon, a deliveryman for Exquisite Cleaners, told the Cincinnati *Post*. He and his customers were using secret passwords to verify his identity.

Despite strenuous efforts, there were few promising leads in the case of Alice Hochhausler's murder, beyond the two-tone 1959 Chevy. Police had already interviewed twenty persons of interest and conducted two lie detector tests, both of which cleared the subjects. Colonel Schott believed that Alice's murder was a crime of opportunity, stating, "The slayer just happened to be in the area of the Hochhausler home and saw his opportunity and struck."

The impact of Alice's murder, coupled with the others, was felt citywide. Accompanying widespread trepidations, resentment was rising in Cincinnati's Black community. Black residents wanted the killer apprehended, just not at the cost of their individual dignity. Dr. Bruce Green, president of the Cincinnati chapter of the NAACP, appealed to the city council, writing, "Citizens, both Negro and white, grow more apprehensive daily about personal safety." Reverend C.L. Connor of the Pilgrim Baptist Church voiced his concern during a meeting with Wichman, saying, "I want it clearly understood that there are as many Negroes interested in the apprehension of this slayer as there are white citizens."

As the city searched for answers, Acting Police Chief York announced that tipsters would not be required to provide police their names, a move aimed at encouraging more people to come forward. By mid-October, rewards for information leading to the capture of The Strangler and the September stabbing murders of the Bricca family exceeded $25,000, with $10,600 earmarked for The Strangler alone. To protect the identity of informants, police devised a system using the serial numbers of dollar bills instead of names. If an informant qualified for a reward, their dollar bill's serial number would serve as proof of their identity.

Sporting goods stores ran out of guns and mace, while hardware stores and locksmiths were overwhelmed with the need for chain locks and deadbolts as women scrambled for protection. Kroger grocery stores distributed 100,000 free whistles, and an Evanston karate studio offered free self-defense classes. Animal shelters struggled to meet the demand for large dogs.

Despite the heightened police activity, Walnut Hills, a predominantly Black neighborhood, saw a spike in assaults and women being chased following Alice Hochhausler's murder. Panic among White women was palpable, but Black women, accustomed to violence in their communities with faint police response, experienced the tension differently. Relations between Black citizens and the police were further strained by the mass questioning of Black men in connection with the murders.

As investigators analyzed the various cases attributed to The Strangler, certain patterns emerged:

- All the victims were women over fifty.

- The attacks involved beatings, strangulation, and rape.

- Different items were used for strangulation: a plastic clothesline, a nylon stocking, a Paisley necktie, and in Alice's case, a bathrobe sash.

- All victims were severely beaten.

- Robbery appeared to be a motive in most of the cases, except for Lois Dant and Alice Hochhausler.

- The attacks occurred in daylight hours, except for Alice's murder, which took place late at night.

Police attention was focused on the search for the cream-and-tan 1959 Chevrolet Bel Air, but progress was slow. By October 17, Homicide Sergeant Jackson politely asked the public to stop calling Station X about two-tone Chevrolets.

One consequence of the focus on the car was a surge in complaints from owners of 1959 Chevrolets who were being pulled over repeatedly by police. A man reported being stopped seven times in three days and pleaded with police to devise a system—such as a window sticker—to indicate that his car had been cleared.

The flood of tips continued - from anonymous letters, to calls to Station X, along with suggestions sent to the FBI. One letter pointed fingers at a Black woman the author suspected, while another detailed a strange encounter with a "colored man" near the Hochhausler home. People wrote with suggestions proposing everything from drastic penalties for sex offenders to dressing male officers in women's clothing to lure the killer.

Among the letters arriving at the Cincinnati FBI office was one telling of a morgue employee who allegedly bragged to his girlfriend that he preferred having "relations with a dead woman than a live one." Another report came from a nurse at Good Samaritan Hospital about being followed by a suspicious man who approached her with the unnerving statement, "I see you're working two jobs." She fled.

Meanwhile, police investigated a new lead involving Elgin Edwards, a fugitive wanted for the murder of Jesse James Brown in May 1966. A tipster reported seeing Edwards hanging around Clifton and Ludlow, not far from the Hochhausler home around the time of Alice's murder. Edwards, described as resembling boxer Cassius Clay (Muhammed Ali), had been on the run since the fatal shooting of Brown outside a home on Valencia Street on Vine Street Hill. Edwards remained elusive until his eventual capture in Phoenix, Arizona, in 1969.

As the hunt for The Strangler continued, the citizens of Cincinnati—both Black and White—remained gripped by fear, desperation, and uncertainty, hoping that the next tip or clue would finally bring the killer to justice.

City officials debated shifting Halloween trick-or-treating to the afternoon of Sunday, October 30, to keep children off the streets after dusk.

At 10:32 p.m. on Sunday, October 23, Station X received a distress call from the Hochhausler household. District Five Lieutenant Hershell Hall, accompanied by two specialists and several district officers, responded quickly.

Beth Hochhausler had answered the phone to hear a voice she identified as a Black man chillingly saying, "This is the killer, this is the killer, I'm gonna kill you."

When police arrived, they found Dr. Hochhausler with Beth and Rita in the living room, all visibly shaken. The Hochhauslers were described as gracious and cooperative. Dr. Hochhausler told the officers that the family was at their disposal, but the Vice Squad chief, Lieutenant Charles Black, corrected him, saying, "No, Doctor, we are at your disposal. In view of the tremendous shock this family has experienced and their present state of upset due to the phone call, should you so desire and should the doctor desire, I will be glad to provide the same detail tonight and for however long you think necessary."

In response, police stationed officers inside the Hochhausler residence around the clock, with a recorder set up to capture phone calls on tape.

As the officers departed the Hochhausler home, they encountered Chic Poppe, a freelance reporter and photographer for local television station WKRC. Poppe had been listening to police radio calls and responded to this one despite its being out as a "305," keeping it within District Five, rather than a system-wide 301, picked up by prying ears. Hall and Black explained what had happened and asked Poppe to keep it quiet, which he did.

Every new assault or murder, accompanied by sensational media attention, contributed to the growing atmosphere of suspicion and helplessness. This sense of desperation was expressed in a letter written by an elderly woman living in an apartment building for seniors, where most residents lived alone.

"What else can be done? Invite the public to offer more suggestions…Please, oh please, tell us what more the public can do."

Enquirer columnist Frank Weikel implored The Strangler "to seek the help you need."

An anonymous writer suggested police reach out to the killer with compassion:

"I am a Negro woman who is interested in the safety of Cincinnati…Perhaps if you compose a letter to this person through radio, television, and NEWSPAPER this will help. I suggest you personally consult a psychiatrist as to the pattern of this very sick person and if you find his pattern, then it will be easy to predict when he will strike again. Appeal to him to give himself up and perhaps during his sane stage he will do just that. Tell him that doctors will cure him or protect him from hurting any more people."

By the end of October, 274 Cincinnati residents had volunteered to help in the manhunt for The Strangler. District Three, which covered the Dant murder and the recent stabbing of a thirty-one-year-old woman in August, had the most volunteers—110. Many of them were retired police officers, firefighters, and military veterans, who were assigned to walk beats or ride unarmed in patrol cars for three to five hours as often as they could.

As Halloween approached, area officials urged trick-or-treating be moved to daylight hours on Sunday, October 30.

Following the Hochhausler murder, Colonel Schott personally delivered sixteen pieces of evidence to the FBI Lab in Washington, D.C. The lab was housed in the Department of Justice building on Pennsylvania Avenue where FBI technicians pored over the evidence. Alice's clothing was laid out on a paper-covered table, while, in another room, materials found beneath her fingernails were examined. Evidence from the Bricca family murders and other Cincinnati cases was also stored in the lab, awaiting further analysis.

From DC, Schott headed to Boston for meetings about investigations into the Boston Strangler who terrorized the city in the early 1960s, killing thirteen women. A suspect, Albert DeSalvo, was held on unrelated charges and later confessed to the crimes while in a Connecticut psychiatric facility. DeSalvo had shared details with another inmate that only the killer could have known. DeSalvo was convicted and sentenced to life in prison in 1967, but his life was cut short when he was stabbed to death in 1973.

On October 20, Sergeant Jackson received the FBI Lab results. "Black hairs of Negroid origin" were noted, some carrying mixed-race characteristics. One hair was artificially colored reddish-brown. Most were Caucasian. Semen containing active spermatozoa was found on Alice's slip, but other samples provided no clues to the perpetrator. No blood or tissue was found in the scrapings from beneath Alice's fingernails. No evidence was found on the piece of concrete collected from the driveway that it had been used to inflict the blunt force upon the victim, as police had suspected.

Dr. Howard B. Lyman, an associate professor of psychology at the University of Cincinnati and a neighbor of the Hochhauslers, was asked by police to examine the four murders linked to The Strangler. Lyman concluded that the killer "may very well be taking his rage out on a mother figure, or middle-aged women in general because of a hatred that such a woman may have engendered in him."

A week after the Hochhausler murder, the city council held an emergency session, approving the registration of retired police officers, firefighters, and military veterans for service in the manhunt. The fire department volunteered its members and equipment to assist in the investigations.

One council member suggested deputizing citizen patrols, meaning they could carry weapons, but the city manager quickly rejected the idea, fearing Cincinnati was already on the brink of mob justice.

An overzealous local newscaster reported a sighting of The Strangler in his two-tone car near Milford, Ohio. Before police arrived, traffic had slowed to a crawl, crowded with cars carrying armed men searching for the killer, without success.

In late October, The Cincinnati *Post* published an

The Cincinnati Strangler

article headlined, "The Cincinnati Strangler...He's a Lot Like Boston's," following the visit of Gerold Frank, author of *The Boston Strangler*. Frank noted the Boston Strangler, Albert DeSalvo, wasn't the brute many expected him to be. Instead, he was "a short, slender, quiet man." DeSalvo's meek manner probably led many of his victims to let him into their apartments without suspicion.

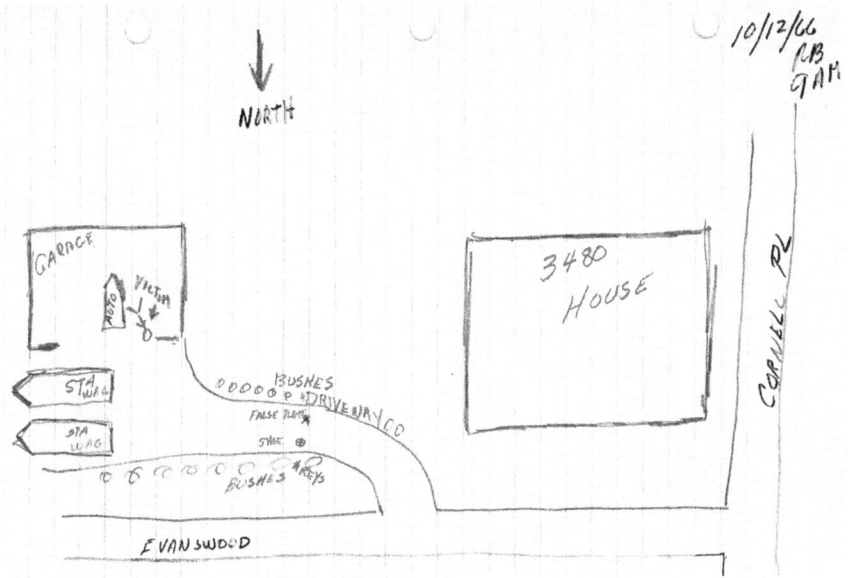

Police sketch of the Hochausler property.

The appearance of a 1959 Chevrolet BelAir drew police attention based on Beth Hochhausler's description of the car that pulled up behind her mother's the night Alice Hochhausler was murdered.

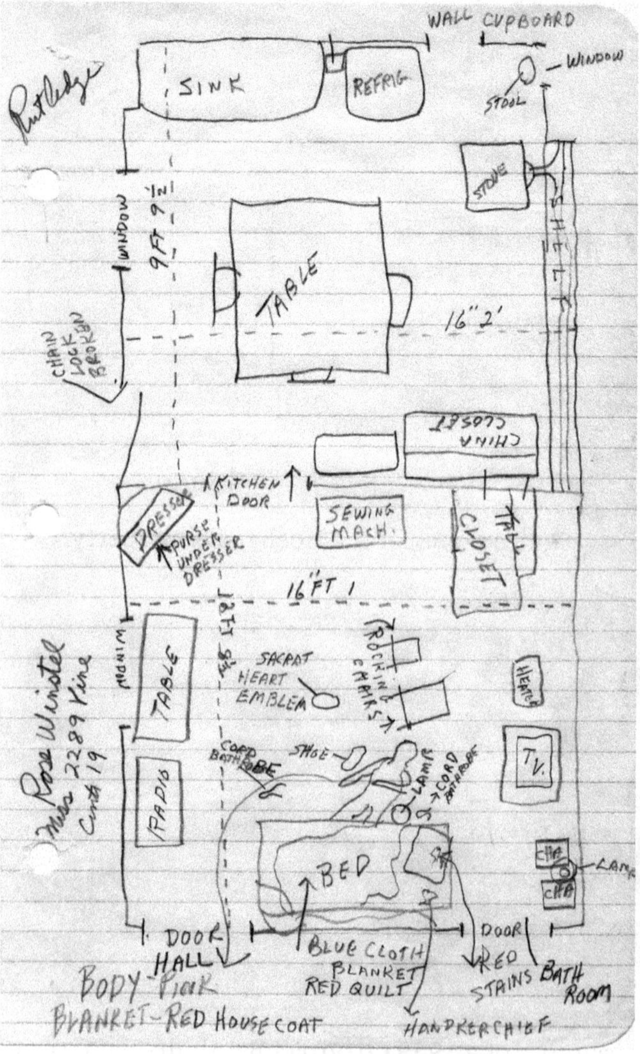

Detective Charles Rutledge sketch of Rose Winstel's murder scene.

Chapter 7
Death Looms Over Vine Street Hill

Thursday, October 20, 1966

The murder of Alice Hochhausler hit a nerve among women in Cincinnati. Many shared a feeling they knew Alice. Perhaps not personally, but Alice was exemplar among friends and neighbors they admired; genuinely nice women dedicated to family, faith, and community. Alice's murder brought the dread into many homes. Across the city, women no longer even cracked their doors for visitors. Strangers walked away unacknowledged. On the streets and driveways, women cast quick, nervous glances over their shoulders as they walked from their cars. From there, they hastened toward the entry door, hands trembling as they fumbled their keys. The sound of locks clicking into place echoed through homes and apartments throughout the city and suburbs.

At 7:40 p.m. on Thursday, October 20, 1966, Patrolman Joseph Lind received a radio call from Station X while patrolling the Northside neighborhood. To avoid putting out a radio call that could alert prying ears, the call was to be discreet. Lind found the nearest callbox on Ludlow Avenue to answer the vague call: "Respond to 2289 Vine Street about an elderly woman not answering calls from family."

The family in question was Frank Winstel, who had grown concerned after multiple failed attempts to reach his aunt, Rose Winstel.

Lind drove the nearly three miles through the neighborhoods touched by previous murders—driving past Beth Hochhausler's apartment on Ludlow at Cornell and Burnet Woods where Mathilda Messer's body had been found.

Reports of family members not responding to phone calls were routine for police, especially in a time of city-wide dread for loved ones and friends. Often, they ended in relief when the unresponsive person was found alive. Or they could result in sadness when the person was found dead. In the case of eighty-one-year-old Rose Winstel, natural causes likely claimed the elderly woman.

What Patrolman Lind found was far more sinister.

Arriving at the dimly lit house at 2289 Vine, Lind approached through a narrow, winding path of concrete stairs. The shotgun-style house stood on a slight incline, separated from the street by a rough-hewn stone wall. After knocking on the front door to no response, Lind noticed a loud television blaring from inside.

Walking alongside the house, the patrolman reached a side door. It had been violently forced open, the frame and locks burst apart from the force of the break-in. Inside, Lind scanned the interior with his flashlight, noting what he initially thought was a pile of clothes in the front room, dimly lit by the flickering television. Upon closer inspection, his heart sank—what lay before him was the lifeless body of an elderly woman, half-dressed, her legs partially concealed beneath the bed.

This was eighty-one-year-old Rose Winstel. Her nephew, Frank, called police concerned about her not answering as he'd been visiting his aunt weekly since the death of her brother, Joe, in June, and her sister, Reva, move into a nursing home.

Rose, nearly deaf and suffering from cataracts, mostly kept to herself in the rough Vine Street Hill neighborhood, part of Clifton Heights, deflecting pleas to move to a safer place; her niece insisting she move into her Price Hill home. Rose remained adamant about staying close to St. George's Church, where she'd been a parishioner for years.

Lind knew immediately he was dealing with more than just a missing person or natural death. He left everything untouched and returned to his patrol car, calling for backup. Soon, Patrolman William Wright arrived, and the two entered the home together. Rose's body was lying at an angle on her back, between a chair and the bed. A pink knitted blanket had been draped over her face. When Lind removed it, they found her face covered in bruises—evidence of a brutal beating. The cord of a red infrared massager was tightly wound around her neck.

Lind used the house phone to call Station X, reporting what appeared to be another strangulation murder. He then had Frank Winstel called to the scene. When Frank arrived, Lind coolly informed him of his aunt's death and asked him to wait outside.

As word spread, a crowd began to gather outside the house. The scene quickly grew chaotic, with neighbors and onlookers swarming around the house; the side yard and back familiar cut-throughs for locals heading to Bellevue Hill Park.

District Five supervisor Sergeant Charles Killinger

arrived with Homicide Detective William Rathman to begin the investigation. Frank Winstel provided them with some background on his aunt, describing her as "sharp for her age, with a wonderful sense of humor." Rose had been aware of the city's growing fears over a killer stalking women, enhanced by a recent break-in to her home when Frank had a new lock installed on her side door.

Rathman and his team quickly went to work. Rathman photographed the scene, while Detective Meiszer and Patrolman Lelias "Lee" Rarden scoured the house for evidence. They collected bedclothes, blanket, pillow, and a raft of other items, placing them into brown evidence bags for sending to the FBI lab. The victim's clothing remained on her body, to be removed later by the coroner, added to the FBI dispatch.

Rose lay naked from the waist down, except for hosiery held up by garters. Her bathrobe, flannel pajama top, and undershirt were torn and left in disarray. Blood on her lower body suggested she had been raped, a conclusion later confirmed in an autopsy, revealing a five-inch laceration running through her vagina, possibly indicating sexual assault with a foreign object.

Investigators noted further evidence of sexual violence. Teeth marks were found on both of her breasts, with deeper impressions on the left. The bed was disheveled, and one of Rose's brown canvas shoes was found between her legs. The other lay about three feet away. A sacred heart scapular was tangled in the fabric of her torn undershirt.

Detectives surmised the killer likely fled through the front door for a quick escape onto Vine Street. The scene was littered with signs of force. The door's chain lock had been broken, and the new Yale bolt lock, which had been installed after a previous break-in, had been violently ripped apart.

Coroner Dr. Frank Cleveland arrived, determining the primary cause of death to be asphyxiation due to strangulation, though the savage beating Rose had suffered was also significant. After Cleveland completed his examination, Rose's body was removed from the home and transported to the county morgue.

Similarities between Rose's death and those of other recent murder victims were noted by police. Colonel Schott pointed out the women were all older, strangled with ligatures, and most sexually assaulted. But some detectives were less than convinced this case was connected to the other strangulation murders. The explosive entry into Rose's home stood out as unusual when compared with the other cases, and Rose was much older than the other victims. While Vine Street had a reputation for violent crime, the other murders had occurred in relatively quiet, residential areas.

As detectives fanned out to canvass the area, the crowd outside the home grew to over a thousand people. Investigators questioned neighbors, some of whom described hearing strange noises and suspicious persons on or around the day of Rose's murder, but none offered serious leads.

Overnight, police rounded up eight suspects for

questioning. Two of them agreed to take lie detector tests. Among the people questioned was Neal Jones, a neighborhood character known for his erratic behavior and for pestering women. Blood and hair samples were taken from Jones, but nothing conclusive was found.

The night Rose's body was found, police rousted a nineteen-year-old man loitering in this car near Rose's house and, finding a length of cord in the car's trunk, held him on an outstanding gang assault warrant. The cord, blood type O, and having driven for Yellow Cab – the young man was a suspect. He told detectives he awoke from a nap after work around ten p.m. and went to the Arcade Bar on Vine where he stayed until closing. His alibi was confirmed by the bartender and three Arcade patrons. He was released.

In June 1966, a Mount Auburn woman called police when a man tried enticing her into his apartment. Twenty-six-year-old Morris Johnson, Jr., was sentenced to ninety days in the Workhouse.

One week after her assailant's September release, the same woman told police of being grabbed from behind and dragged into a building entryway where she was raped by Johnson. She then began receiving telephone calls at the Frisch's Big Boy restaurant workplace, the caller telling her: "You identified me and I'm going to get you and bite your tits off."

Johnson was charged with rape but acquitted in June 1967, thanks to his alibi that he'd been with friends in a café at the time.

On October 6, a forty-eight-year-old woman was

assaulted as she walked into the elevator in the basement of her apartment building at 2324 Park Avenue, the Parkland Apartments, next to Elizabeth Kreco's Verona apartments. She was coming home from the beauty parlor and walked from her car in the basement garage to the elevator. A man, described as Black, a medium-build, about twenty years old, forced his way into the elevator and tried looping a rope over her head, getting tangled in her glasses. The elevator doors opened, the woman screamed, and the man fled.

Benny Bailey arrived in Cincinnati by misfortune and an odd route. Three days before Rose's death, Bailey appeared in the office of George Bement in the Hamilton County Welfare Department. While traveling from New York to California, during a stopover in Cleveland, three men waylaid Bailey and robbed him of $1,100. Still holding his bus ticket, Bailey traded it for a ticket to Cincinnati, despite his having no friends or family in the city.

Born in Georgia, Bailey went to high school in Souda, New York. The twenty-seven-year-old, six-foot-five, 180-pound Bailey said he'd worked in his uncle's construction business in Lyons, New York, telling the social worker he was a member of three trades unions in New York having worked in Brooklyn and Manhattan.

Now he was penniless, friendless, and in need of a job and place to live in a strange city.

After spending nights in a shelter on the city's outskirts, Bailey said he registered with the state unemployment agency and was referred to a job with a painting contractor.

Bement arranged a room for Bailey at 2121 Vine, blocks away from Rose's home. It was a two-room apartment for fifteen dollars a week rent. Bement provided vouchers for one week's rent and a week's worth of food.

Throughout their conversations, Bement thought Bailey odd as he was always looking down, acting dull-witted, and rather indifferent.

On October 21, the day after Rose Winstel's murder, Patrolmen Lowell Allen and Rick Rhodes of the Vice Squad responded to a call Bailey was behaving wild and violent. Refusing to calm down, Bailey was arrested for failure to cooperate. After briefly holding Bailey, he was transferred to the Rollman Psychiatric Institute.

Detective Kersker visited Rollman's on October 26 to interview Bailey, but his social worker and psychiatrist said Bailey had worsened and he was heavily sedated. Kersker returned the next day.

Bailey was conversant, Kersker also noted Bailey acting passive and dim-witted while constantly looking down at his shoes. Bailey told Kersker on the day of Rose Winstel's murder he was visited in his apartment, where he was reading and listening to music, by the building owner hanging curtains and a man working on the space heater.

Police sent Bailey's fingerprints to the FBI without a match. Still, Bailey remained a suspect.

The detectives continued combing through the evidence. Pubic hair samples were mixed—some Negroid, others Caucasian. Fingerprints lifted from a beer can found on the hillside behind Rose's house did not match

The Cincinnati Strangler

any of the suspects.

In the end, despite the massive effort to find Rose's killer, the investigation struggled to gain traction. The neighborhood was rife with potential suspects, but no single lead stood out to investigators. As police worked overtime, combing through clues and following leads, life on Vine Street Hill hardly missed a beat.

Cincinnati Police bulletins sent to departments across the country netted reports of similar cases, some meriting a follow-up, sprinkled with confessions from some claiming to be The Strangler.

As the local investigation dragged on, the sense of fear in the community deepened. Residents were left to wonder when, not if, the maniac terrorizing their city would strike again.

People in Cincinnati suddenly felt trapped in a nationwide downward spiral of violence they'd seen on TV and read about in newspapers, but those were faraway big cities, certainly not Cincinnati.

Why is this happening?

Electric massager and cord from
the murder of Rose Winstel

Detective chief Jacob Schott and Detective Kenneth Davis comb the hillside where Mathilda Messer's body was found. (Cincinnati Enquirer)

Part II: Investigation

City of Cincinnati

W. C. WICHMAN
CITY MANAGER

DEPARTMENT OF SAFETY
DIVISION OF POLICE
CINCINNATI, OHIO 45214

HENRY J. SANDMAN
DIRECTOR OF SAFETY

STANLEY R. SCHROTEL
POLICE CHIEF

& OFFENSES
STRANULATION HOMICIDES 1965

KRECO........OCT.12,1965   FULL MOON CYCLE...OCT.10,1965

                    51- DAYS

HARRINGTON..DEC.2,1965   "   "   "   DEC.8,1965

              ~~STRANGULATION HOMICIDES 1966~~

                            124
DANT....APRIL,4,1966   "   "   "   APRIL,5,1966
                        ~~66-DAYS~~ 67

MESSER.JUNE,10,1966   "   "   "   JUNE,3,1966

                       66-DAYS   12
BOWMAN,AUG.15,1966   "   "   "   AUG.~~20~~,1966

                     ~~59-DAYS~~ 134

HOCHHAUSLER,OCT.12,1966   "   "   "   OCT.13,1966

        CALCULATED TIME OF NEXT STRANGULATION HOMICIDE IF SUSPECT NOT APPREHENDED

DECEMBER 10,TO 15,1966   "   "   "   DEC.11,1966

REASON FOR EXTENDED PERIOD OF TIME BETWEEN DECEMBER 2,1965 AND APRIL 4,1966,POSSIBLE
CONFINEMENT,OR SUSPECT OUT OF TOWN.

NO STRANGULATION OFFENSE OCCURRED AFTER 15,DAY OF ANY MONTH.

Winstel — Oct 19-20 — 7 days

Chapter 8
Help In the Stars

In the mid-1960s, the world of the paranormal was in vogue. Extrasensory Perception (ESP), parapsychology, astrology, and even Ouija boards captivated the American public, and Cincinnati was no exception. With eyes turned toward the skies of the Space Age, psychics also garnered the interest of those seeking guidance and answers, including police.

One resident of Madeira, a Cincinnati suburb, wrote to the Homicide Squad, telling them she was receiving ESP impressions about The Strangler. While sitting alone in a darkened room, she saw a man in her mind spending time in sewers, watching people and places. Her visions painted a picture of a young man with "hair less tightly curly than most negroes," a face not unpleasant, with beautiful eyes, a short nose, and an unusually large jaw. Homicide did not respond.

In the 1960s, Peter Hurkos, a Dutch psychic known for assisting criminal investigations, gained fame after Boston police consulted him in their Boston Strangler cases. His work impressed skeptical local police and citizens alike, leading to public calls for Cincinnati to seek psychic help in finding the local killer. However, Colonel Schott dismissed the idea, saying, "I just can't see us going into court with a case solved by ESP."

Meanwhile, WCPO-TV's general manager, Robert D. Gordon, took matters into his own hands. He contacted another well-known Dutch clairvoyant and psychic detective, Gerard Croiset, enclosing a transcript of a September 28, 1966, feature on the Cincinnati murders. Croiset was well known in the U.S. from the popular television program, The Baffling World of ESP, hosted by Basil Rathbone. Croiset acknowledged the request but replied he was not available to assist as he was occupied investigating the disappearance of the three Beaumont children in Australia.

A group of concerned Cincinnati housewives also penned a plea to Croiset, begging for his assistance. "Please help us find a murderer at large here in Cincinnati," they wrote. "Where does he live? Where should the police look for him? What's his name? Can you answer these questions for us? If the police won't call on you, we'll take matters into our own hands."

Beyond psychics, and over official departmental skepticism, Homicide Sergeant Russ Jackson, a well-respected investigator, did look to the heavens for answers, studying phases of the moon in the search for patterns among the murders. Balding and stocky, Jackson was known as a tenacious detective dedicated to leaving no stone unturned. His resemblance to FBI Director J. Edgar Hoover often garnered whispers at crime scenes. "FBI's here," fellow officers would joke. Despite the teasing, Jackson was highly respected across ranks.

Jackson's fascination with lunar cycles was triggered by a letter from J.S. Gunderman, an advertising manager at Dubois Chemicals. Gunderman wrote of seeing "interesting patterns" among the murder dates. He laid out a theory examining days of the week: the first murder occurring on a Thursday, the second on a Monday, the third

The Cincinnati Strangler

on a Friday, and the fourth on a Tuesday. Each day was spaced four days apart, forming a strange symmetry.

Intrigued, Jackson developed his own chart, starting with the full moon of October 10, 1965, two days before the attempted murder and rape of Elizabeth Kreco. Fifty-one days passed before the Harrington killing on December 2, 1965. Another 124 days led to the murder of Lois Dant on April 4, 1966, the day before the full moon. Jackson speculated confinement or other absence led to the lapse of time.

Sixty-seven days passed before the death of Mathilda Messer on June 10, a week after the full moon. Sixty days later, circled and marked with a question mark, was the August stabbing death of Barbara Bowman, three days after the full moon. A lengthy 134 days elapsed before the October 12 murder of Alice Hochhausler, the day before the full moon. Seven days after her death, Ruth Winstel's body was found.

Jackson's theory hit a snag with the Winstel murder being only seven days after Hochhausler's death, defying his moon-based timeline.

Gunderman proferred a prediction the next murder would occur on December 17, 1966. Jackson agreed, extending his predictive window that the next murder would fall between December 10 and December 15, noting that no strangulation murder had ever occurred after the 15th of any given month. He missed that target by just a day.

"I am not generally superstitious, but I am beginning to get that way," Gunderman told Jackson.

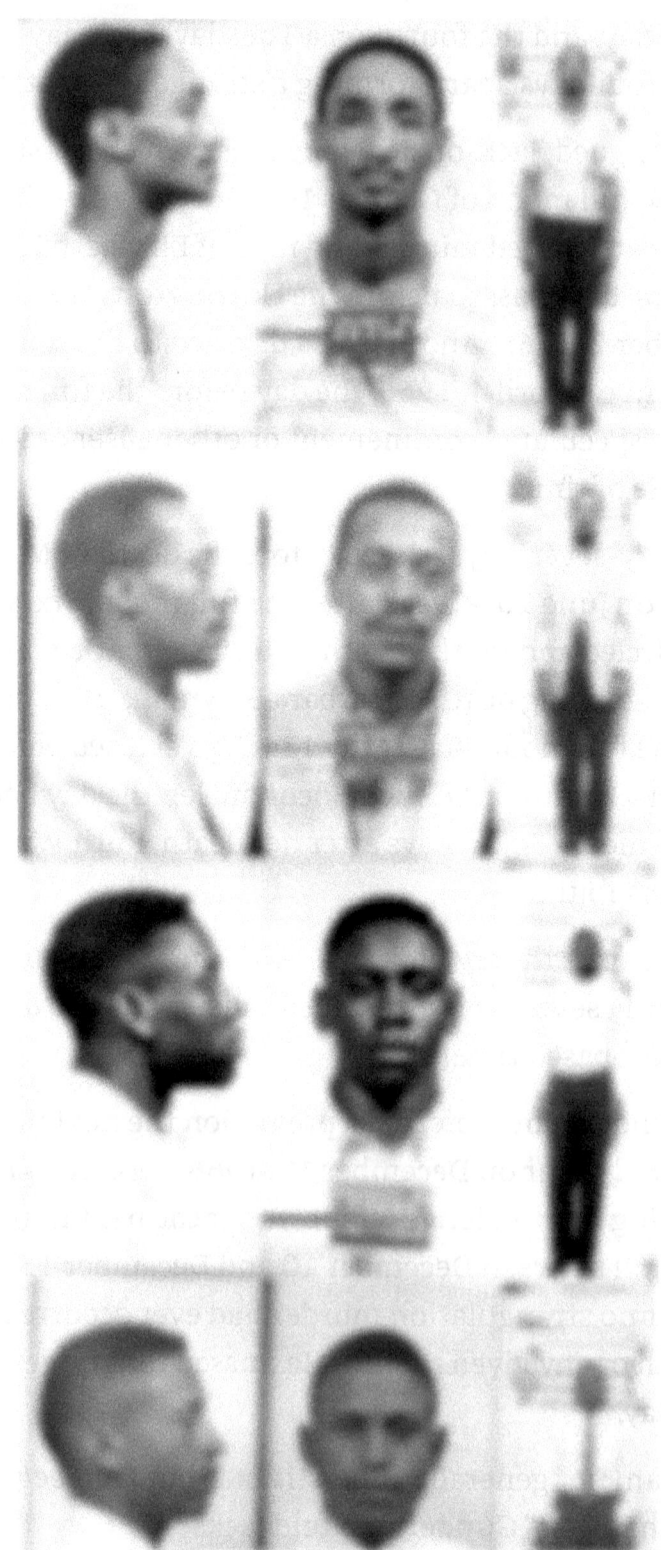

Chapter 9
Dragnet

5000-Man Posse Beefs Up Hunt For Sex Maniac

Sensational front page headline of the October 14, 1966 Cincinnati *Enquirer* following the death of Alice Hochhausler. (Newspapers.com)

Detectives John Huber and Robert Groppe were tasked with organizing the evidence from the Winstel murder for shipment to the FBI. Both men were seasoned veterans of the Cincinnati Police Department—Huber joining the force in 1941, and Groppe in 1949 after serving in the Navy during World War II. Tagging and bagging evidence was a routine job, but it provided a welcome break from the relentless pressure of the murder investigations that had consumed the department for nearly a year. Groppe's widow's peak and intense gaze lent him a sharp, probing demeanor during interviews with suspects, while Huber's broader, easygoing face helped him play the role of the "good cop."

After shipping the Winstel evidence, Huber and Groppe returned their attention to the murder of Lois Dant. They joined Sergeant Jackson at the Crime Bureau to review the case files. Though there was no need to re-canvass the neighborhood, certain neighbors and businesses, particularly those employing Black men, warranted another visit. For Huber, this case was personal—he had grown up in Price Hill, close to the Dant apartment, and now lived across the street from Carson Elementary, the school he attended as a child. Murder had struck his childhood neighborhood, and he was determined to find answers.

Their first stop was to talk with Regina Albers, the wife of the custodian at Dant's apartment building. Albers was painting the unit across from where the Dants had lived. She told the detectives that the building's owner, George Emmick, did not hire Black men for odd jobs.

The detectives then looked into records from companies and subcontractors involved in building the United Dairy Farmers convenience store at the corner of Rutledge and Glenway six years earlier, specifically information on Black employees. This led the detectives to eight men, by this time in their late twenties to early sixties.

A roofing subcontractor from the construction project provided three more names, including one worker who had previously worked at The Verona apartments.

Another lead took the detectives to Jewish Hospital to speak with their security office about Percy Lee Brooks, a man whose photo had been selected by witnesses from the Lark Café as something of a look-alike to the suspect. Brooks, a tall, thin World War II veteran, had a 1958 mugshot from a burglary charge that failed to clear the grand jury, his only note in police records. There was a suggestion that the FBI sketch artist used this mugshot as the basis for one of their renderings of the killer.

James William Delaney, who drove a Yellow Cab for

a month in 1965 before being dismissed after three suspensions, also drew the investigators's attention. Delaney had a clean criminal record, but photographs taken of him during the time he was brought in for questioning may have been the model for another police sketch. Two years later, he was arrested for drunkenly hurling epithets at the District Seven police officers and firefighters at Engine Company 16 on East McMillan, one officer telling a reporter, "Every time he gets loaded, he makes the rounds." Delaney merited thirty days in the Workhouse for his bluster.

Huber and Groppe returned to Alma Cox, the neighbor across Rutledge from the Dants whose ringing doorbell went unanswered the morning of the slaying. Now, eight months later, Cox remembered waiting for a bus across Glenway from Rutledge between 10:30 and 10:35 a.m. when she saw a Black man in his early twenties, light complexioned, five-seven to five-nine, about 130 pounds, wearing a three-quarter-length dark car coat, a dark bebop hat with a small brim, carrying a light blue sweater rolled up under his arm, running up Rutledge Avenue to Glenway. From her vantage point, he stopped at the corner, looked over each shoulder before running across Glenway, and hopped into a car. She could not describe the car and had never seen the man in the neighborhood. Cox told the detectives she'd been overly excited when she previously spoke with them, causing her to forget, but she might be able to identify him under similar conditions. Groppe showed her a mugshot array, and Cox picked out a man who looked somewhat similar.

The detectives revisited Myrtle Wilhelmy, who had

been driving along Glenway Avenue the morning of the Dant murder. Wilhelmy recalled seeing a two-tone pinkish-and-tan car with two distinctive black spots on the right door and fender. When she was shown a photo of a 1959 Chevrolet, the car identified in the Hochhausler case, she said it wasn't the car she had seen. She thought the car she saw looked more like a 1954 Chevrolet.

The next day, the detectives spoke with a bread truck driver who had been making deliveries in the area around the time of the Dant murder. He didn't recall much but directed the detectives to potato chip or milk trucks that might have been in the area.

Huber and Groppe tracked down the milk truck driver, who remembered seeing a car parked on Glenway between a café and a chili parlor, but didn't recall any cars in the United Dairy Farmers lot. He did remember a dog running across the lot with its chain still attached.

The detectives also met with John Faust, the head of custodians for Cincinnati Public Schools, who provided a list of former janitors at Carson Elementary. The detectives also spoke with Bill Powell, the head janitor at Carson who'd worked there since 1959. Powell mentioned a few temporary workers, telling the detectives none of the men seemed capable of the murders. The one inescapable factor to police was the color of their skin.

Next, the detectives returned to Reidy Janitor Service, located across Rutledge from the Dant apartment, to talk with the owner, Ben Reidy. They sought the names of men responding to Reidy's help-wanted ads posted in The Cincinnati *Enquirer* during August 1966. The ad read:

"JANITOR Must know all phases of cleaning and janitorial services and must pass strict security. Call for interview. REIDY JANITOR SERVICE." What stood out to the detectives was the ad asking applicants to "apply after ten a.m.," the time Lois Dant's body was found.

Reidy provided the names and contact information for former employees, as well as those he'd fired over the years. Despite the ads running months after Lois Dant's murder, the detectives pursued this lead, recording lists of names and numbers from Reidy's notes.

The pair employed deception in their telephone canvass of Reidy's numbers. Without identifying themselves as police officers, they asked to speak with the individual, saying they'd received an out-of-state communication for someone with the man's name and were seeking to confirm if he was the intended recipient. They also asked for birth dates and occupations to help verify their identities.

From the canvass, police brought in one man, with no criminal record, for questioning about his knowledge of Rutledge Avenue and Price Hill. Another man, five-foot-ten and 143 pounds, who did not own a car, was questioned about his knowledge of Price Hill. A forty-six-year-old construction worker whose photograph was picked by Reidy from a mugshot array was also questioned. In another case, a fifty-six-year-old janitor who stood under five-foot-three and weighed 186 pounds had no connection to Reidy or Price Hill. In all of these cases, the detectives collected head and pubic hair samples to send to the FBI for analysis.

Though Reidy was eager to help police, perhaps over-eager as he proved to be an unreliable witness. Plus, much of the contact information he provided was outdated, making it virtually impossible to track down the individuals.

The man picked from a mugshot array by Alma Cox was forty-year-old Hiawatha Johnson, a Navy veteran from World War II. Johnson came to the Crime Bureau for an interview. He was five-foot-eleven, weighed 195 pounds, and had been drinking before his arrival. Johnson knew Reidy from working with him at Arlan's discount store and frequently picked him up at his Rutledge Avenue home. The interview ended with detectives collecting head and pubic hair samples from Johnson for FBI analysis.

Reidy's information was typical of the quality of leads police were receiving—minor, non-violent incidents at worst, with ages and dimensions varying wildly. The only consistency was race. Public fear, stoked by police and media, placed enormous pressure on the investigators to find the killer. But the lack of clear evidence drove them into desperate roundups, terrorizing Black neighborhoods and inflaming already heightened racial tensions during a period of social unrest.

Despite the fruitless leads, Huber and Groppe continued interviewing men connected to Reidy's janitorial service while also preparing for the grand jury hearing on the October murder of Virginia Wolpert.

A visibly drunk and nervous man walked into the Town and Country Restaurant on Dixie Highway in

Northern Kentucky late in the morning of October 26 seeking a room. Told he was in a restaurant and not a motel, the man wrote a note that he handed to the cashier. "Call police. Tell them to check apartment 18 at 2985 W. McMicken Ave. Tell them they'll need an ambulance."

Patrolman Giles Frost was dispatched to the apartment where the caretaker opened the door to apartment #18 where Frost found the lifeless nude body of Virginia Wolpert. The forty-seven-year-old widow had been badly beaten about the face, but there was no immediate sign of strangulation.

Wolpert lived in apartment #14 and was hosting her eldest son, Joseph, a Navy electronics specialist, his wife, and two children as they were visiting during Joseph's move from the West Coast to his new posting at the Great Lakes Naval Station. They were staying in his mother's apartment while she spent the night in the apartment of her paramour.

The next morning, Virginia did not show up at work and there was no answer at the door of apartment #18. The report from the Northern Kentucky restaurant gave the answer.

As police converged, a crowd gathered outside the apartment complex. Everyone was certain this was another strangulation murder.

Veteran journalist and copy editor at The Cincinnati *Enquirer*, Eugene Fiske, was arrested in a motel near the restaurant. The White divorced father of three told detectives he'd been drinking and was jealous Wolpert had been paying too much attention to other men. Fiske admitted he "slapped her around a bit to straighten her out."

Fiske was tried on a second-degree murder charge, first-degree homicide ruled out lacking evidence of premeditation or another crime. Fiske pled guilty to first-degree manslaughter and was sentenced to five years of probation, an outcome that remained in the minds of many Cincinnatians.

Groppe met with Aelred Birkemeier, the caretaker of Rapid Run Park, which was near the Dant apartment. He inquired about any Black employees Birkemeier might have had, but Birkemeier said his two employees had always been White. However, several Black teenagers had been sent by the Youth Corps. Birkemeier provided their names and addresses.

Groppe and Huber's unscientific pursuit of suspects based solely on skin color was unusual for them, given their reputation as technological pioneers within the police department. Groppe was fascinated by investigative technology, while Huber developed databases for tracking criminal behavior and indexing firearms. However, the investigation's lack of direction, along with immense pressure to catch the killer, led them and others down increasingly desperate paths.

Assistant Chief Schott directed the entire police force not to hesitate stopping suspicious persons, adding that if they don't give the right answers, bring them in. Schott promised officers the full support of the department, backing them "one-thousand percent."

Among those swept up was a forty-two-year-old

man accused of following an elderly White woman in the West End in October. He had been a day janitor at the University of Cincinnati since 1945 and worked at the Kroger Building at nights, but, as the detectives reported, "we could not eliminate him from any of these homicides through his work record." Additionally, he owned a brown and white 1959 Chevrolet, which added to their suspicions.

In Price Hill, a man approached Captain Howard Rogers at an intersection, telling him about following a 1959 Chevrolet driven by a Black man with scratches on his face. Police followed up, but the tip went nowhere.

The detectives followed up on a disturbing 1962 incident at Good Samaritan Hospital, where an attendant had been caught sexually assaulting a corpse. A cleaning woman had reported finding the man fondling the breasts of a deceased female, and several weeks later, she discovered the same man sexually abusing another corpse. The man had been fired in 1962 and reportedly moved to Los Angeles in 1964. Despite the time elapsed, Huber and Groppe considered the possibility that this man could be connected to the current murders.

Cincinnati's Black community was not immune to anxiety over the roving killer, while all too familiar with police inattention to their neighborhoods. Specialist Jack Browning of District Four responded to a call from a resident of Kennedy Heights, a predominantly Black neighborhood. The woman was upset because she had been reporting sightings of a two-tone 1959 Chevrolet slowly cruising her neighborhood, studying houses over four months without any police response.

The NAACP's local president, Dr. Bruce Green, continued his appeal to the Black community to come forward with information about the killer. Reiterating his offer to act as an intermediary between citizens and the police, Green made a heartfelt plea on local TV: "Surrender to me or any other leader in the Negro community." He knew that catching the killer would benefit everyone, regardless of race.

Tensions between Black residents and White law enforcement escalated. At an October meeting with civil rights leaders and community organizations, City Manager William Wichman agreed that representatives from these groups would meet weekly with Captain Elmer Reis, head of the Cincinnati Police Community Relations Bureau, to improve relations. Aside from the promises heard before, participants expressed frustration over the heavy-handed police tactics generating a climate "dangerous to Negroes in the city."

Police exhausted their search of the 15,000 registrations of 1959 Chevrolets in their quest to find the car identified by Beth Hochhausler. As Huber and Groppe focused on the Dant case, Detectives Rutledge and Meiszer turned to the murder of Barbara Bowman, the Yellow Cab passenger stabbed to death in August. They narrowed their search based upon descriptions of the suspect with registered cabdrivers. From this, Rutledge and Meiszer culled fifteen photos of current and recently separated cab drivers, supplementing this collection with another thirty mugshots for potential witness review.

By November, the investigation was losing momentum. Money for extra policing ran out, and officers re-

The Cincinnati Strangler

turned to regular eight-hour shifts at the beginning of the month. The department's focus on The Strangler had delayed the appointment of a new police chief, as candidates were too consumed by the investigations to prepare for the Civil Service exam required for the job.

Walter Evans, an ex-convict who had served three years for forging a $155 government check, was anxious to stay on Detective Meiszer's good side. Evans told Meiszer about Levi Kemper who'd been arrested for the rape of his own sister. Evans befriended Kemper in prison where Kemper "seems to have a problem with his sex activities with these other women." Though Evans had little concrete information, he hinted that Kemper had bragged about his luck with women in recent months. In exchange for this tip, Evans asked if the detectives could help him out of some unpaid parking tickets?

Despite Evans's questionable credibility, Kemper became a suspect, particularly because of his September arrest for rape. Reddish-black hairs recovered from Kemper's coat were found to match hairs discovered at the Hochhausler crime scene, drawing further suspicion.

Tips continued flooding in. One woman wrote about how her husband had tried strangling her in 1958. An anonymous caller informed Station X that her husband had not been home on the nights of the murders, describing him as a cruel man. Employees at a printing company and at a produce business each reported a Black employee who had been absent on the days of the killings. Another tip came from a post office worker, who said his Black co-worker was writing a book about sex and middle-aged women. A woman called to remind police of the teenager who beat her badly enough to lose sight in one eye, but was only fined and released.

Amid this frenzy, there were also false reports. A forty-two-year-old woman falsely claimed she had been lassoed around the neck with a piece of rope in the early hours of the morning. The report prompted a massive response—twenty-eight patrol cars, thirty officers, and two canine units—but it was later revealed to be a fabrication. The woman admitted she had made up the story to get attention from her children and was sentenced to six months in the Workhouse.

Another false report came from twenty-eight-year-old Betty Ruth Ross, who claimed that a man had tried to strangle her in the basement of her North Fairmont home with a wire. Sergeant Jackson suspected she wasn't telling the whole truth, especially after she and her children suddenly disappeared. They were later found in Atlanta, Georgia, where police concluded that the attacker was likely an ex-boyfriend of Ross's mother-in-law.

In November, a fifty-year-old Black housekeeper, Ruby Gore, was returning to her employer's home on Elmhurst Place in the O'Bryonville neighborhood. Ruby grew up in the West End, but was working and living in her White employer's spacious home. Gore had been shopping in her employer's absence when she realized she was being followed. Walking along the driveway toward the front door, a soft-spoken voice called out, "Hey, you remember me?" Gore turned to see a young man dressed in light-colored clothing advancing toward her holding a length of rope. She screamed and the man fled. The police response included canine units searching the

The Cincinnati Strangler

area for hours without finding anyone but they did find a fifteen-inch length of rope on the steps to the home.

Jackson dismissed Gore's attacker as a "frightener," not the killer terrorizing the city. Too often, reports from Black Cincinnatians were discounted by police.

As false reports and panicked rumors swirled, violent attacks continued. A thirty-five-year-old Black mother on Mulberry Street was raped by a man who had hidden in her bathroom. He knocked her to the ground, choked her with a piece of clothesline, and assaulted her. The victim managed to bite him several times before passing out. She described him as Black, in his mid-thirties, about six feet tall, and wearing checked brown boots and a stocking cap. Despite the use of a clothesline, police dismissed any connection to the string of murders, calling it "incidental to the attack."

As 1966 was drawing to a close, solid leads eluded police and Jackson feared that his predictive calendar was correct—the killer would strike again soon.

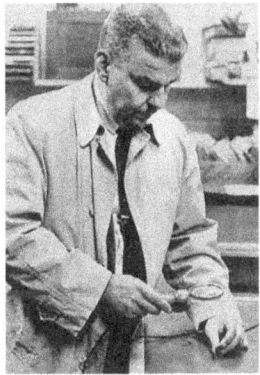  

Three of the lead detectives working the Strangler cases, from left, Charles Rutledge, Bernie Kersker, and Robert Meiszer. (Rutledge & Meiszer - True Detective; Kersker family)

Kenner Toy Company facility at 912 Sycamore Street where Sandra Chapas worked. (Barbara and David Day)

Chapter 10
Pursuit

Midnight, Friday, December 9, 1966

Christmas was approaching, and twenty-two-year-old Sandra Chapas was working the night shift at the Kenner toy factory on Sycamore Street, near the Hamilton County Courthouse. Her job that night was to place the knobs on Easy-Bake Ovens, Kenner's most popular toy for Christmas 1966.

The night shift suited Sandra. It allowed her to spend days with her infant son, while her husband, George, a Macedonian immigrant, worked as a painter. But that night, George didn't show up, forcing Sandra to do what she had been repeatedly warned against—walking home alone at night through the dark, empty streets of downtown. Her shift ended as the calendar flipped from Thursday, December 8, to Friday, December 9.

Sandra crossed Sycamore Street onto narrow East Court Street. To her right loomed the six-story courthouse, while to her left stretched a long row of three-story apartments, followed by an empty, foreboding six-story warehouse. A slight turn to the right on East Court brought her to the open area in front of the courthouse. There, the covered vendor stalls of the Court Street Market stood along the sidewalk, eerily quiet. As she neared Vine Street, where East Court becomes West Court, she knew her apartment was only a short walk away.

Just then, Sandra noticed a cream and tan two-tone car—possibly a Chevrolet—parked in a lot on Court. A man sat behind the wheel. When she glanced his way, the man started the engine and drove off.

Sandra quickened her pace toward her apartment, located on the fourth floor of a walkup. As she climbed the first flight of stairs, she heard footsteps on the stairs behind her but couldn't see who it was. Sandra felt certain it was the man from the two-tone car.

Her heart raced along with her feet up the stairs. Reaching her door, Sandra banged until her mother unlocked it,. She slammed it shut and locked it behind her. Safe at last, but rattled.

With his prey out of reach, the man looked around, seemingly confused, before running down the stairs, fleeing the building.

The commotion roused Ethel Hall, a resident on the floor below Sandra's, whose door was slightly open awaiting her husband's return home from work. Hearing the noises, she peered into the hallway and saw a short, slightly built Black man looking around her floor and then quickly exiting down the stairs.

At the same time, Ethel's husband, Lawrence Hall, approached the building just as the man ran out of the front door and sprinted toward his car. The late hour and the Black man's frantic behavior piqued Lawrence's curiosity. As the man jumped into a two-tone car and sped off, Lawrence made a mental note of the license plate: Ohio 3097AA.

Chapter 11
"There's a dead lady in your elevator"

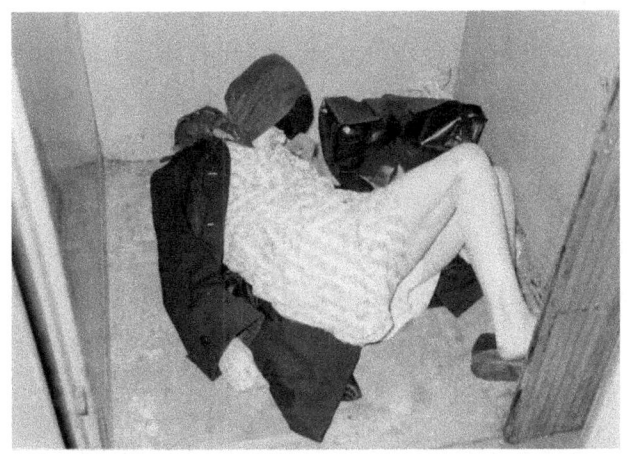

Lula Kerrick in The Brittany apartments elevator.
(Cincinnati Police Department)

Friday, December 9, 1966

Rain fell on this unseasonably warm December morning as police cars filled West Ninth Street in front of The Brittany apartments. Inside the building, four blocks from where Sandra Chapas lived, an old woman lay dead on the floor of a small elevator, a stocking drawn tight around her neck.

Residents were baffled, none knowing who the woman was. Her identity was obscured by a black lambswool hat pulled over her face. Few residents knew the victim anyway.

Eighty-one-year-old Lula Kerrick was a reclusive longtime resident in The Brittany. Those who did know her were principally aware of her devout Roman Catholic faith. Lula attended 6:30 a.m. Mass at St. Peter in Chains Cathedral every morning, often returning in the afternoons to pray the Rosary. Her commitment to her faith drove Lula to make the daily quarter-mile walk to the cathedral, despite it becoming increasingly difficult for her to do so.

That morning, Lula left her fourth-floor apartment before six a.m., long before the sun broke the horizon. A light, warm rain was falling, so she covered her hat with a plastic brown rain bonnet tied under her chin. Despite the warmth, she wore a red-checked wool scarf around her neck, tucked beneath her black raincoat. Underneath, Lula was wearing a simple white smock patterned with flowers and vines.

At Mass that morning, Philip Muldoon, a caseworker in the Hamilton County Probation Office, took note of the elderly woman seated in front of him. She appeared frail, struggling to kneel and then stand.

"She put her hands down on the floor to push herself up from the kneeling bench at the communion rail," Muldoon later recalled. "Then she grabbed her back as if there was a hitch in it. She struggled to her feet and walked slowly back to her seat."

After the service, Monsignor Francis Kennedy noticed Lula praying in a side chapel. She left the cathedral around 7:30 a.m., exiting through the righthand transept door to Eighth Street. She faced the towering Romanesque granite structure of city hall before turning right, reversing her earlier route. Walking east on Eighth, she crossed Elm Street under the shadow of the grand Isaac M. Wise Temple with its distinctive minarets.

Making her way to Ninth Street, as she often did, Lula stopped at Edith's Grocery, a small market at the corner of W. Ninth and Elm Streets where she picked up a few provisions.

Edith's was owned and operated, from seven-to-seven, six days a week, never on Sundays, by fifty-five-year-old Edith Graven. Edith stood at five-three and weighed about ninety pounds, but she feared nothing and no one. A small grocer made little money off the likes of Lula; the exterior signs reflected the lion's share of Edith's business – Beer & Wine. She was known as a feisty old bird in her grocery who wielded a can of Lysol to get rid of unwanted customers, but gentle as a lamb at home. She was also known for giving to the truly needy. Someone once wrote in chalk outside Edith's, "This woman will feed you."

Local and national celebrities came into Edith's and Izzy Kadetz kosher restaurant catercorner from the studios of WLW, home of the popular chat and entertainment shows of Ruth Lyons, Paul Dixon, and Midwestern Hayride.

Edith lorded over her store at the cash register beside the front door where she stood on a platform to keep an eye on everything. Her coal-black hair fell barely past her shoulders when down, was set into a bun atop her head every Sunday. She typically wore a white button-down blouse with pearls and a sweater, always wearing long navy or black pants, or long skirt with white shoes and socks.

As patrons at the Belmont Café across Race Street attested to Cincinnati *Post* reporter Polk Laffoon for a 1977 feature, "Edith knows more about what's happening than Johnny Bench knows about baseball."

Like Lula, Edith also grew up in Kentucky, giving the pair a shared experience, mutual comfort, and a familiar twang. Lula had no friends and no interest in making friends, but Edith was different.

Lula gathered enough foodstuffs to fill a medium brown paper bag, Edith twisting the top and fitting it inside Lula's large black leather tote. Lula slowly lifted the long handles of the bag with her thin, boney right hand, quietly leaving the store with a nod and thank you.

As Lula trudged along Ninth Street toward her apartment, Stanley Brandt, a fellow resident at The Brittany, passed her on his way home from his overnight shift at the post office. He said hello, but Lula, true to form, kept to herself.

"She never bothered anybody," her niece Anne O'Brien Adams would later recall. "She didn't mix with anybody; she just wanted to be by herself."

Walking slowly along Ninth Street, Lula reached the stone steps leading to the building's front door. Stooped under the weight of her large bag, she struggled up to the front door. A man came behind her, offering to hold the door. Lula bristled at the unsolicited help but said nothing. The man asked her where he could find the custodian. Again, Lula didn't respond, continuing down the long hallway toward the small, European-style elevator at the end. As the man followed, Lula grew increasingly uncomfortable, though remaining silent. She pressed the elevator button, and when it arrived, the man held the door open for her.

As soon as she stepped inside, the man struck. With

a sudden, brutal blow to the back of her head, Lula was sent crashing into the elevator's wall. Her false teeth clattered to the floor beside her crumpled body. The man pulled a stocking from Lula's leg and quickly fashioned a garrote, tying a knot in the center. Wrapping the stocking around his fists, he yanked hard, the knot digging into Lula's throat as her feet kicked helplessly against the elevator's doorframe. Her last breath escaped in a raspy death rattle as the man loosened his grip. Lula's legs hung limply over the threshold.

The killer rummaged through Lula's bag, finding her meager billfold. But before he could escape, the elevator buzzer sounded. Startled, he quickly tucked Lula's legs inside the elevator, closed the scissor door, and slammed the outside door shut, fleeing through the building's front entrance. The elevator rose to the third floor, carrying Lula's lifeless body.

At eight a.m., third floor resident Charles Minor opened the elevator door to the horrifying sight. Shocked, he quickly retreated to his apartment to call police. The doors closed and a minute later, the buzzer sounded again, dispatching the elevator to the fifth floor where Sam Collins made the same gruesome discovery as Minor. He, too, called Station X.

The Brittany soon swarmed with police. Outside, Sergeant Moore directed officers to canvass the area, especially focusing on the onlookers gathered across Ninth Street. Outside the entryway, Homicide Detective Bernie Kersker slipped past the growing crowd of reporters. Always well-dressed in a dress shirt, necktie tied tight, and sport coat, Kersker was the picture of a professional detective. A short-brimmed felt Fedora was perched on his head and the stub of a stogie stuck out from the corner of his mouth.

Kersker, a no-nonsense investigator and former Merchant Marine, was unfazed by the rain. He'd crossed the treacherous Atlantic uncounted times during World War II, supplying fighting forces around the Mediterranean. Kersker was a genuine character, an excellent investigator who'd seen it all and was always happy to share war stories with young beat cops who all looked up to him. Not all detectives were tolerant with young police officers but Kersker always took time to impart lessons on rookies, many inspired to follow the experienced detective's path to Homicide. New detectives taking a ride with Detective Kersker were in for a musical treat as Bernie, an avid barbershop quartet singer, would serenade a passenger with tunes evoking a time gone by, amid the aroma of cigar smoke.

Today, his focus was on solving this heinous crime and brining the killer to justice, and Detective Kersker was regarded as the best. His attention to detail was legendary and his notes always kept investigations on track. His control of crime scenes included one where he chastised the chief of police who quickly left the scene.

Kersker entered the long, narrow hallway of The Brittany's lobby. He glanced toward the elevator, where detectives Robert Groppe and Wilbert Stagenhorst were already at work, using portable spotlights and flashlights in the search for evidence. Stagenhorst waved Kersker over for his thoughts. After briefly conferring with his colleagues, Kersker headed up the old staircase to begin interviewing residents, as Moore directed.

Kersker began his inquiries by speaking with seventy-four-year-old Charles Minor, the third-floor resident who had first called Station X. Next, he interviewed Sam Collins, a retired electrical supplies salesman, who had been unfortunate enough to discover the body moments after Minor. Collins had called for the elevator just after Minor's discovery and was, likewise, deeply shaken by the sight of the woman sprawled inside. Like Minor, Collins rushed to his apartment to call the police after the grisly discovery.

Lula's body remained in the elevator until patrolmen arrived to remove her on a gurney. With calls coming from both the third and fifth floors, Kersker faced the challenge of determining where the murder had actually taken place. As was the case in all strangulation cases, evidence was absent on where the attack occurred. Detectives still did not know the name of the victim. This spread Kersker's attention over the three possible floors of The Brittany's six-stories.

The detective was especially frustrated no one could identify the victim due to her hat being pulled down over her face. Sam Collins believed he recognized her but couldn't recall her name. To confirm the victim's identity, Kersker sought out Charles and Anna Marshall, the long-time caretakers of The Brittany. The Marshalls had worked in the building for twenty-nine years, so Kersker hoped they might know the elderly woman who had been murdered.

Preparing Mrs. Marshall for the grim task ahead, Kersker asked, "What kind of nerves do you have?"

"I've got good nerves," she replied.

In response, the detective deadpanned, "There's a dead lady in your elevator."

After evidence had been gathered and photographs taken, detectives removed the hat from the victim's face. Mrs. Marshall immediately recognized her: it was eighty-one-year-old Lula Kerrick.

Louisa "Lula" Kerrick was born in 1885, the eldest of eight Kerrick children in Payneville, Kentucky—a small rural town about 150 miles southwest of Cincinnati. After leaving the family farm, Lula moved to the outskirts of Cincinnati during World War I to work in an ammunition factory. Following the war, she returned briefly to Kentucky before moving to Norwood on Cincinnati's outskirts with her sister Grace. When Grace married in 1926, Lula relocated to downtown Cincinnati, living above Frank Kieswetter's shoe repair shop on Vine Street.

Over the years, Lula moved around several Over-the-Rhine locations in the city's basin, but the neighborhood was becoming increasingly unsafe for an elderly woman. One memory that lingered with Lula was the mugging she suffered in 1960 at her Elm Street apartment, when a man knocked her to the ground and stole her purse, containing only $1.50. After that incident, Lula, then seventy-five, moved into The Brittany, believing the area to the west of OtR safer and close to St. Peter in Chains Cathedral, where she attended Mass daily.

The Brittany, though once home to professionals due to its convenient downtown location, had fallen into disrepair by the mid-1960s and was mostly occupied by elderly tenants, like Lula. The six-story red-brick building's once-pristine appearance had deteriorated. The thick Chinese Red paint on the interior walls and trim was chipped, and the tiled floors were grimy from age and neglect. The mailboxes lining the wall next to the elevator had been broken into over time and stood unrepaired. A towel was stretched across the threshold of the rear hallway door to block the wintry air.

Lula and her sister Grace shared an interest in real estate, investing together in properties, including a three-unit house on Warsaw Avenue in Price Hill that they bought in 1947. Ironically, this property was the other half of the duplex where Barbara Bowman lived.

Despite the increasing danger downtown, Lula was reluctant to leave. She hated the idea of being far from her beloved church, but Grace was concerned for her sister's safety. She begged Lula to move in with her in Price Hill. Lula finally relented, promising to make the move in the coming weeks.

Before she could make the move, Lula's story came to a tragic end.

On December 15, 1966, Lula's funeral was held at St. Mary Magdalen Catholic Church in Payneville where she was laid to rest in the church cemetery among her family members.

As the initial investigation into Lula Kerrick's murder continued, word leaked to the press that police had made a significant breakthrough. Reporters were eager to hear about the latest developments, but Lieutenant John

McLaughlin cautioned them not to jump to conclusions, emphasizing that any suspect at this point could not yet be considered "a prime suspect."

The murder of Lula Kerrick came almost exactly one year after the discovery of Emogene Harrington's body in her apartment building on December 2, 1965. Emogene's murder remained unsolved, along with, now, the other five victims. Now, Cincinnatians feared that the city's phantom strangler had struck again.

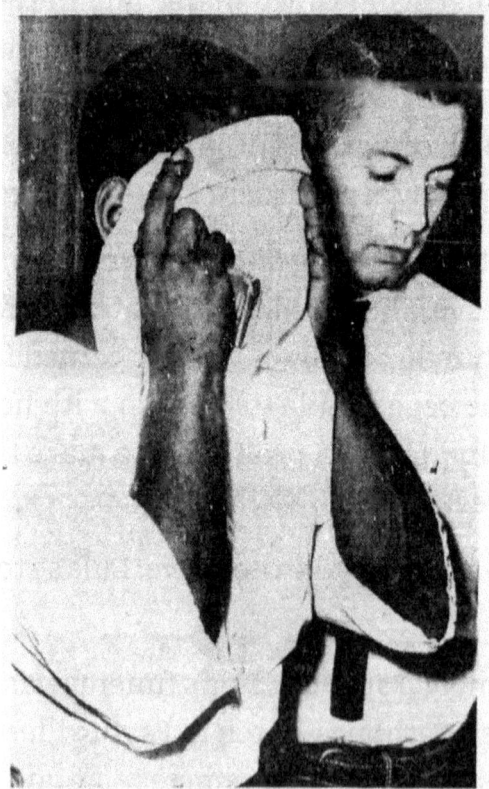

Suspect Covers His Face
... he's Posteal Laskey, 29

The Cincinnati *Enquirer* on December 10, 1966. From the day of his apprehension throughout the trial, Posteal Laskey and the Cincinnati Strangler were daily news. (Newspapers.com)

Chapter 12
Apprehension

Friday, December 9, 1966

This morning's 7:30 a.m. roll call in the Homicide Squad show-up room was anything but routine. As detectives clattered into their wooden school desks scattered about the room in front of the line-up stage where Detective Chief Schott focused their attention on the owner of the automobile license plate number reported from the attempted assault of a woman on West Court Street after midnight. He was driving a two-tone car; meaning, this could be the killer.

Unbeknownst to detectives as they met, eighty-one-year-old Lula Kerrick was walking home from St. Peter's Cathedral, past City Hall where detectives were meeting in the basement, just blocks from her fate.

When the call came in about the discovery of another potential Strangler victim, a surge of urgency swept through the squad. Solving these murders and putting an end to the terror was the top priority of the investigators who were clinging to a hope that this new incident could finally bring a close to The Strangler. But experienced detectives knew better than to rush to conclusions that could vanish in a blink.

Detectives Robert Bluhm and Paul "Skip" Morgan were assigned to follow up on the license plate of the two-tone car tied to the attempted assault on Sandra Chapas. The news of another strangulation murder enhanced the importance of the suspect they were seeking. Perhaps the two incidents were connected? They occurred only blocks and hours apart.

Leaving the basement headquarters in city hall, Bluhm and Morgan set off for 1820 Freeman Avenue, the West End address of Posteal Laskey, Jr., the registered owner of the car bearing Ohio license plate number 3097AA.

The detectives arrived at the three-story, freestanding row house where a woman answered the door. They asked for Laskey but the woman, who identified herself as Posteal's mother, told them he wasn't home. He was working at the Adam Wuest mattress factory. Thanking her, the detectives returned to their car to visit the Wuest warehouse, also located in the West End.

From Freeman Avenue, the detectives drove along Gest Street, a major commercial thoroughfare traversing the western basin, to the Wuest mattress warehouse. The detectives pulled into the rear parking lot where they spotted the two-tone 1962 Oldsmobile Holiday Coupe, license plate Ohio 3097AA. While to two-tone color scheme matched the car police had been seeking, the design of the Olds was wholly unlike the 1959 Chevrolet with its distinctive tail fins police assiduously sought.

Bluhm and Morgan entered a small doorway dwarfed at the base of the six-story, 19th-century red brick factory and warehouse. They climbed a set of old, creaky wooden stairs to the office of superintendent, Art Hunsicker, who called Laskey to his office. Laskey was a "floater," filling in wherever needed. Checking his time card, the detectives saw Laskey arrived for work at 8:07 A.M.

The Cincinnati Strangler

Coming from the second floor, Laskey stepped from the slow-moving freight elevator dressed in a blue and black-checked button-down cardigan sweater, and white t-shirt. Identifying themselves, Bluhm and Morgan told Laskey they wanted to speak with him about a matter they'd rather discuss at the station. "Am I under arrest?" Laskey asked. They assured him he wasn't, explaining it was a routine matter. They promised to bring him back to work as soon as things were cleared up.

There was no need for handcuffs as they escorted Laskey to their unmarked car for the drive to detective headquarters. On the way, Bluhm and Morgan noted in their report, advised the suspect of his Constitutional right not to speak with them, a result of the recent Supreme Court decision in Miranda v. Arizona.

Circling City Hall, the detectives drove past St. Peter's Cathedral where Lula Kerrick attended Mass earlier that morning.

From Ninth, they passed through a stone portico and into the open-air interior courtyard of City Hall, parking their vehicle outside the double doors into the Crime Bureau and Detective Headquarters.

The single-room Homicide office was inside the larger Crime Bureau in the basement of city hall, next to the offices of Chief of Police Stanley Schrotel and his assistant chiefs.

The windowless office, blue walls stained with smudges, scrapes, and nicotine, was only eleven by twenty-two feet in size with barely enough room for the desks of twelve Homicide detectives, piled high with case files.

While The Strangler cases were THE top priority, they shared desktop spaces with stacks of other murder cases – shootings, stabbings, domestic rage, and life gone awry.

As telephones rang amid the banter of detectives as they clattered away at manual typewriters churning out reports while trying to weave evidence and witness interviews into a narrative telling the story of the crime and circumstances.

Paperwork was soul-crushing and the seriousness of their daily tasks weighed heavily upon the minds of Homicide detectives, but the collegial back-and-forth and bawdy jokes helped break the mix of monotony and tension; the grinding routines and horror scenes. Detectives loved the hunt, the investigations, and interrogations, despite being witness to relentless inhumanity, a victim's blood, horrible wounds, the tears of those left behind, and witnesses in shock from what they had seen. The crude arrogance of murderers and rapists who cared little for anyone beyond their own emotions and carnal drives piled on the shear exhaustion, and growing cynicism from listening to endless pleas of innocence from the guilty. Homicide detectives suffered the daily horrors in silence beyond talking with other detectives, careful not to bring the job home. Some fell prey to alcoholism, mental illness, and the vices too often plaguing the generation of Great Depression survivors and wartime veterans amid the seismic cultural upheaval of the 1960s. Police, once regarded as cornerstones of the community were now being eyed with suspicion and resentment. Cooperation with investigators was rapidly evaporating.

Two primary detectives were assigned to each of the

strangulation cases, while also carrying their responsibilities for investigating the daily sturm und drang of homicide and manslaughter, death and misery, interviewing witnesses, checking leads, writing reports, and appearing in court.

Nothing remains of the police offices in the City Hall basement today but it was the inspiration behind the police department scenes in John Huston's 1950 noir masterpiece, The Asphalt Jungle. Huston and the film's art director, Randall Duell, traveled to Cincinnati to scout locations and were attracted to the basement setting. Unable to shoot in the tight confines of a working police department, Huston and Duell had the Cincinnati headquarters reproduced on a Hollywood soundstage.

Located across the courtyard from the City Jail, Laskey was led into a small interrogation room in the corner of Homicide.

Bluhm and Morgan led Laskey into a small interrogation room on the corner of the Homicide office. It was a spartan setup: a steel table, a few chairs, and a leather recliner for suspects who agreed to take lie detector tests. Though inadmissible in court, police would tell suspects that taking a polygraph could prove their innocence. When offered the test, Laskey declined.

Lieutenant John "Mac" McLaughlin, head of the Crime Bureau, kicked off the questioning at 1:30 p.m. McLaughlin knew Laskey well—he'd arrested him before, back in October 1965, for the brutal assault of Judy Buckner in Clifton. Laskey had received probation for that crime, and McLaughlin was still holding that against him. While McLaughlin tried to keep his contempt for Laskey under wraps, his questions dripped with suspicion.

The interrogation continued, with Lieutenant Colonel Schott, Sergeant Jackson, Sergeant Moore, and Detective Kersker joining the session. They were Homicide's best interrogators, but Laskey remained quiet, offering only firm denials. He did offer details of where he was the previous night.

To the detectives, Laskey's demeanor seemed almost indifferent—detached. A musician by trade, his encounters with police taught Laskey the importance of silence under pressure. Those run-ins stretched back to youthful truancy and petty theft, escalating in later years into violence, particularly targeting women.

In March 1957, Laskey was discharged from the army with less than honor following the assault of a female German civilian in a bar. He was in constant trouble for going AWOL and a variety of misconduct charges culminated in a court martial on the assault charge and discharged. Trouble followed Posteal Laskey back to Cincinnati.

Returning to his hometown, in November Laskey was arrested for the violent assault of fifty-nine-year-old Celia Purvis in her Hyde Park apartment. Found guilty of Assault with Intent to Kill in February 1958, he was sentenced to the Lebanon Correctional Institute and remained there until his release in February 1962. He served his final year on parole.

Christmas Eve 1963 found Laskey in trouble again,

this time arrested in Covington, Kentucky, for stalking a twenty-four-year-old woman and stealing her purse. He served two years in the Kentucky State Penitentiary before his release on August 21, 1965. Barely more than a month later, Laskey was arrested for the brutal assault of twenty-six-year-old Judith Buckner outside her Clifton apartment. Two days after that assault, Laskey was taken into custody, admitting to attacking Buckner, while claiming he had no recollection of why. In November 1965, he was sentenced to three years of probation, something prosecutors would use to their favor in 1966.

Now, under the intense scrutiny of the city's top investigators, Posteal Laskey, Jr. remained cool and collected.

Despite their suspicions, the detectives knew they didn't have enough to keep Laskey in custody indefinitely. But with mounting evidence and rising public pressure, they also knew this interrogation wasn't the end—it was just the beginning of something much bigger.

Inside the interrogation room the questioning turned to Laskey's 1962 Oldsmobile, the two-tone vehicle parked at his workplace with the license plate matching the one reported from the early morning attempted assault. Detectives asked if anyone else had driven the car, to which he responded that, no, he was the only one driving the car. Volunteering information about his whereabouts, Laskey told them he had been practicing with his band, Tiny Charles and the Rocking Outlaws, at the Playboy Bar on Colerain Avenue in the West End. He left the bar with "Tiny" Charles Bullock around 10:30 p.m. and headed to Bullock's apartment on Reading Road. Laskey recalled leaving the apartment around 11:45 p.m., driving through the city and passing the Arcade Bar at Green and Vine, as well as the Elm Inn on Elm Street, without stopping.

Next, Laskey said he briefly visited Club Ramon, a known musician hangout on Stark Street in the West End, where he spoke with two unnamed women before leaving after just five or ten minutes. He claimed to have gone to Chums restaurant in Walnut Hills for a cup of coffee, but since he didn't recognize anyone there, he left and returned to the apartment he shared with Brenda Jackson on Reading Road. When Brenda came home around 3:00 a.m., she woke Laskey to tell him she was leaving for Florida with some friends.

When asked about the strangulation murders, he shook his head, maintaining his innocence with a slow, deliberate motion. As the line of questioning shifted from his car to the murder of a woman found strangled just blocks from the attempted assault, Laskey sensed the interview was turning into something more serious than a routine inquiry. The detectives's demeanor hardened and their smiles disappeared, signaling the gravity of the situation. Realizing the interview had transitioned into interrogation pointing to murder, Laskey went completely silent.

In the end, Laskey was officially arrested on a misdemeanor charge of attempted assault. Detectives noted having reminded him again of his right to remain silent and to have an attorney present. He initially asked to call his mother but then changed his mind, saying, "I'll wait awhile and see what happens." A misdemeanor charge meant he'd be released.

Detectives Bluhm and Morgan left the interrogation room to visit the victim, Sandra Chapas, while Detectives Paul Ellis and Marvin Lacy drove to confirm Brenda Jackson's whereabouts with her father, Warren Jackson, who verified that Brenda had indeed left for Florida.

Fingerprints were taken and mugshots snapped. Laskey was then placed in handcuffs and escorted across the courtyard to the City Jail. His paperwork was handed to the front desk patrolman who entered Laskey's details by hand into the jail's logbook. Hair and blood samples were taken for analysis in both the police and FBI labs for comparison with evidence from The Strangler cases.

Laskey would be held overnight to face a hearing in Police Court the next morning. He was taken to a heavy, wrought-iron gate within a wrought-iron wall at the jail's entrance. A guard, called the turnkey, used a large, old skeleton key to unlock the door. The sound of the gate slamming shut behind him resonated with the finality of incarceration. Though he tried to remain calm, the sound of the closing gate was too familiar—the sound of separation from the outside world.

To his left was a stairway leading up to the courtroom where he would face his initial hearing the next morning. To his right was a barred window through which he was ordered to hand over the contents of his pockets to the guard on the other side. The items were logged: a brown leather wallet, a "green yellow gold wristwatch," a Ronson lighter, keys on a chain, a yellow gold man's signet ring, and thirty-four cents.

At the far end of the corridor was another iron gate, identical to the first. After passing through, Laskey was taken into the main holding area of the jail. There, he was handed a blue Workhouse inmate uniform and a large brown paper bag to store his personal clothing, which would later be sent to the FBI for forensic analysis. Detectives were particularly interested in comparing the samples of Laskey's blood and hair with the evidence found at the crime scenes. Laskey's blood type—A Positive—did not match the Type O blood central to the early police investigations. No longer would this suspect be released simply because his blood type did not match their assumptions.

Posteal's brother Dave and their mother brought a fresh set of clothes for his court appearance: a gray sport jacket, slacks, a white shirt, dress shoes, and clean underwear. They entered the imposing west entrance of city hall, under the stone arch where Cincinnati Police Department was chiseled, but were not permitted to see Posteal. His family members were told only that he had been arrested for assault and would be arraigned the following morning.

Meanwhile, Laskey sat in his small jail cell, convinced he could handle the assault charge. Even if it resulted in a probation violation, the most he expected was a short stint in the Workhouse.

On Saturday morning, Patrolman George Pille drove to the Wuest factory to tow Laskey's car into custody, but the parking lot gate was locked. The vehicle would have to wait until Monday.

The Cincinnati Strangler

Inside the City Jail, Laskey, along with other detainees awaiting arraignment, was allowed time to change into his court clothes. Laskey would ascend the staircase to the courtroom where he would face an uncertain fate.

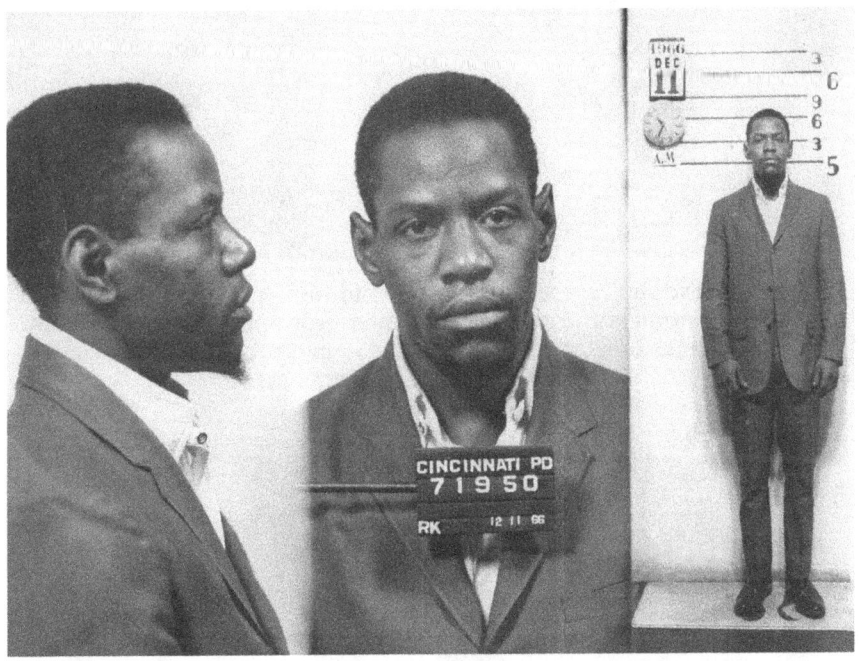

Posteal Laskey, Jr. mugshots at the time of his December 1966 arrest for assault in the pursuit of Sandra Chapas and probation violation. (Cincinnati Police Department)

Left, sketch made by FBI specialist Carl C. Mumford, Jr. from descriptions by Lark Cafe customers and cabdriver Sol Thompson of the man with whom Barbara Bowman left. On the right is a 1965 mugshot of Posteal Laskey, Jr. (Cincinnati Police Department)

Absent crime scene evidence, police rounded up known criminals, along with young, old, fat, thin, short and tall men sharing only the color of their skin. Eyewitness accounts and public tips led police in different directions.

Chapter 13
Probable Cause

Saturday morning, December 10, 1966

Police Court was a whirlwind of bravado and fear. Car thieves, embezzlers, and small-time crooks filled the morning's docket. Some defendants had lawyers, most did not. Posteal Laskey, Jr. was among the latter.

When his name was called, Posteal stood before Judge George S. Heitzler who asked if he had legal representation. Laskey replied that he did not. The judge motioned for Cincinnati's lone public defender, Eddie Fidler, to step forward.

Fidler, a familiar face in Police Court, was always overwhelmed by the sheer volume of cases he was asked to handle. As the city's only public defender, his resources were stretched thin. His office, tucked away in a forgotten corner of City Hall, was little more than a repurposed elevator shaft and storage closet, a relic of a bygone era.

After briefly consulting with Laskey, Fidler entered a plea of "Not guilty" on the assault charge stemming from the attempted attack on Sandra Chapas. When asked if he wanted a jury trial, Laskey declined, hoping that a swift resolution would clear his path forward.

Assistant prosecutor Donald Hardin presented Sandra Chapas's complaint, amplifying the community's collective angst over the past year. Hardin painted Laskey as a dangerous figure capable of violence, emphasizing the anxiety gripping the city as women lived in fear of the Cincinnati Strangler. Judge Heitzler agreed and found Laskey guilty of assault, not an attempt to assault. Heitzler said Laskey's actions clearly instilled fear and posed a direct threat, enough to warrant the straight assault finding.

Heitzler sentenced Laskey to six months in the Workhouse for the assault, adding $200 in costs. He also ordered him held without bond on the probation violation from his 1965 conviction. The sharp rap of the gavel hit Laskey's ears like the slamming of the jail's iron gate.

Judge Heitzler, a gaunt figure with a balding head, was a former prosecutor and staunch Republican, known for his stern demeanor. His time as a prisoner of war in Germany during World War II left its mark on him, shaping his no-nonsense approach to the law. Now presiding over Hamilton County Municipal Court, he handled misdemeanors and referred felony cases to the Court of Common Pleas.

Informed that Laskey was a target of a murder investigation, Heitzler appointed two defense attorneys to represent him in his assault appeal: Donald Roney and Burton Signer, both former assistant prosecutors. A murder charge warranted dual representation.

Judgment on the probation violation was deferred until a December 20 hearing, pending the outcome of Laskey's appeal on the assault conviction. Delay or not, Laskey knew his fate was sealed in a system stacked against him.

The six-month Workhouse sentence, plus extended detention for the probation violation, provided police

The Cincinnati Strangler

and prosecutors time to keep digging.

After sentencing, Laskey was handcuffed and escorted downstairs to change into his prison uniform, and then across the courtyard to the Crime Bureau, to face a lineup.

Posteal Laskey, Jr., third from the left, in a December 1966 lineup.
(Cincinnati Police Department)

# Part III: Death and Justice

Yellow Cab 870 disabled at Ring and Grand, where Barbara Bowman was murdered. (Cincinnati Police Department)

Chapter 14
Taxi Into Darkness

Police felt certain they had their man. They were convinced he was the elusive killer terrorizing the city. However, the lack of physical evidence from the murder scenes left them with little to definitively tie him to the crimes. In collaboration with Hamilton County Prosecutor Melvin Rueger, detectives turned their focus to the August 1966 murder of Barbara Bowman as a possible breakthrough in their investigation. The key connection between Laskey and the murder was his experience driving a Yellow Cab in 1962.

Saturday, August 13, 1966 – Sunday, August 14, 1966

It was a miserable night, turning into the early hours of Sunday. Thirty-one-year-olds Charlotte Barnhart and Eileen Aultz found themselves navigating through a dark and rain-soaked Price Hill, desperately searching for the Summit Apartments. The two had been driving around unfamiliar streets after attending a birthday party in the western suburbs, hoping to find their friend's new apartment for a late breakfast.

Charlotte drove a maroon 1957 Oldsmobile while Eileen did her best to navigate. After stopping short of Grand Avenue, they asked a passerby for directions, but he didn't know where the apartment was located. Frustrated, they turned left on Grand, realizing the neighborhood of small bungalows didn't seem like the right place for a big new apartment building. Still lost, they turned south toward Warsaw Avenue.

It was then that Eileen spotted a Yellow Cab parked along the street. Hoping for guidance, Charlotte pulled up next to the cab, and Eileen rolled down her window, shouting, "Sir, could you tell us where the Summit Apartments are?" Peering through the rain, they saw no driver behind the wheel, but instead, a Black man leaned over the front seat from the back.

Eileen repeated her question, but the man remained silent. Slowly, he climbed over the front seat on the passenger side, while a White woman suddenly sat upright in the backseat. "My God, that's a White woman!" Eileen exclaimed to Charlotte, alarmed by the sight.

The driver still didn't answer Eileen's repeated questions. Instead, he slid into the driver's seat, his face cloaked in dim light, his furtive movements conveyed panic. Turning the ignition key to start the engine, his left hand gripped the steering wheel while his right shifted the car into reverse, his head turned away as the looked out the rear window. Penned in by a curb to the right, a parked car ahead, and Charlotte's car to the left provided the man with only one escape route – in reverse. The cab sped up the hill, its tires squealing on the slick pavement.

Confused and certainly not fully grasping the situation, Eileen chuckled nervously. "Well, you know what he's probably doing," she said, and Charlotte continued down Grand, away from the fleeing cab, in search of the Summit Apartments. After asking for more directions from a group of boys outside Red's Deli, they were told the new apartment building was on Lehman Road, the very street they had already passed earlier.

The Cincinnati Strangler

As they traversed Grand again, they noticed the Yellow Cab parked sideways across the entrance to Ring Place. The cab's headlights were off, and no one was inside. Not wanting to get further involved, they drove on.

What Charlotte and Eileen didn't see, however, was what had happened just moments before. After the cab sped away in reverse, the driver skidded to a halt just over the hilltop. The driver realized he'd be dangerously flying into Glenway Avenue in reverse, a bad idea even at this early-morning hour. As the vehicle stopped, the rear door swung open, and the terrified passenger tumbled out onto the rain-slicked pavement. Dazed and disoriented, she kicked off her as she scrambled barefoot toward the darkness of Ring Place. Her eyeglasses also fell to the pavement as she ran, leaving her practically blind. In terror, she stumbled over the curb at Ring where she fell face-first onto the asphalt.

The driver, startled by her sudden escape, quickly weighed his options. Should he let her go, or ensure she would never be able to identify him? He chose the latter.

The cab surged forward, its wheels thumping over the first curb, nicking a stop sign before bottoming out on the second curb, breaking the cab's tie rod, rendering the vehicle uncontrollable. The massive vehicle rolled over the woman's outstretched leg, shattering her right ankle and leaving the bones protruding grotesquely from the skin. She screamed in agony, unable to move as the driver approached. He pulled out a knife and stabbed her repeatedly in the neck—once, twice, seven times—before fleeing into the night.

At around two-thirty that morning, nineteen-year-old Ruth Ann Bailey was returning to her mother's home on Ring Place after spending the evening with Raymond "Bud" Walker, the forty-year-old owner of the Broken Drum Café. Ruth Ann, married since age fourteen, was lonely as her husband was serving in Vietnam an a U.S. Army medic and was spending the weekend with her mother on Ring Place.

As the couple neared Ring in Walker's 1965 Simca, they found the street blocked by a Yellow Cab. Lying beside the cab, in the pouring rain, was a woman. Her leg appeared broken, and she was clearly in distress. Walker and Bailey assumed it was a car accident and that the driver had gone for help. The woman was moaning in pain, her crumpled dress riding up to reveal her undergarments. Despite the seriousness of the accident, help had not arrived.

A man driving a 1958 Chevrolet Impala pulled up and asked, "Where's the police?" Walker told him they thought the driver had gone for help. The man offered to drive to the nearby police station to report the accident.

As the Impala drove away, Walker knelt down beside the injured woman, asking, "Did the taxi hit you?" She tried to respond, but her words were unintelligible, her eyes, staring directly into Walker's, were filled with silent pleading. Blood flowed away in the rain and into darkness.

Minutes passed, and the man in the Impala had yet to return. Growing concerned, Walker and Bailey decided to drive to the District Three police station themselves, just a quarter mile away on Warsaw Avenue.

Meanwhile, Sol Thompson, a Parkway Cab driver, passed the scene carrying a fare. He saw the abandoned cab but did not stop, continuing on his route.

At the District Three police station, Walker and Bailey reported what they still believed to be an auto accident to the desk officer.

Thomas Tomaseck, the man in the Impala, had driven in the wrong direction but eventually found his way to District Three where he could see Walker and Bailey inside. He returned to the scene at Ring Place, finding no one had yet arrived to help the woman.

Sefton was on duty at District Three at 2:45 A.M. when Walker and Bailey arrived to report an auto accident. Sefton called the Traffic Bureau to report an accident involving a taxi with an injured passenger and put out a radio call for officers to respond as he left the station.

Sefton arrived at the scene in a scout car, a station wagon equipped with a gurney for transporting an individual to the hospital or morgue.

Patrolman Richard "Fish" Salmon was pulling onto Grand from Warsaw when the call went out for assistance, arriving at the same time as Sergeant Virgil Hall, about three minutes after the radio call, and just ahead of Patrolman Robert Ramstetter. Sefton was pulling the gurney from the scout car when Salmon arrived to help lift the victim onto the gurney and into the back of the car. Sefton had tried enlisting Tomaseck to assist, but it proved too upsetting as Tomaseck began vomiting and asked to be excused.

Blood was running down the street in a foot-wide stream, washing away in the rain, making it difficult to identify the source of the flow. The victim was barely conscious, groaning as she was lifted onto the stretcher and into the scout car. She began furiously kicking, requiring her being strapped down. To the officers, this was an auto accident, as reported by Walker and Bailey, an assessment officers brought to the hospital with the victim. To investigators, there were tire marks on the curb, extending across the victim's leg. The taxi's fender was dented, and a mark on the stop sign indicating an accident, but the bleeding around her upper torso confounded the initial assessments.

As Sefton and Ramstetter were taking the victim to the hospital, Sergeant Hall opened the closed cab and sat in the driver's seat. The key was in the ignition of the Checker Marathon, so Hall started the engine and tried moving the cab to clear the intersection, but the steering wheel went round and round without engaging the wheels.

Patrolman Salmon opened the back door where he observed a Sunday *Enquirer* on the back floor and necklace beads scattered across the backseat.

Sergeant Rupert Meiering arrived from the Traffic Bureau shortly thereafter, noting the damage to the cab and the victim's extensive injuries. But something wasn't adding up. He began to question whether this was merely an accident.

"How in the devil can she have got hurt so bad with

so slight of damage to the cab? Maybe she'd fallen out?" Where were her shoes and purse? And, where's the driver?

Meiering climbed into the back seat of the cab on the passenger side, closed the door, and then pushed on the heavy steel door to see if it possibly could have flown open on its own.

"You couldn't push it open with your shoulder," Meiering reported, later assuring investigators, "I didn't touch anything inside the cab." Meiering wasn't sure if anyone had touched anything in the cab. His conclusion was a "hit-skip," a hit-and-run incident.

Sol Thompson, the Parkway Cab driver, returned to the accident site a few minutes before three o'clock and Salmon asked Thompson to examine the taxi. What stood out to Thompson was the absence of a trip sheet. He radioed the dispatcher that Yellow Cab #870 was in an accident and had been abandoned. Thompson's supervisor, Harry Burks, came to the Ring and Grand where he told police Yellow Cab #870 had not been checked out that night.

Thompson left on a call at three-fifteen to pick up another fare at the nearby Queen's Tower for a location at the base of the hill. A woman in her thirties, wearing a blue raincoat, got in, saying only, "thirteen-hundred block of Bowman, please." Bowman Avenue and its surrounding streets remain today a ramshackle collection of houses and wooded thickets along the hillside of a tough White neighborhood where a Black cabbie would feel uneasy in the early morning darkness.

Dropping off his fare, Thompson drove on Bowman to a right turn on Mistletoe when he heard the whistle of someone hailing a cab. Stopping, he saw no one, so Thompson started to leave when the right rear door swung open, and a Black man jumped in.

"Take me to Brighton," was all he said.

Making a left on State Avenue from Mistletoe, the fare slid across the seat directly behind Thompson, making him nervous fearing a robbery, so he asked the man to move.

Driving toward the two-tiered Western Hills Viaduct, Thompson asked his fare – upper or lower?

"Take the top deck," the man replied, handing Thompson two soaking-wet one-dollar bills, Thompson looked in the rearview mirror but the man's deep-set eyes were hidden in darkness, his image flickered under passing streetlights.

Reaching the traffic signal at the end of the viaduct, Thompson asked, "Now which way?"

"Up Central to Baymiller," so Thompson turned right on Central Parkway toward downtown to a quick right on Short Colerain to Central Avenue, cutting across Brighton Corner, and then Baymiller into the West End.

On Baymiller, as they approached Bank Street and Bloom School, across the open space of Dyer Park, Thompson noticed a police car a block away on Freeman. Thompson assumed his passenger also must have spotted the patrol car as before the cab came to a full stop at the intersection, the man opened the door, saying, "This is good enough," and ran away, disappearing between two residential buildings on the southwest corner. Thompson put the two soaked dollars covering the $1.40 fare in the glovebox.

Feeling uneasy about the combination of an accident involving a stolen taxi, and then picking up a drenched Black man in an area one would never expect to find a person of color, Thompson recounted the events to his dispatcher who called police while Thompson continued working. The dispatcher radioed Thompson that police wanted him to come to St. Mary's Hospital in the West End.

Doctors at St. Mary's Hospital fought desperately to save the woman found lying in the street, but her injuries and blood loss were too severe. Her jugular vein had been severed among seven deep stab wounds to her neck. The attending physician, Dr. Rodriguez, noted the wounds had been inflicted by a sharp instrument, likely a knife. There were also marks around her neck, suggesting a possible strangulation attempt. Despite the best efforts of the medical staff at St. Mary's, the woman whom no one knew was pronounced dead at 4:30 a.m. The cause of death: exsanguination—she bled to death.

Thompson arrived at the hospital where he told police about the man who rode in his cab earlier that night. He estimated the man to be between twenty-five and thirty years old, five-foot-eight, and weighing 140-155 pounds. The man had a thin build, dark complexion, and spoke with a raspy, rough voice, as if he had a cold. He was wearing a hip-length black leather jacket, a navy-blue knitted watch cap, dark pants, and black shoes.

Thompson distinctly remembered the man was soaking wet when he got into the cab.

Police searched Thompson's vehicle, but found no evidence linking the passenger to the murder. There were no signs of blood or mud in the backseat to indicate the man's involvement in a murder. The only clues to his having been in the cab were two wet one-dollar bills in Thompson's glove compartment.

Back at the intersection, Patrolman Sefton returned from the hospital and was instructed to call Homicide. Detective Ken Davis, Cincinnati's first Black Homicide detective, was roused from his sleep to respond. A towering six-foot-two man weighing 250 pounds, Davis was a gentle soul. He'd broken many barriers placed in his way, joining at a time when White officers refused to even stand next to Black officers in photos. A veteran of the Marine Corps and the Negro Baseball Leagues, Davis endured relentless internal racism, but his accomplished police work earned him a place in the Homicide Bureau.

Davis arrived at the same time as fellow detectives Tom Gardner and Sergeant Charles Berghausen. The rain had eased in the early morning darkness to a crime scene poorly lit by a single streetlight. Their flashlights were insufficient in the search for clues, so Berghausen requested floodlights from the fire department to improve visibility.

Under the brighter lights, the detectives began finding crucial evidence. Sergeant Karl Schulz discovered a folded five-dollar bill and a set of keys lying in the gutter, streaked with blood. The items were passed along to Sergeant Hall, who handed them to Patrolman Salmon for safekeeping in his pocket. As the search continued, Sergeant Meiering spotted a broken paring knife in the grass about ten feet from where the body had lain. Two shoes were found scattered along the west side of Grand, thirty feet apart from each other. Glasses lay on the opposite side of the street.

Meiering carefully measured the scene:

The victim laid six feet from the sewer on Ring Place and nineteen feet from Grand Avenue.

The knife was found about fifteen feet from the body and just one inch from the sidewalk.

Her eyeglasses were nearly 106 feet away on the east side of Grand.

Her right shoe was found about forty-three feet away, directly across from the glasses.

The left shoe lay fifty-six and a half feet from the right.

The two shoes were thirty-two feet, ten inches apart.

As dawn broke, Detectives Fritz and Cortland searched along Ring Place where they found more items—a pocketbook on the sidewalk and a billfold a short distance away. Nearby, at the corner of Ring and Underwood, they found a rope entangled with beads. The layout of the evidence suggested the driver fled into the darkness of Ring Place, tossing away the pocketbook, billfold, and rope as he escaped.

The billfold revealed victim's identity: thirty-one-year-old Barbara Rose Bowman of 2500 Harrison Avenue.

In daylight, Homicide Detective Bernie Kersker retraced what appeared to be the killer's escape route from the evidence found along the way. From Ring, stogie dangling from his lips, the detective walked right on Underwood Street, so narrow it was little more than a path. As he continued down steep Underwood, Kersker speculated the killer turned into the darkness of Stoddard and Kingston Places leading to Warsaw Avenue toward the panoramic mirage on the horizon of the urban basin.

Over a half-mile from where Kersker started, a staircase to the left offered a shortcut from Warsaw down to Wilder known as the Peerless Street Steps. Cincinnati's steep hillsides are laced with some four-hundred concrete staircases built to facilitate travel up and down the vertical inclines. At Wilder and Glenway, the killer was close to the freedom of the dark, flat, industrial basin. Just four-hundred feet ahead lay Gest Street, an industrial flatland leading to the labyrinth of the West End.

Instead, if the killer was the man who jumped into Sol Thompson's cab at Bowman and Mistletoe, he would have traversed the face of the hill, in a racially hostile area, for another half-mile, instead of disappearing into the urban flats.

Patrolman Sefton brought photographs from the victim's billfold to 2500 Harrison Avenue, a six-bedroom house in Westwood, broken into six individual apartments. The caretaker remembered Bowman living there some three to four years before but had no idea where to find her. Joan Birch, a first-floor resident, remembered

Barb Bowman and that she had a friend living nearby at 2887 Harrison, a garbage-strewn property owned by a notorious hoarder, Karl Kleve. Bowman's friend, Frances Baird, a teller at Welfare Finance, told Sefton that Barb was living at 2909 Warsaw Avenue, four blocks from Grand and Ring. Baird and Birch accompanied Sefton to the morgue to identify their friend.

Detectives entered the side entrance of the clapboard duplex where Bowman lived to reach her second floor apartment where they used the key found at the murder scene to enter. Inside, police found a purple octopus doll sprawled across the patchwork quilt atop her bed, China cats of all shapes and sizes were arrayed about the apartment, with houseplants sitting on windowsills and tabletops.

Barb's landlord, Cliff Sizer, told the *Enquirer*, "She was a very lonesome person, I know this." According to Sizer, Barbara was "a very desirable tenant – clean, neat, and a nice person," telling the Cincinnati *Post*, "She went to church twice a week, if she possibly could."

"I really think if somebody had married her and settled down, he would have had one of the best of wives," *Enquirer* reporter Margaret Josten quoted Sizer as saying. "She wanted affection – that's what she really wanted."

Another second-floor resident, an unnamed graduate student, said Barbara typically went out on weekends, though he never saw who she went out with, he had the feeling she was dating an entertainer, possibly named Norbert.

According to the grad student, Barbara typically

arose around 6:30 A.M. to get ready for work and she returned home around 5:30 P.M., keeping a punctual routine.

Bowman's apartment offered scant clues, other than the contact information for her parents and that she worked at Mehl Manufacturing. Max Anderson, personnel manager at Mehl, said Barbara Bowman worked as a secretary at Mehl since October 1964. She was a quiet, diligent worker without any personnel matter of note.

Barbara's parents, John and Edith Bowman, lived in Beechgrove, Indiana, near Indianapolis, about one-hundred miles from Cincinnati. They told police Barbara was born in Indianapolis in 1934 and grew up in Cincinnati where her father was a machinist for the New York Central Railroad. Barbara attended Western Hills High School and graduated from the cooperative work experience program at Woodward High School in 1953.

"Barby is a 'bright-eyed" girl – Has a nice big smile and pleasing disposition," read the note in her high school yearbook.

In 1962, Bowman's father was transferred back to Indiana. After six months, Barb returned to Cincinnati, when she lived with Frances Baird and Joan Birch on Harrison Avenue. She moved into her Warsaw Avenue apartment in June 1965. From her friends, police gathered Bowman dated frequently but never any Black men, as far as anyone knew.

Police also found that, in June 1964, Bowman had given birth to a child at Good Samaritan Hospital and the infant was placed into adoption. The father was reportedly a man named "Pedro." Police connected Pedro with Pete, the author of a strange letter found in Bowman's tidy apartment. Dated March 20, 1966, "Pete" outlined the last time he'd been with Barb.

"Dear Barb," Pete's letter opened with an apology for the way he behaved last time she was in Indianapolis, explaining when he got off work, he drank "2 cans of beers and a half of a half of a pint of V.O. on my way to get you. Then we went to Don's and I drink there."

Returning to his place, Pete kept drinking until, as he wrote, "really hit me all at once. The bed was going round & round and after you left, I really felt sick. I know you didn't have a nice time and again I say I am sorry."

He then mentioned his poor finances, implying he needed money, but was willing to pay for Barb's return to Indianapolis, "If you like to come home this weekend I'll pay for your bus ticket."

Pete added, "P.S. By the way how was our sex we had the last time I do remember you saying about did I have some rubber. I said no but I did have some."

Pete was never identified in the investigation.

At her apartment, Sizer helped Barbara's parents pack their daughter's belongings for return to Indiana.

John Bowman retired from the railroad in 1970 and passed away the following year, Edith Bowman saying at the time of his death, "He never got over Barbara's murder. Barbara was all we had."

John Bowman was buried next to his daughter in the West Point Cemetery in Liberty, Indiana.

With Posteal Laskey in custody, police turned their full attention to pinning he tragic and senseless death of Barbara Bowman to this man whom they believed was the Cincinnati Strangler.

Barbara Bowman's shoe, billfold, glasses, and newspaper left at the murder scene. (Cincinnati Police Department)

Yellow Cab #870 parked in the police department impound garage. (Cincinnati Police Department)

Chapter 15
A Killer's Trail

How did Barb Bowman end up on the pavement at Ring and Grand, bleeding to death next to a wrecked taxi?

Detectives Ken Davis and Tom Gardner began their investigation by visiting the West End offices of Yellow Cab, located in the 1100 block of Kenner Street, in the shadow of Cincinnati's Art Deco-style Union Terminal train station. There, they spoke with Arthur Scholl, a taxi maintenance man, and Harry Burks, the overnight supervisor who had responded to Sol Thompson's call about the abandoned cab.

Twenty-two-year-old Artie Scholl was responsible for gas and oil servicing of the taxi fleet. He told the detectives about an incident that occurred on the night of Friday, August 12. Close to midnight, Scholl heard a door slam on one of the new 1966 Plymouth cabs. Burks also heard a slamming door. Both saw a man in the lot neither recognized. Scholl called out for the man to stop, but the stranger only momentarily turned before briskly walking away across the lot. Scholl started after him, but Burks called him back, telling him to forget it.

As Scholl turned to walk away, he glanced back and saw the man stop directly beneath a light, about thirty feet away before walking on. Moments later, a 1956 Buick emerged from a nearby street. Scholl believed it was a light-colored sedan, though he wasn't certain. He estimated the time of the incident to have been around 12:10 a.m.

Scholl described the man as between twenty-four and twenty-seven years old, about 5'9", weighing between 155 and 170 pounds, with broad shoulders, a square face, dark complexion, and close-cropped hair. The man was well-groomed, his hair shaved straight across the nape of his neck, "like a lot of Negroes." He wore dark trousers and a loud checked shirt with white checks on a yellow background. Scholl wasn't sure if he had any facial hair, but he said he could recognize him if he saw him again.

When shown an array of mugshots, Scholl selected none. Included in the array was a photo of former Cincinnati Police patrolman Thomas W. Fisher who was dismissed in 1963 after being accused of making forcible advances toward a woman. At the time of the incident, Fisher had also worked off-duty as a taxi driver. Fisher came to mind as, after three years of appeals, the Black patrolman's dismissal was upheld in 1966.

Yellow Cab and Parkway Cab, both jointly owned, shared the same parking lot. Yellow Cab operated a fleet of fifty Checker Marathons. Citywide, there were over 1,150 licensed taxi drivers, with more than five hundred actively driving in August 1966. Investigators began combing through taxi driver registrations going back ten years, cross-referencing them with criminal records.

Harry Burks confirmed that Yellow Cab #870 had been stolen. He told the detectives the cab had not been in circulation since June 19 and only sixty-three miles had been registered on its odometer since then, showing $11.00 in fares.

The Cincinnati Strangler

Vincent Taylor, the dispatcher on duty at Yellow Cab that Saturday night, was called in by investigators. Together with fellow dispatcher David Shanklin, Taylor handled taxi dispatch calls that night. The pair kept a log of calls while also recording their back-and-forth with drivers.

Culling through the callsheet, detectives discovered that one driver's call number—#186—did not match any vehicle currently in service. This meant the driver of cab #870 had been identifying himself as #186, taking calls for six fares over the course of the night. In the Yellow Cab system, drivers were known only by their call number, the vehicle number, and not by name, making it difficult to immediately identify who was behind the wheel.

The first recorded fare for #186 occurred at 11:52 p.m., with a pickup on Chatham Street in Walnut Hills. The next call came at 12:03 a.m., for a fare at the Guild Theater on East McMillan Avenue. The driver picked up August Kramer, an employee at the Guild, and dropped him off at 26 East McMillan near the University of Cincinnati campus.

At 12:37 a.m., cab #186 responded to a call from 1675 Gellenbeck Avenue in Price Hill, picking up James Curtis and taking him home to 1705 Vine Street in Over-the-Rhine. The driver then picked up a fare from Bill & Bob's Café on Beekman Street at 1:03 a.m.

The final recorded call for #186 was to the Lark Café in Corryville at 2:00 a.m.

Though the call logs recorded times, drivers often "sharp-shot" one another by arriving at pickup points first, so the logs were not always reliable.

The detectives also listened to the recording of the night's dispatch calls. The voice of the man claiming to be driving cab #186 was described as "an educated voice but with somewhat of a Negroid accent." Detectives played the recording for dispatchers and drivers across the city, but no one could identify the man behind the voice.

Detectives focused on the last call for #186, the Lark Café, where Barbara Bowman was last seen alive. The Lark was a bar near the University of Cincinnati, owned by Clyde and Maggie Vollmer. Clyde, a former Cincinnati Reds baseball player, confirmed that Bowman had been in the bar that night, along with a pair of friends known only by their nicknames, Mickey and Bert.

After three years of appeals, the patrolman's dismissal was upheld in 1966.

At the time, Fisher also worked off-duty hours driving a cab. His photo was included in the array viewed by Scholl and Burks, neither selecting him.

Scholl later viewed another array at the Crime Bureau, picking Sam Jackson, who was neither a former cabbie nor suspect; rather, a current Yellow Cab driver.

Parkway and Yellow cabs were jointly owned and shared the same parking lot. Yellow Cab operated fifty Checker Marathons on the lot. Citywide, there were 1,152 licensed taxi drivers, with over five hundred actively driving in August 1966.

Investigators waded through ten years of taxi driver registrations at the Public Utilities office, cross-checking them with criminal records at the Bureau of Information.

Burks confirmed Yellow Cab #870 had been stolen, as he reported when visiting Grand and Ring. Number 870 had not been in circulation since June 19, driven sixty-three miles since then, showing $11.00 in fares.

Burks called in Vincent Taylor who had been on duty as dispatcher handling Yellow Cab calls Saturday night into Sunday morning alongside fellow dispatcher, David Shanklin. They recorded the calls and pickups from the previous night, both in a call log and in an audio recording of the back and forth with drivers.

Culling Taylor's timesheet, matches were made between drivers and cabs, only one driver's call number, #186, did not match vehicles in service. That meant, the driver of cab #870, the number painted on the cab, was identifying himself as cab #186, handling six calls over Saturday night and Sunday morning. Drivers were known only by their cab number, not their names.

The first reported fare of #186 was at 11:52 P.M. to Chatham Street in Walnut Hills, quickly followed by a 12:03 A.M. call to the Guild Theater on East McMillan Avenue, also in Walnut Hills. August Kramer, a Guild employee, was going home to 26 East McMillan near the UC campus.

At 12:37 A.M., cab #186 picked up James Curtis at 1675 Gellenbeck Avenue in Price Hill for a ride home to 1705 Vine Street in Over the Rhine.

At 1:03 A.M., #186 responded on a call to Bill & Bob's Café at 2735 Beekman Street in the Fairmont bottoms along Mill Creek where Art Baldrick was going home to

Tafel Street in Clifton.

At 1:15 A.M., #186 responded to a call from a phone booth at Central and Colerain, but no one was there.

His next, and last call, was at 2:09 A.M. for the Lark Café at 3001 Vine Street in Corryville.

The logs recorded the time calls went out to drivers, but drivers regularly "sharp-shot" one another by reaching the pickup point first, making the logs an unreliable source.

The recording of that night's dispatch calls held the dialog between the driver identifying himself as #186 and dispatcher Taylor. The tape was played to every taxi dispatcher in the city, as well as drivers, to see if anyone recognized the voice, but speculation was the best they garnered. Detective Rutledge described the driver's voice as, "an educated voice but with somewhat negroid accent."

Monday night, police arrived at the last call of cab #186 – the Lark Café in Corryville, near the University of Cincinnati, where they interviewed owners Clyde and Maggie Vollmer.

Clyde was a well-known Cincinnati native who'd played for the hometown Reds. The Vollmers confirmed knowing the victim, whom they only knew as Barb, and that she was in the bar with friends on Saturday night. Clyde was tending bar where Barb was sitting with her girlfriends, Mickey and Bert, known only by their nicknames.

Clyde remembered the cabbie as a very dark-complected Black man, about five-foot-six to -seven, weighing 160 to 170 pounds, not wearing a hat, and having short hair. Clyde recalled Bowman taking a Sunday *Enquirer* with her as she followed the cabbie out the door.

Maggie recalled Barb arriving around 9:30 p.m. with a couple she didn't know. The three sat at the bar until Mickey and Bert showed up.

The couple moved to a table in front of the bandstand where Charlie Secrest was playing piano that night, joining another couple. Detective Hillman asked Maggie if Secrest dated Barb, responding she didn't know for certain, but Charlie seemed to show an interest. This last Saturday night, Secrest left with his girlfriend.

Maggie had been waiting tables and remembered Barb making a telephone call around two a.m., recalled as the time when the music stops. About five minutes later, a very dark complected Black man, "he was a Negro; very, very black," standing about five-foot-seven, broad shoulders, burr haircut, a dark, rather than loud, checkered shirt, and not wearing a hat. He went to the bar and said, "Cab." He bore no distinguishing marks, Maggie summarizing her impression, "I wouldn't have went out with him."

Claudia Vollmer, their eighteen-year-old daughter, arrived at her parents's bar at 12:30 a.m., saying hello to Barb and her friends, Bert and Mickey. She'd known Barb as a Lark customer for the past three or four months.

A little before two a.m., Claudia saw a very dark complected Black man enter the typically all-White bar. He was around thirty and stood about five-foot-eleven (later telling Hillman he was five-foot-seven) and stocky. He wore a dark, large-checked shirt, no hat, dark trousers, and short-cropped hair. Claudia saw the man enter but did not hear him say anything. She knew Barb walked out behind him carrying her Sunday paper, later telling Hillman that Barb was also carrying a rain scarf.

Another Lark customer, Ken Mullins, came to the Crime Bureau on August 20 to meet with Detectives Kersker and Rutledge. Mullins had been sitting at a table about fifteen feet from the door, describing the cabdriver as standing five-foot-seven to five-foot-eight, weighing 145-150 pounds, "medium complexion for a colored guy," dark green or black jacket, black pants; overall "clean looking." He put the man's age between twenty-five and thirty, but could have been older. Mullins said his very small head was hatless, Mullins emphasizing the man was not "shortneck," but "his head just seemed like it was smaller." Mullins said he was too far away to see any facial hair.

Mullins heard the man ask, "Does anybody want a cab?" sounding clear, not guttural or mumbling. He described the man throwing his head back when he entered and "walked with sort of a what I call a cocky walk." Certain the man was a cabbie, Mullins turned his attention to his date and did not see Bowman leave.

Detectives asked Mullins, "Did he have negroid features from the side view or did he have more like a white person's features?"

"He didn't have, um, big lips. He was more or less on the white. I mean he had small lips and didn't have a real large nose."

Mullins responded to a question about anything distinct about the man's face or head, "Well, the only thing that, ah, that I observed was like … his head seemed a little smaller than what a normal person's, I mean, colored person's, would be for that size of his body."

Mullins hinted to detectives he'd heard Barb had intercourse, triggering questions about Bowman's promiscuity; Mullins also saying he'd never seen her leave with anyone. He described Barb as a very friendly person who "always conducted herself in a very womanly way, from my estimation."

Specialist James O'Brien interviewed Lark patron Ray Holstein who'd been seated next to Barb at the bar.

"He didn't say nothing, just walked up between these people and I noticed him walking up there and I was sitting right there. That's why I asked Barb if someone called a cab."

Insisting the man said nothing, Holstein only noticed him, "because he was colored and there's no colored ever comes in here and, ah, that, ah, he was probably a cab driver. So, I said to Clyde, 'Did someone call a cab?' Before Clyde could respond, this girl jumped up saying, 'I did'." Holstein later told O'Brien, "I was the one, I said, 'cab, Clyde did someone call a cab?'"

Holstein described the man as being in his early twenties, wearing a dirty white shirt, and had one of those little peaked caps, a Be-Bop hat, saying it was like a tam with a little peak and a short brim. The man had a normal forehead and hairline without any distinguishing marks or scars.

"He looked dirty, hard-looking."

Holstein provided the man's height being about three inches taller than the people seated at the bar, about five-foot-ten, and weighing about 160 pounds.

He described Bowman as walking first before turning around to glance at the guy before heading out the door, "sort, to me, like she was sort of, was thinking about riding with him, you know."

Another Lark patron, Frank Smith, recalled someone remarking, "Oh, she's not leaving with him?"

A message to call a woman about the Bowman murder was on Detective Hillman's desk when he returned to the Crime Bureau. Betty Beckman telephoned Station X when she heard about her friend's murder. She would reveal how Barbara Bowman came to the Lark on Saturday night.

Beckman lived in Price Hill, on Elberon Avenue, not far from Barb's apartment, and was going out with Larry Goody that night. Betty sometimes went to the Lark with Barb, so she asked Goody if he would mind giving her friend a ride to the bar, promising she would not be a third wheel. Goody agreed, and they picked up Barb at the corner of Grand and Warsaw at 8:40 p.m. The trio arrived at the Lark a few minutes after nine.

Beckman recounted sitting with Bowman at the bar until Barb's friends, Bert and Mickey, arrived when she and Goody moved to a table in front of the bandstand to join another couple. She, too, did not know Mickey and

Bert's full names.

Barb came to their table sometime between one and two asking if they were going to get something to eat when they left the Lark. Thinking her friend would find her own way home, Beckman curtly answered she didn't know, to which Bowman replied she didn't feel like eating and would get a cab home. "OK," Beckman replied, "I'll talk to you tomorrow."

Beckman was aware Barb called a cab but didn't see the cabbie arrive, nor did she see her friend depart as she and Goody were busy talking and dancing. She assumed Barb called Parkway Cab as that's who they typically called when they went out together. Sometimes a Yellow Cab might appear. On occasion, they might have the same driver two weeks in a row but neither of them ever requested a specific driver.

Asking Beckman about a relationship between Barb and the piano player, Beckman said Barb never dated Secrest but he may have shown some interest. Hillman then asked if she knew a man by the name of Norbert. She recognized the name as someone Barb had dated, but Beckman had no idea about his identity.

Ending the call, Betty asked Hillman if her name could be kept out of the news, "because if there's a crackpot around here, he's liable to be looking for me. I live by myself and I'd be scared to death."

Beckman provided the detective the full names of Barb's friends –Miriam "Mickey" Uchtman and Alberta "Bert" Walther, but neither provided useful insights.

Lark patron, Josephine Herald, told Detective Gardner, "this guy came in and hollered for a cab." Herald described the man as a dark-complected "big guy," over six feet tall, with bushy black hair in loose curls. He weighed close to two-hundred pounds and wasn't wearing a hat, but he had a dark waist-length coat. She didn't notice him smiling or his mouth open, but thought she saw the man had gold teeth on the right side of his mouth when he spoke. It was close to two a.m. when the man came in but, other than her brief look, Herald lost notice of him.

Gilbert Alten, another Lark customer, remembered the man having bushy hair, "longer than most Negroes."

The following Saturday, another Lark customer, Virginia Young, came downtown to talk with Detectives Kersker and Rutledge. Young lived across the street from the Lark and knew Bowman by sight, but no other details about her. Young recalled the cabbie as a soft-spoken Black man about thirty-years old, standing about five-six, and weighing between 140 and 150 pounds. He was not wearing a hat, revealing bushy hair on top with close-cut sides. Then, Young changed her description to the man having a flattop burr haircut.

Young described the driver wearing a dark, lightweight, waist-length jacket zipped up the front, walking with his chin in the air. She selected a photo from an array detectives knew was not the man.

She couldn't see his shirt but added, "now, they're talking about a plaid shirt, I never saw anything like that."

"He walked in and had this arrogance about him, he turned his head from one side to the other and, naturally because he was a Negro, we all looked, we thought maybe he was coming for a drink, cause they do come in once in a while."

Another patron held an empty beer bottle beneath the bar, just in case there was trouble.

The FBI sent sketch artist Carl Mumford to Cincinnati to create a composite drawing of the suspect based upon eyewitness descriptions. Meeting with Lark patrons and Sol Thompson, Mumford produced a sketch of a hard-featured Black man between twenty-five and thirty-five years old, with a dead expression and close-cropped hair. A second sketch placed a knitted skullcap perched on the back of the same man's head. The sketches were distributed to local media, and police canvassed the area with them, setting off a new wave of citizen calls to Station X with sightings of the killer.

Police compiled lists of current and former taxi drivers, attuned to Black drivers and on-alert for any with criminal records. They checked backgrounds and conducted interviews of men who'd worked on the taxi lot dating back to 1957. Police focused on men with knowledge of taxi operations and dispatch, especially at Yellow Cab, who would know one key could open and start any Checker Marathon parked in the lot. Local cabbies fully cooperated with police, angered the killer was ruining business.

Police were perplexed as the killer was employing different methods to fulfill his deadly desires. Violent assault, strangulation, and rape had been the killer's modus operandi, changing from indoors to outside; but Barbara

Bowman's death added the violence of running over her supine body with stolen cab and then inflicting multiple stab wounds with a knife. The killer's methods were evolving.

Amid the investigation into Bowman's murder, violence and racial tensions kept the city on edge. Until Laskey was taken into custody, police had no evidence or suspects in the Bowman case.

At the end of August, a forty-year-old Price Hill housewife, Rose Thompson, was attacked in the basement of her three-family house after hanging laundry on a clothesline in the backyard around two in the afternoon. Startled as she entered the basement, the assailant threw a cup of bleach in her face, grabbed her neck while twisting her arm, breaking her necklace, and tearing open the top button of her blouse. As the struggle ensued, her little fox terrier, Bouncey, bit the man's leg, evoking a string of curse words with the threat, "I'll kill you," Thompson thinking was intended for Bouncey, not her. Thanks to the little dog's bravery, Thompson seized the opportunity to break free and call for help. As she ran screaming up the stairs, she saw the man run from the property. A neighbor responded to her screams and pulled Thompson inside her apartment to call police. A resident of Glenway Avenue saw a man run into the woods at Lehman Road, not far from the scene of Barbara Bowman's murder.

She described her assailant as a big man with a mustache, thirty to thirty-five years of age, five-foot-eleven, weighing 185 to 190 pounds, and wearing a short-sleeved maroon shirt. She noted the back of his head was very greasy with a big wave in his hair. Thompson managed to grab a ballpoint pen from the man's pocket and police checked the red plastic cup holding the bleach for prints, but no prints were found on the cup. The pen was imprinted with "Golden Gate Casino, Las Vegas," but it turned out a student nurse at Good Samaritan Hospital had handed out hundreds of the pens sent to her by her brother who owned the casino.

A Black man working at a West Side auto dealership called police for assistance when a group of youths taunted and threatened him, accusing him of being The Strangler. When police arrived, they took the man in for questioning.

Later that afternoon, a forty-nine-year-old Black man from Avondale was driving along Warsaw Avenue in Price Hill when he was stopped by James Noble, a nearby resident, who pointed a .38-caliber revolver at the driver as he flagged down a passing police cruiser. Noble proudly told the officer he'd captured The Strangler. Instead, his handgun was confiscated, while the accosted driver opted not to press charges.

Deadly violence continued into September as the month closed with the gruesome stabbing murders of the three members of the Bricca family in their suburban Bridgetown home on the west side of Cincinnati, investigated by the Hamilton County Sheriff's Department, not Cincinnati Police. There was no connection with The Strangler attached to the Bricca murders, other than the mounting fear of violence gripping the city.

Chapter 16
Charges Mount

Inside City Jail, Laskey was summoned to the iron gateway where he stood face-to-face with a woman on the other side who scrutinized him intently. The woman, forty-six-year-old Virginia Hinners, a mother of four and a "unity teacher" at The New Thought Unity Center on East McMillan Street, had been assaulted and robbed in her office on September 21, 1966. Hinners identified Laskey as her attacker, telling the police, "That's him."

Following this impromptu stand-up, Specialist Howard Oberschmidt escorted Laskey across the courtyard to the Detective Bureau. There, a group of witnesses awaited: Lark Café patrons Clyde Vollmer, Virginia Young, and Ken Mullins, along with Eileen Aultz and Charlotte Barnhart, the two women searching for the apartment building the night of th Bowman murder. According to his attorneys, Laskey was led handcuffed and fully visible to witnesses who would soon be asked to pick the man they saw last August from a police lineup.

Inside the Crime Bureau's show-up room, the same space used for morning roll call, two banks of footlights blinded suspects from seeing the witnesses, standing toward the darkened back of the room. Four men stood across the brightly-lit platform, staring straight ahead, height lines on the wall behind them. Three microphones on stands were placed in front of them, and according to Laskey's attorneys, each man was instructed to say, "Cab."

The lineup included Ernest Mosley, standing on the

far left, about the same height as Laskey but with a distinct pompadour haircut making him appear taller. Mosley also wore glasses. Next to him was nineteen-year-old Joseph V. Jones, who stood over six feet tall. Lawrence Roland, another nineteen-year-old with a pompadour hairstyle, stood to the right, dressed in a red University of Cincinnati sweater. Standing barely five-six, Laskey stood third from the left, wearing his gray sport jacket, slacks, and a white shirt without a tie.

The results of the lineup were mixed. Clyde Vollmer tentatively identified the third man from the left, Laskey, but he wasn't positive. Virginia Young said none of the men matched her recollection. Ken Mullins, like Vollmer, hesitantly picked the third man from the left, while Eileen Aultz confidently selected Laskey.

The process was repeated several times throughout the evening, with each lineup yielding different reactions. By the following morning, The Cincinnati *Enquirer* ran the headline: "Six Witnesses Tentatively Identify Suspect in Strangulation."

A month earlier, before Laskey's arrest, Lark customers Ken Williams and Virginia Young viewed an array of forty-five mugshots, picking two: Posteal Laskey and Odell Lyons. Young and Mullins had previously been shown the same photos but selected neither. Two weeks later, Sol Thompson, the Parkway driver, was shown the same photos, choosing none. Returning to the Lark, the detectives passed the photographs around and witnesses positively picked a father of six employed by General Electric.

Among mugshots cataloged in police records as, "Been in or eliminated," the October 1965 mugshot #71950 – Posteal Laskey, Jr., was included.

Laskey's criminal record of violent assaults on women and his experience driving a Yellow Cab provided the circumstantial evidence, but it was the eyewitness identifications that linked Laskey directly to Barbara Bowman's murder. Like police, Prosecutor Rueger was certain Laskey was the phantom strangler but he was content to focus on building evidence against Laskey in Bowman's killing to net a death sentence, effectively closing the books on the entire series of strangulation murders.

"We think he's the guy," Detective Chief Schott told reporters, adding that there was "a definite tie-in of the Kerrick slaying with other strangulations in the city," reiterating their continued belief in a single killer.

Amid the whirlwind of lineups, Laskey twice met

with his court-appointed attorneys, at 2:15 and again at 8:00 p.m. The meetings took place in a small, cramped room where Laskey and his lawyers sat shoulder to shoulder. During one of these sessions, a photographer from the Cincinnati *Post* snapped a shot of the three together. The resulting image showed a blasé but cool, cigarette-smoking Laskey flanked by his over-eager lawyers leaning into their legal action poses.

A week earlier, Laskey's attorneys were forced to resign from their assistant prosecutor positions over financial misdeeds. Posteal Laskey's case would be their first, a high-profile trial to launch their private practice. Their former boss, Hamilton County Prosecutor Melvin Rueger, was happy to second their appointment to defend Laskey as he would be prosecuting the case.

By Sunday morning, another lineup was arranged. Laskey stood alongside three men of varying ages—one nineteen, another thirty-two, and a fifty-year-old. The witnesses this time included Clyde Vollmer, his wife Margaret, and Joan Hudson Craig, another Lark Café patron. It's unclear whether any positive identifications were made, but Margaret Vollmer's 2017 obituary boasted, "Mrs. Vollmer's testimony helped convict Posteal Laskey, Jr., the 'Cincinnati Strangler'."

That Sunday, Laskey was transferred from the City Jail to the Workhouse—a grim, three-story Romanesque-Gothic castle built soon after the Civil War. The building had changed little over the past century. The 550 four-by-eight cells were without electricity or plumbing. Prisoners used slop buckets that were emptied into troughs in the towers at the ends of the building. The heating system, comprised of bare cast iron pipes, offering little heat. There was no cooling in hot months.

Upon arrival at the Workhouse, prisoners surrendered their personal belongings. In return, they were given a Bible and a blue Workhouse uniform. This imposing structure, a relic of another era, would be Laskey's new home.

On Monday morning, Patrolman Pille returned to the Wuest lot to tow Laskey's car into police custody. Meanwhile, Detective Howard Smith spoke with Herbert Wuest, president of the Adam Wuest Mattress Company. Laskey was an all-purpose laborer working at Wuest, on and off, since August 1965. Wuest provided Smith with Laskey's time cards, showing his attendance on the days corresponding to the murders:

October 12, 1965 (Elisabeth Kreco): Off

December 2, 1965 (Emogene Harrington): Laid off

April 4, 1966 (Lois Dant): Not at work

June 10, 1966 (Mathilda Messer): At work (arrived at 6:59 a.m.)

October 11, 1966 (Alice Hochhausler): Off work (arrived October 12 at 6:55 a.m.)

October 19-20, 1966 (Rose Winstel): Arrived late at 8:36 a.m.

Time cards, however, are not a reliable source as employees often clocked in and out for each other.

At Wuest, Detective Smith also spoke with Charles Banks, a Wuest employee and Laskey's brother-in-law.

Banks had been married to Posteal's older sister, Mollie Ann, until her death in 1957 at the age of twenty-five.

Mollie Ann Laskey Banks had been living with Charles and their two children in the Laskey household at 1820 Freeman. At 4:27 A.M. on March 16, 1957, Mollie was rushed to General Hospital for excessive bleeding. Transfusions sought to replenish Mollie's lost blood, but physicians were unable to stem the flow. Mollie told Dr. Stephen Horstein that a woman had inserted a rubber catheter into her womb to induce an abortion. Mollie died the next evening, the cause of death noted as Criminal Septic Toxic Abortion.

Sixty-nine-year-old Roberta Starks was arrested by Homicide Detective John Huber the following day. Known as Ma Starks and Little Mam, she had already served two years in prison for a 1950 abortion. Starks told Huber she performed the abortion on her Sixth Street kitchen table using an old-fashioned fountain pen inserted into Mollie's womb, advising her to take a physic post-op, a laxative traditionally used as a purgative cleanser in cases of unwanted pregnancies.

Banks told the detective he'd met Posteal in the early fifties roller skating, continuing until the past year when Banks quit skating due to a back injury. They remained close friends, spending work lunch breaks together, either bringing their own or ordering carryout from Lou Weiland's Café across Gest Street. Sometimes they'd drive to various places over lunch where they'd park and eat before returning to work. Smith neglected to ask Banks what neighborhoods they visited, including Ring Place on the precipice overlooking the Wuest warehouse.

He described Laskey as a loner, saying he didn't know Posteal's friends, except for Brenda Jackson, who Banks described as "shapely" with red hair.

Referring to Laskey by his nickname, Junior, Banks said he never gave any reason for suspicion; insisting Posteal incapable of committing such acts.

Detective Smith walked away from the interview convinced Banks knew more than he was saying, certain he was lying to cover up for Laskey.

The prisoner was driven from the Workhouse to City Jail for his hearing in Police Court on the assault and robbery charges brought by Virginia Hinners. Judge Clarence Denning granted a continuance to January 4, ordering Laskey held without bond.

Following his court appearance, another lineup was held at 10:15 A.M. when Clyde and Margaret Vollmer identified Laskey, third from left in a four-man lineup.

Two hours later, Artie Scholl from Yellow Cab identified Laskey in four-man lineup. At this same time, Eileen Aultz identified Laskey from the lineup photo, saying for the record that Laskey was the man she saw in the rear seat of a Yellow Cab parked on Grand Avenue facing Warsaw Avenue with a white woman.

As Laskey was busy in court and standing in lineups, a team of detectives, led by Sergeant Moore, descended upon the Laskey home at 1820 Freeman Avenue in the West End with a search warrant issued by Judge Denning that morning. The three-story freestanding townhouse where the Laskey family lived in five rooms on the first floor was described from a 1962 visit by his parole officer,

David D. West, as being in "poor condition in an old run-down part of Cincinnati."

Dave Laskey kept an eye on detectives as they removed a variety of items from their home. A clothes line and plastic sash were removed from the rear bathroom. Two wood-handled knives were taken from a wash tub in the cupboard. A dry-cleaning label, an Ohio chauffeur badge #569117, and four keys, along with a black leather jacket. Detective Bluhm added three more knives with wooden handles from the kitchen. In the basement, they removed a white dress and smock in the toilet area; wrapping up at 11:10 A.M.

Fifteen minutes later, the team arrived with a warrant to search the Reading Road apartment Posteal shared with Brenda Jackson. As she was opening the apartment to detectives, the landlady told them that Laskey left at 7:40 A.M. Friday morning, the last time she saw him.

Their search netted twenty items from apartment twelve, including a black tam. They wrapped up at 12:30 P.M. and returned to headquarters with three large brown paper bags full of items from the two residences.

At 2:30 P.M., Laskey was moved to City Jail where, starting at 4:35 P.M., he was called again to stand behind the bars of the entry gate for viewing by August Kramer, a passenger in cab #870 from the Guild Theater to his home the night of Barbara Bowman's death. Next up was another Cab #186 passenger, Art Baldrick, followed by Lark customer Mickey Uchtman. These witnesses had earlier been shown the photo array of suspects, including Laskey's mugshot, without picking him, the same result in this exhibition.

During the afternoon and evening, Detectives Rutledge and Robert Wolff retraced Laskey's professed activities on the night of Sandra Chapas's pursuit. Their inquiries were balanced between the Chapas case while seeking insights into Laskey's life and associates.

At the Playboy Bar, the detectives spoke with Phyllis Tanner, the "very cooperative" club manager, who told them Laskey was practicing with his band when she arrived at 9:00 p.m. and was certain he left around 10:30 with other members of the band. She remembered the time as when the band leader received a telephone call.

The detectives also spoke with the leader, "Tiny" Charles Bullock, who told them he arrived at the bar with other members of the band, including Posteal, between 7:45 and 8:00 p.m., and didn't leave until almost midnight when he and Laskey took a couple of girls, one named Diana, to the RB Café on Spring Grove. Next, they went to Bullock's apartment on Reading Road sometime between 12:15 and 12:20 A.M., Laskey stayed until shortly after one a.m. Bullock said his girlfriend, Mattie Showes, was also at the apartment.

Showes accounted for Laskey up to 12:30 A.M., confirming they arrived at Bullock's Reading Road apartment around 10:40 P.M. Rutledge and Wolff considered Showes truthful, perhaps since she thought Laskey capable of The Strangler crimes. Showes described Laskey as a loner and strange, and that his girlfriend was a "girl lover" who'd approached her just the week before.

Tuesday, December 13, opened with another court

appearance, this time Laskey was transported from the Workhouse to the Hamilton County Courthouse to appear before Municipal Court Judge William S. Mathews on the charge of violating his probation. Mathews presided over Laskey's November 1965 conviction for the assault of Judy Buckner when he sentenced him to three years of probation. Now, Laskey would appear before the same judge for the violation.

Phil Muldoon, Laskey's probation officer, testified that Laskey reported every Tuesday and had worked regularly over the past year. Judge Mathews asked Muldoon if the defendant had complied with the order to keep "reasonable hours," be home by 1:00 a.m. on weekdays and 2:30 on weekends, Muldoon responded that, as far as he knew, Laskey did comply.

The previous Friday, it was Muldoon seated behind Lula Kerrick at Mass in Saint Peter's Cathedral.

Laskey's attorneys sought to have the probation violation dismissed entirely, arguing that without proof of an actual assault, grounds for probation violation were invalid. They reminded the court that Laskey's assault conviction was under appeal. The judge rejected the motion while admitting he "was of the mind" that Laskey was guilty of the violation. Laskey would continue being held on the probation violation.

This setback pushed Laskey's defense team to begin preparing for what they knew would be a broader battle—a change of venue. Roney argued the atmosphere in Saturday's Police Court was, "so hostile because of Friday's strangulation murder that it was impossible to get a fair trial." Judge Mathews responded he had neither seen nor heard of such conduct, and would have quickly quashed it, had he known.

That morning's *Enquirer* quoted an "unimpeachable source" that police would be charging Laskey with first-degree murder. Hamilton County Prosecutor Melvin Rueger quickly told police to slow down, continue gathering evidence, and leave the prosecution to him.

Safety Director Henry Sandman and Rueger released a joint public statement supporting Rueger's lead in charging Laskey: "After consultation with the prosecutor's office, the Safety Department and the Police Department, we decided to follow procedures recommended by the prosecutor's office." Rueger alone, would lead the prosecution.

To ensure control of the narrative, Rueger planned to bypass a public arraignment, ostensibly to avoid a media spectacle. Instead, he would take the case directly to a grand jury.

"After we reviewed all the evidence, we felt that because of the many witnesses involved and the great amount of publicity given to the case and keeping in mind the recent U.S. Supreme Court decisions on pretrial publicity, that it would be in the best interest of justice to present the matter directly to the grand jury."

An *Enquirer* editorial agreed the prosecutor was being forced to yield to the "anxieties generated by a fear of overstepping the bounds defined in a series of Supreme Court decisions."

Defense attorney Burt Signer noted Rueger's tactic

had last been employed in 1914.

Rueger's gambit prevented the defense a pre-trial presentation of the prosecution's case. Instead, prosecution witnesses would reinforce the prosecution's case with evidence presented without question or objection by the absent defense; the proceedings cloaked in a sacred secrecy. An arraignment opened the case to public scrutiny and media attention, along with defense objections and counterpoints. The only word to leave the grand jury room would be indictments for first-degree murder.

Laskey faced another lineup on December 13. Standing third from the left in a four-man group, again viewed by Clyde and Margaret Vollmer. This was two days before, presumably, they would appear before the grand jury. Identities of testifying witnesses was cloaked in the secrecy.

Following the lineup, Laskey stood before Delle Ernst, the seventy-year-old East Walnut Hills assault and robbery victim attacked in October. Yes, it was Posteal Laskey who knocked her to the ground and ran off her purse. After the viewing, Ernst filed charges of assault and robbery against Laskey.

The case against Posteal Laskey, Jr. was ready for presentation to the grand jury for an indictment of the first-degree murder.

On December 14, seventy-nine-year-old Anna Scales was beaten in the basement hallway of the Walnut Hills apartment building at 2315 Kemper Lane where she was caretaker. Anna was struck multiple times about the face and her head was slammed against the concrete wall

The Cincinnati Strangler

outside her basement apartment. She described the man as Black, between thirty-two and thirty-five years of age, and wearing a cardigan sweater. He'd come to her door asking about renting a room when he suddenly attacked.

In the days leading to the grand jury hearing, *Enquirer* columnist Frank Weikel poked fun at pronunciations of the prime suspect's name: "The radio contest people missed a golden opportunity last week. A thick bundle of trading stamps might have been offered for the listener who unscrambled Posteal Laskey, as the name was fogged up by the newscasters. The oftener it was heard, the deeper the confusion became."

By New Year's Eve, The Strangler had been reduced to a punchline, as columnist Ollie James wrote in *The Enquirer*:

"We absolutely refuse to believe any man in this area would be so darned ungentlemanly, but C.C. Lee of Latonia, a guy hearing the doorbell, answers it to a man standing there saying, 'I am the Cincinnati Strangler'."

"Oh, he says, and calls to his wife, 'it's for you, dear."

At nine a.m. on Thursday, December 15, the fifteen-member grand jury gathered in the Hamilton County Courthouse, seated should-to-shoulder along three rows of benches with a desktop before them for note taking. A judge would not be present at the hearing, rather the prosecutor would control the proceeding. To achieve an indictment, twelve of the fifteen grand jurors would have to concur.

The prosecution laid out their case to grand jurors without defense questions or objections, buttressed by multiple eyewitness accounts of seeing Posteal Laskey at critical times on the night of Barbara Bowman's murder. Laskey was seen in the Yellow Cab lot on Friday night and, on Saturday evening, he was the cabdriver who needed reminding to start the meter. In the early morning of Sunday, Laskey was the taxi driver walking from the Lark Café with Barbara Bowman. In the rain and darkness, it was Laskey who jumped into a cab near the scene of Barbara Bowman's murder.

Beside the eyewitness accounts in the murder of Barbara Bowman, Rueger also presented evidence in the assault and robbery of Virginia Hinners, surprising observers by adding the October assault and robbery of Delle Ernst.

The identities of witnesses testifying before the grand jury were held secret and remain so today. They likely included:

Five witnesses from the Lark Café: co-owner Margaret Vollmer, sans her husband, Clyde, who could not identify Laskey as the cab driver; Ray Holstein, Carl Stiegleiter, Kenneth Mullins, and Virginia Young.

Parkway Cab driver, Sol Thompson; Art Scholl, the Yellow Cab maintenance man; Eileen Aultz, who asked the cab driver for directions; Virginia Hinners, the victim of an assault and robbery in September; and Delle Ernst.

Grand juries typically reported on Fridays but, in this case, they quickly handed down three indictments the same day as the hearing, submitting them to Common Pleas Judge William R. Matthews:

Indictment #88695: Murder 1st Degree – Barbara

Bowman

Indictment #88696: Robbery and Assault to Rob – Virginia Hinners; September 21, 1966; $28.00

Indictment #88697: Robbery and Assault to Rob – Delle S. Ernst; October 4, 1966; theft of a purse and contents.

Upon receipt of the grand jury recommendations, Judge Matthews issued a sharp admonishment to local news media about reporting the grand jury proceedings:

"I deeply regret that I have heard on the radio and television and read in the newspapers about matters being considered by you after I instructed you that your proceedings were to be secret. I realize that this information was not released by any of your members and that you are not at fault…The law does require that your investigations remain a secret even though the various news media have informed the entire community not only whom you are investigating but have even indicated what indictments you would probably return and when."

"I can imagine your difficulty in remaining silent when your husbands or wives ask questions of you. But the law does require that your investigation remain a secret. It is regrettable that this has occurred. I apologize."

Reporting on the indictments, The *Enquirer* reinforced Laskey as The Strangler: "Police also consider Laskey a suspect in the city's six unsolved strangulations of middle-aged and elderly women."

In his December 15 *Enquirer* column, Frank Weikel wrote of receiving a telephone call from Della Buckner,

Undated photos of Barbara Bowman, left, and Judith Buckner. (Cincinnati Police Department)

the mother of Judy Buckner, speaking of her frustration with police who were disregarding her calls pointing them to Posteal Laskey after the murder of Barbara Bowman. She recounted telling the court in her daughter's 1965 assault case that Laskey was likely to attack again if released. Buckner said her daughter and Barbara Bowman knew one another, Bowman once staying in their home. The two shared remarkably similar appearances. Della told Weikel, fourteen months after the attack, Judy still refused to go outside at night.

Laskey's arraignment on the indictments was scheduled for Monday morning before Judge Matthews, but Roney and Signer requested additional time to review the indictment before entering pleas. Matthews granted the continuance, without objection from Assistant Prosecutor Calvin Prem.

Monday brought the announcement that Lieutenant

The Cincinnati Strangler

Colonel Jacob Schott was selected to be Cincinnati's next police chief, filling the role left by Chief Stanley Schrotel when he retired in September. Schott, who joined the police force in June 1937, had steadily climbed through the ranks. With his close-cropped hair and muscular build, Schott carried a look of all business. Schott was well-dressed in a rugged sort of way but his soft, mannerly style of speech belied the visage of a tough cop.

On Wednesday, Rueger surprised everyone when he convened the same grand jury for a second hearing featuring potential defense witnesses. An unnamed court observer was quoted in The *Enquirer*, described calling additional witnesses before the grand jury after indictments had been handed down, "has never happened before in Hamilton County." Rueger acknowledged it as, "unusual."

Such a hearing held no sway as indictments had already been issued, but the hearing provided prosecutors unbridled insights into Laskey's alibi and defense witnesses. Counter to the finger-wagging from Judge Matthews to local media about the sanctity of grand jury proceedings, the full names and addresses of all testifying witnesses appeared on newspaper front pages and in broadcasts. These included three members of Posteal Laskey's immediate family – his mother, Nancy; brother, Dave; and sister, Patricia Jordan.

The grand jury convened under that morning's front page *Enquirer* headline, "Laskey's Family Called Before Grand Jury Today," naming Posteal's family's names with their addresses. So much for the sanctity of grand jury proceedings.

Posteal Laskey's family members, from left, Patricia Jordan, David, Laskey, and Nancy Laskey. (Cincinnati *Enquirer*/Newspapers.com)

Along with widespread public exposure, the Laskeys were forced to sit in the public hallway outside the grand jury room where photographers popped flashes in their faces and reporters asked invasive questions. The three Laskey family members sat on a long bench, Patricia, holding her nine-day-old infant daughter, a scarf wrapped around her head. Dave, seated between Patricia and his mother, staring straight ahead as flashbulbs popped. His mother, Nancy, was impassive, wearing glasses, a tight white scarf over her ears, and a checked winter coat.

"I know he's innocent," Nancy Laskey was quoted as saying while she sat dry-eyed and stony-faced awaiting her appearance before the grand jury.

The other nine witnesses were also publicly exposed: girlfriend Brenda Jackson; brother-in-law Charles Banks; musicians Thomas Lomax, Harry Darks, "Tiny" Charles Bullock, and James Brown; booking agent Joseph N. Riley; and the women with Laskey and Bullock on Friday the ninth, Vernetta Sargent and Mattie Showes, all potential alibi witnesses at trial.

A grand jury hearing can be something of a free-for-all, absent courtroom formalities. The omission of the defendant and his counsel from the proceedings meant they flowed without objections or questions contrary to the prosecution's argument. Jurors were encouraged to ask questions and press prosecutors on evidence.

Nancy Laskey was the first to testify, telling the grand jury she couldn't recall when her son was at home on the night of August 13-14, but on Sundays, she typically visited her younger sister, Jean, after church, and Posteal frequently drove her. Likewise, when asked about Posteal's whereabouts at the times of The Strangler murders, Nancy told the jurors she could not recall. She provided the background of her son dropping out of old Woodward High School and that he "played bass fiddle in a band," an instrument he kept in the trunk of his car.

Jurors inquired about clothing – Do you wash his clothes? Sometimes. Have you ever noticed any soaking wet clothes? No. Was he in the habit of getting rid of clothes? No. Another juror asked about the assault of Virginia Hinners, a question rooted in the secret grand jury hearing when a member asked, "Did your son ever work for an AC company?"

"No."

Posteal's brother, twenty-three-year-old David Laskey, spoke of the people living in their house. His mother, cousin Russell, and boarder Benjamin Johnson, whom Dave referred to as his step-father, lived at the Freeman

Avenue address, along with Junior. Their father, Posteal Laskey, Sr., passed away in June 1966, having been separated from their mother for more than a decade.

Dave told of being a professional jazz guitarist who could be on the road for, "five weeks, two weeks, or two days," so he couldn't say for certain his brother's whereabouts on the various dates of the murder and assaults.

He said he was very close to his brother, describing Junior as always calm, holding his emotions, and never getting excited. He portrayed him as a neat dresser who often wore a tam. No, Junior did not own a leather jacket, and he'd always, for as long as Dave could remember, had a thin mustache and goatee; thin because he couldn't grow thick facial hair. A juror asked if the three boys exchanged clothing, Dave saying Junior was too small to fit in any of his or cousin Russell's clothing.

He told jurors how his brother had moved from Freeman Avenue to an apartment on Oak Street and then to 2201 Reading Road with Brenda Jackson, whom Dave described as not Junior's exclusive girlfriend.

Joseph Riley, a post office employee and musical booking agent, was questioned next. Riley said Dave was a member of Cincinnati's Local #814 of the American Federation of Musicians, the union for Cincinnati's Black musicians, a remnant of past segregation in the Cincinnati music business. White musicians belonged to AFM Local #1, the first musicians union in the country. Some White jazz musicians also belonged to Local #814.

Riley booked Tiny Charles and His Rocking Outlaws over Friday, Saturday, and Monday nights, but their contract expired in July 1966.

Riley was followed by "Tiny" Charles Bullock, saxophonist and leader of the Rocking Outlaws, a rock, soul, rhythm and blues band.

Bullock told the jury the band had no gigs during August, but were booked at the Soul Lounge in Madisonville and Playboy Bar on Colerain at Alfred Street. Bullock said Posteal also played with the Soul Twisters who performed in reviews across Indiana and Michigan.

Bullock described Laskey as quiet, someone who kept to himself. When asked about Posteal's alcohol consumption, Tiny said his bassist might have a couple of drinks before performing to help face the audience, but he was never intoxicated.

The band typically wore matching outfits, suits, white shirts, cummerbunds, and bow ties; donning dinner jackets when playing at nice clubs.

Posteal's sister, Patricia Laskey Jordan, took the stand holding her infant daughter, telling the panel her mother regularly attended the First Reformed United Church of Christ at Hulbert and Freeman, across the street from their home, and that she had separated from her father thirteen years earlier. The Laskey family, sans Posteal, Sr., had been living at 1820 Freeman Avenue for the past ten or eleven years, with Benjamin Johnson who'd been there since their parents separated. She said her brother had been staying at 1820 Freeman when he wasn't living with Brenda Jackson.

Charles Banks, Posteal's brother-in-law and Wuest co-worker, said Posteal worked as a "floater" at Wuest, earning $1.82 per hour. Banks said he spoke with Posteal about the murders, telling grand jurors Laskey said the man was nuts.

Brenda Jackson

Next to appear before the grand jury was the elusive Brenda Jackson. She told of leaving for Miami on the morning of Friday, December 9 and returning by Greyhound bus on December 16, meaning she did not participate in the December 15 grand jury.

According to Brenda, Laskey was home Thursday when she returned from work sometime between two and three a.m. She told of regularly dancing at Club Riverview on Lawrenceburg Road in Harrison, at Club Riviera in Ross, Ohio, the Red Room, and at Herbie's in Walnut Hills, earning $15 a night dancing, plus tips.

It was then she told Posteal she'd be leaving for Florida with her brother Warren, his girlfriend, and two friends in her friend's Volkswagen.

Brenda had known Posteal since 1962. They renewed their friendship when she returned to Cincinnati in November 1965 after living in Los Angeles. In February 1966, they were living at 730 Oak Street in Walnut Hills, but returned to their respective family homes in August as bills were piling up as income was not.

When Brenda was asked if she remembered the murders, she replied she didn't. "I don't. I mean, it's so much of this stuff going on." Still, she bought a "gas gun" for protection, Posteal warning her not to go out alone.

She described Posteal as, "a tender man, a calm man. He's quiet and really didn't like a lot of people."

Brenda revealed she had been interviewed at length by Sergeant Jackson, the only police detective to interview her, also saying she spoke with Burt Signer on December 20.

Brenda Jackson's words ended recorded testimony as Volume Two of the testimony is presumably destroyed.

This second grand jury session served only to benefit the prosecution at the expense of the defense.

As the same time the grand jury was meeting, the scheduled hearing on the defense Motion to Suppress the Indictment on Constitutional grounds was held in Common Pleas Court before Judge Matthews.

Originally scheduled for January 19, the same day as the surprise grand jury hearing, Matthews agreed to a delay into the following week on Friday the twenty-third.

The defense subpoenaed twelve witnesses to speak about Posteal's first days of confinement and possible violations of his Constitutional rights.

The first witness was Workhouse Superintendent George Studt. He did not know when Laskey arrived at the Workhouse, but knew was there as of December 12.

Studt told of Laskey's comings and goings, most without court orders or in the presence of counsel. On December 12, he was transferred to the Crime Bureau, not returning to the Workhouse until late the next day when he was taken to the courthouse for his probation violation hearing.

Laskey's visitation log during those first days in Studt's custody revealed an array of police, and strangers, unknown to Studt who said it was customary not to record specifics.

Police Chief Jacob Schott testified that he signed an order for Laskey's removal from the Workhouse to Sergeant Jackson, with the approval of Safety Director Henry Sandman who oversaw all city jail facilities. Schott said Laskey was brought in for several people to have a look at him, specifically instructing detectives that no questions be asked without the presence of counsel.

Homicide chief Jackson saw Laskey but told the court that it was Detective Charles Rutledge who was the only one with Laskey late in the afternoon of the 12th but Rutledge could not testify as he'd been hospitalized.

Schott said Rutledge brought in cab #870 passengers August Kraemer and Art Baldrick to view Laskey in the Crime Bureau. That same evening, Lark patron Micky Uchtman came to headquarters where Laskey was brought to the cellblock gate for viewing through bars.

Detective Robert Meiszer told the court he brought two men to the Workhouse to view Laskey, Robert Corwin "Corky" Short and an unknown friend, Judge Matthews siding with Rueger's objection blocking Meiszer from telling the court why Short, a twenty-six-year-old Cincinnati Art Academy student, was brought in to identify Laskey. Laskey and two other prisoners had been told to step to an iron gate where Short viewed the three men.

At that time, Meiszer brought Laskey's beret and had him put it on. Short was not mentioned again.

Detective Tom Gardner escorted Laskey from the City Jail with Detective John Huber across the courtyard to the show-up room for viewing by two female witnesses on the 12th. Laskey, with three others – one police officer and two civilians, were placed in a wire cage, as he described it, with lights shining on them and the room darkened to leave witnesses anonymous. Bluhm said he didn't hear anyone yell "cab." Detective Huber, on the other hand, told the court he heard Laskey and the others say the word "cab" before five witnesses.

Huber described the walk from the cellblock to the show-up room via a public corridor to the entrance of the Bureau of Identification, about a two-minute walk. Signer neglected to ask Huber about witnesses seated in the corridor with a full view of the prisoner being escorted, asking only about officers in the show-up room, which Huber did not recall.

Detective Harry Hillman spoke of passing Laskey in the hallway as he was being taken to the show-up room. Again, Signer neglected to ask about witnesses in the hallway.

Detective Ken Davis saw Laskey only on the 13th with Detective Gardner when they brought a witness to City Jail for viewing Laskey with two others behind the iron bars. The witnesses stood ten to fifteen feet away.

Signer grilled Homicide Detective Albert Williamson, over Rueger's repeated objections, about papers he was holding prior to testifying. Williamson said he was holding them for Sergeant Jackson while Jackson was testifying, describing the contents as photographs taken of the defendant posing with his two attorneys, as requested by defense counsel for press distribution.

The final witness was Ronald Charles Gutmann, deputy clerk of courts, who provided a transcript from the December 10 proceedings in Police Court.

Did Judge Heitzler enter an order for Laskey to be removed from the Workhouse and taken to the Crime Bureau? Gutmann pointed to an undated entry into the log with the word, "Warrant," handwritten by the prosecutor.

Signer requested a recess for the defense to depose Detective Rutledge on the events of December 12, but Rueger objected. After a lengthy back and forth, Judge Matthews denied the request. Judge Matthews, who also oversaw the grand jury proceedings, declared the warrants Constitutional and the arraignment would proceed as scheduled when the defendant would enter his plea on each of the three indictments.

On Friday, December 23, fifteen defendants appeared for the regular arraignment call in Judge Matthews's fifth-floor courtroom before the judge would read the murder, assault, and robbery charges against Posteal Laskey, Jr., each replied to with a plea of innocence or guilt. Once entered, the cases would be remanded for trial.

Laskey arrived at his arraignment hearing carrying a copy of Reader's Digest that he held in his lap throughout the brief proceeding, silent and emotionless.

Common Pleas deputy clerk, Eugene Montesi, read

the murder indictment, asking Laskey, "How do you plead?"

Roney, responded, "The plea is not guilty," repeating the mantra for the other two charges.

With the pleas entered, Judge Matthews refused to set a bond on any of the charges, meaning Laskey would remain in custody. The hearing lasted only minutes.

Local criminal defense attorney, Eugene Smith, commented to *Enquirer* columnist Weikel about the crowd gathered outside the courtroom hoping to catch a glimpse of Laskey, "I'm glad I don't have to defend him. People want to believe he is guilty," adding that due to the fear in the community, defendants have the book thrown at them, "if they happen to be Negroes."

The same day, Judge Matthews denied the defense motion on Constitutional violations during Laskey's incarceration.

The defense also filed a motion on the 27th for a transcript of the grand jury proceedings but that, too, was overruled two weeks later.

In the meantime, Laskey's defense team faced the ongoing challenge of securing their key alibi witness, Brenda Jackson. She initially agreed to testify but was proving difficult to track down. By the time of the next court hearing, Jackson was once again missing. Despite Roney's complaints that police had taken her into custody for questioning, no one, not even her father, seemed to know her whereabouts.

Police Chief Schott repeated that Brenda Jackson had

voluntarily walked into Detective Headquarters where she spoke with Sergeant Jackson. But her failure to appear at the hearing only deepened the mystery surrounding her role in the case.

Posteal and his lawyers appeared before Judge Heitzler for another continuance for Brenda Jackson to appear but Heitzler refused to grant the additional time.

"Police took this witness into custody yesterday (Monday) for interrogation and we don't know where she is," Roney complained after the hearing.

Schott told reporters Brenda Jackson had voluntarily walked into Detective Headquarters and spoke with Homicide chief Jackson, adding, as far as he knew, Jackson did not appear at Tuesday's hearing "of her own volition."

Public pressure was bearing down upon the judicial process as Roney recounted to Judge Heitzler, as he had Judge Mathews following his client's first appearance in court, of being confronted outside the courtroom after the hearing, shaking their fingers at him for defending him. "Some had the attitude of, 'Let's get along with the hanging'." Heitzler, like Mathews, said he knew nothing of any such demonstration.

Throughout this turbulent period, local newspapers continued to paint Laskey as the lone suspect behind a string of unsolved strangulations, despite there being no formal charges tying him to other cases. The *Enquirer* repeatedly reminded its readers that Laskey remained the "prime suspect" in the deaths of six Cincinnati women.

The long Christmas weekend brought a brief respite from headlines. Laskey's name didn't surface again until

The Cincinnati Strangler

Tuesday, December 27, when Frank Weikel's *Enquirer* column sparked controversy by reporting rumors circulating in the Black community. According to Weikel, there were claims that the grand jury which returned Laskey's first-degree murder indictment was all-White. While the actual composition of the jury wasn't entirely White, the statement added fuel to the already tense atmosphere.

In an attempt at levity, Weikel also noted that Laskey had received a Christmas card from Brenda Jackson, but it had been withheld until the five-cent postage was paid.

As the year came to a close, The *Enquirer* published its list of the top ten stories of 1966. The Cincinnati Strangler topped the list, followed by the Bricca family murder in third place. The murder of Barbara Bowman was ranked sixth. A separate survey of local high school students also ranked The Strangler as the year's biggest story, with one student remarking that "Because of all the riots between the white and Negroes, something had to be done to calm this down."

On January 3, 1967, Laskey was back in court as Judge Matthews heard another round of arguments regarding his removal from the Workhouse to appear before witnesses without legal representation. The defense again requested access to grand jury records, but Matthews quickly denied the motion, citing a longstanding Ohio Supreme Court ruling that forbade such access unless overturned by higher courts.

The following morning, columnist Weikel gleefully reported on Laskey's mounting troubles. This time, his financial woes took center stage as news surfaced that

Laskey's car had been repossessed by a finance company for non-payment.

Then, on January 12, 1967, the FBI returned its analysis of the physical evidence gathered from Laskey. One significant finding was a brown pubic hair with Caucasian characteristics, discovered in Laskey's athletic supporter. The report stated that this hair appeared to match some found at the Winstel murder scene, sharing similar microscopic characteristics. The results added another layer of suspicion but still fell short of conclusive evidence.

By mid-January, the FBI had conducted over fifteen hundred microscopic tests for the Cincinnati Police in their search for The Strangler. Despite the effort, clear connections remained elusive.

On January 28, Sergeant Leonard F. Dehn of the Indianapolis Police Homicide unit said William Lester, owner of the Embassy Club in Indianapolis, reported Tiny Charles and His Rocking Outlaws playing over three weeks in August 1966:

August 1, 4 and 6

August 8, 11 and 12

August 22, 25 and 26

A weekend entertainment guide in The Indianapolis *Recorder* trumpeted, "Tiny Charles and the Rocking Outlaws are jumping like mad at this northside playspot Monday Thursday, Friday and Saturday nites," but the opening two Saturday nights were canceled due to the drummer's absence.

Chapter 17
Setting the Stage for Trial

On March 3, 1967, a hearing was held to set a trial date for the first-degree murder charge against Posteal Laskey, Jr.

Outside the courthouse it was a warm, sunny spring day; inside, the prisoner was escorted along the grey iron and concrete cellblock on the top floor of the building by Burt Signer. A local newspaper photographer documented Laskey, untethered by handcuffs or leg irons, walking beside his attorney past cell bars. He was holding a copy of *The View from Pompey's Head*, a 1954 novel about the arrogance, class divide, and racial prejudice in Pompey's Head, South Carolina.

Wearing a gabardine suit, white shirt, and light brown tie; looking as though returning from a nightclub engagement, the defendant entered the courtroom through a door beside the judge's bench. The light grey jacket and pants Posteal wore throughout the initial proceedings were incinerated in a February 1967 Workhouse fire that destroyed the clothing of all 557 prisoners. The city compensated each five dollars for their loss. Posteal's family provided a new set of clothes for the trial.

Judge Simon Leis stepped to his bench, his round, white balding head was surrounded by his black robe and high-backed black leather chair.

Judge Leis would preside over the trial and set March 27 as the opening day over strenuous objections by defense attorneys insisting they needed more time to prepare their case.

"There are only two of us," Signer told The Cincinnati *Post*, "while the prosecutor has 900 policemen to assist him in his investigation," asking for a delay until mid-April.

This was immediately denied.

The next day, Laskey's attorneys filed an appeal in the First District Court of Appeals, asking the three-judge panel to delay the trial. The appeals panel set a hearing date of March 27, the same day as the trial opening.

Judge Leis ordered all motions be filed by March 13 when the defense submitted four motions: to suppress evidence, inspect physical evidence, require prosecutors to provide a grand jury witness list, and for the prosecution to provide the names and addresses of their witnesses.

One week later, Judge Matthews overruled all four in one sweep.

The trial would proceed on schedule.

The players in this courtroom drama, from the judge through defendant, would dominate headlines and consciousness for the coming weeks of the trial.

Judge Simon Leis

(Cincinnati Library/*Enquirer*)

Judge Simon Lawrence Leis was born on August 16, 1896, in LaCrosse, Wisconsin, making him seventy years old when the trial opened.

Attending law school in Cincinnati, Leis passed the Ohio bar in 1922 and married Ida Jane Pilger in 1927. Active in Hamilton County Republican circles, Leis netted an assignment as special prosecutor for the State of Ohio, chasing down voter fraud and dog racing in the 1920s and 30s. During the 1940s, Leis pursued the numbers racket in Youngstown, Ohio and corrupt public officials in Springfield, Ohio.

Days before his 1927 wedding, Simon Leis represented John Rucker, a Black man accused in the shooting death of Cincinnati Police Patrolman Joe Franken. Rucker was convicted of first-degree murder and sentenced to death in the electric chair over the pleas of defense counsel Leis that his client had been at a liquor party in Newport, Kentucky and was so "drug-crazed" that he did not know what he was doing when he ran amok with a shotgun and pistol shooting two people, and frightening a woman so badly she died of heart attack. Rucker was executed on November 30, 1928, with Stanley Charles Hoppe, known as the Toledo Clubber, arrested in the death of a seven-year-old girl and confessed to five other clubbing deaths. The news headline announcing Rucker's death read, "Toledoan and Negro Die at Ohio State Prison."

By 1937, Leis was an assistant Hamilton County prosecutor who participated in the prosecution of Anna Marie Hahn, a serial killer who murdered four men by arsenic poisoning. Hahn was the first woman to die in the Ohio electric chair on December 7, 1938.

Elected to the Common Pleas Court bench in 1955, Leis enjoyed an uninterrupted tenure to the Laskey trial.

A lifelong health enthusiast, Leis was renowned for his daily seven-mile walks from his Westwood home in the western hills to the courthouse, sometimes hiking up the eastern hill to Mt. Adams and back at the start of a day.

He also was known as a gruff old curmudgeon who suffered no nonsense in his courtroom, preventing lawyers, "to stray from the straight line in the courtroom, or I put them back where they belong." Attorneys appearing before Judge Leis were aware of the thin line to walk, succinctly keeping to the legal points. On the other hand, Leis had his own straying ways from higher court rulings where he disagreed, especially those he deemed interfering with police functions. Outside the courtroom, Leis was regarded as kind-hearted.

At seventy years of age, Leis was at the limit for judges but this would not disqualify him from presiding over the Laskey trial. The age limit did block Leis from running for re-election in 1970. Throughout, Leis steadfastly resisted calls for his retirement. The local Republican Party wanted to make the change while Republican James Rhodes was still Ohio governor and before Democrat John Gilligan assumed the governorship in January 1971. Leis finally acquiesced in announcing his retirement on Christmas Eve in 1970 with a promise that his son, Simon Leis, Jr., would gain a judicial appointment.

The wheels turned and prosecutor Rueger was appointed to Leis's Common Pleas bench by Governor Rhodes, as directed by the Hamilton County Republican patronage machine. It would take months for Leis's son to be named Hamilton County prosecutor.

Prosecutor Melvin Rueger

(Courtesy James Rueger)

Born in 1917, Mel Rueger spent much of his life on the far west side of Cincinnati on the family farm in Delhi on Mount Alverno Road. Years later, Mel and his younger brother, Harris, built homes on parcels carved from the original Rueger farm.

Mel worked as a bookkeeper for a paint wholesaler before enlisting in the U.S. Navy in 1942. He rose through the ranks from yeoman to lieutenant, junior grade while stationed in Washington, DC and South America. Likely, the young officer served with the Special Intelligence Service (SIS), the U.S. intelligence operation run by the FBI monitoring German espionage activities in the Western Hemisphere.

After the war, Rueger graduated from Chase Law School in Cincinnati and immediately joined the prosecutor's office specializing in litigating property cases.

The Cincinnati Strangler

In August 1949, then-prosecutor Carson Hoy transferred Rueger to the Criminal Division where he handled a large caseload from the start.

In May 1956, Rueger was named assistant county prosecutor C. Watson Hover, in office since Hoy moved to the bench 1951.

In 1955, he assisted Hover in the prosecution of Robert Lee Jackson for the first-degree murder of Cincinnati Police Detective Walter Hart. Emotionally addressing the jury, tears welling in his eyes, Rueger's voice quavered as he told them: "Walter Hart was a friend of mine. I knew Walter Hart for a few years. He was a friend of yours as a public officer. He was a friend of everyone. He was a friend of the law.

"It's about time we call a halt to this kind of thing. Let other Jacksons sit up and take notice that we have laws and juries that enforce those laws."

It was left to chief prosecutor Hover to close the case for the death penalty:

"I demand on behalf of all of us that if you carry out your sworn duty you have no choice but to have Jackson suffer the strongest penalty the law permits."

Rueger's emotions may have overtaken him in the Jackson trial, but his typical courtroom demeanor was calm and reasoned; determined but dignified. Rueger was known for presenting evidence in clear narrative, connecting the dots for a jury. His son, James, later said his father "took no pleasure in dealing in human misery," and that he never brought his work home.

The triggerman, Lemuel Sam Trotter, and Willie Barnett entered the Grey Eagle Café where Trotter held his gun on patrons as Barnett rifled the cash register; Robert Jackson acted as lookout. Detective Walter Hart happened to be a patron of the downtown tavern that night and ended up in a shootout, wounding Barnett before being shot dead on the sidewalk. Jackson and Trotter were executed in the electric chair on the same date, July 7, 1958, eighteen minutes apart in the Ohio State Penitentiary.

Rueger was a master of the rules of evidence and criminal procedure. Leading criminal defense attorneys all spoke highly of him, his honesty, and his integrity. Rueger was not a big man in physical size, rather known for his intellectual and ethical stature.

Rueger was named prosecutor in July 1965, succeeding William S. Mathews when he was appointed to the Municipal Court. Rueger was elected prosecutor the month before Laskey's arrest. In 1972, he would be named a Probate Court judge where he remained until his retirement in 1990.

An avid golfer and champion of parks, Mel Rueger died in 2010 at the age of ninety-two, his obituary cited the prosecution of Posteal Laskey, saying: "He brought to justice the serial killer and rapist known as the Cincinnati Strangler." The obituary also noted Rueger's role the infamous 1958 murder trial of Edythe Klumpp and the 1969 robbery of the Cabinet Supreme Savings and Loan that ended in the shooting deaths of four women.

Assistant Prosecutor Calvin Prem

(Courtesy Kenton County Library)

Calvin Warren Prem was born on September 22, 1924, to Austrian-immigrant parents living on Main Street in Over the Rhine, next to The Woodward theater. His father, Adolph, died in 1927 after the family moved to the eastside suburb of Oakley, and the year following Adolph's naturalization. Gisela was left a widow with two young sons – Cal, not quite three, and his infant brother, Ronald, who would grow up to be a Cincinnati firefighter.

Cal's mother pushed him hard, the lessons she impressed upon him about good appearance remained with him through his life, despite enduring a childhood with other kids taunting him for his prim appearance. As an adult, Cal was always a sharp dresser, wearing crisp white dress shirts, C.W.P. monogrammed on the cuffs, closed with gold cuff links; a gold watch underneath. His appearance was accentuated by his alert eyes and arched eyebrows.

In 1952, Cal married Lee Jones, a popular radio and television singer. Lee arrived in Cincinnati from Chicago in 1950 to work at WLW radio, billed as "Lee Jones, the Singing and Yodeling Cowgirl." Her radio performances included a children's musical hour, and commercials before moving to top billing on Midwestern Hayride, a popular regional television country music variety show, as the winsome young cowgirl. Lee was born in Muhlenberg County, Kentucky, the daughter of Kennedy "Jonesie" Jones, a coal miner and pioneer in thumb-picking guitar style, and an influence on many well-known country guitarists. Lee's star grew when she was paired with Bonnie Lou on Hayride as the Yodeling Cowgirls. Lee's brother, Kenny, played guitar in the house band, The Hayriders.

Cal Prem was Mel Rueger's righthand man on high-profile criminal cases, making him heir to the prosecutorial seat. The two worked in successful tandem garnering shared experiences they brought into the Laskey trial. Prem was known as a gifted litigator who cared deeply about every case, striving for perfection beyond a doubt, getting it right the first time to avoid retrial or loss on appeal. He advocated for his client, the state or, later, in private practice, as zealously as legally and ethically possible, within the bounds of the rules. Once, Cal was asked how many people he'd sent to jail over thirty-five years? His answer: None. His job was to present the facts and leave the final decision to the judge and jury.

Cal was a folksy individual, never looking down others, even those he was prosecuting. According to his son, Prem never took pleasure in seeking the death penalty, regarding it as a tremendous responsibility. Both of Prem's sons became lawyers, following their father into roles as assistant prosecutors.

Cal's favorite opponent in the courtroom was locally renowned defense attorney Bernard Gilday, playing Perry Mason to Prem's Hamilton Berger. Prem regarded trying a case akin to tennis or football where you try like hell to offset your opponent, but afterwards you sit down for a drink together, the relationship enjoyed by Prem and Gilday.

When Mel Rueger assumed his judgeship and Simon Leis, Jr. was appointed prosecutor, Prem resigned. Tradition held that when the prosecutor moved to the bench, the first assistant prosecutor was promoted to prosecutor, abandoning nineteen years in the prosecutor's office for private practice as a criminal defense attorney.

Defense Counsel – Donald Roney and Burton Signer

Posteal Laskey, Jr. flanked by his attorneys, Donald Roney, Left, and Burton Signer during his 1967 trial. (Cincinnati *Post*/Newspapers.com)

Donald Francis Roney was born in 1915 and graduated from the Cincinnati YMCA College of Law in 1946. Roney was a second lieutenant in the Army Reserves during the Second World War. He worked in insurance before graduating law school.

Burton Robert Signer was a political animal born in 1930. In June 1951, Burt married Arline Harriet Schwartz, daughter of Benjamin Schwartz who, in 1956, was appointed Juvenile Court judge in Hamilton County and was a force in local Republican politics. Signer netted his first patronage job in 1953 as a constable in the Common Pleas Court, graduating law school four years later.

Roney and Signer were appointed by Judge Heitzler to represent Posteal Laskey, what they hoped would jumpstart their new law practice. Heitzler knew both lawyers from their support of his re-election campaign and as active local Republicans.

Before their appointment, Roney and Signer were assistant Hamilton County prosecutors working under Mel Rueger. Roney had been with the office for sixteen years, serving as the chief investigator for the office, Signer for three.

Hangdog Roney was the point of the prosecutor's investigative spear working within police ranks on major criminal cases. His tactics were often a headache for the prosecution as his aggressive style resulted in not guilty verdicts or high-profile cases overturned. Roney could turn his good cop/bad cop personae on and off. He might bring drinks and sandwiches to an interview, or apply unrelenting interrogative pressure upon a suspect. Roney was infamous for getting suspects to confess to the crimes.

Signer, on the other hand, had little trial experience outside lower-level cases. His greater interest laid in real estate and finance. Signer parlayed his standing in Cincinnati society and legal circles, his father-in-law easing his way to prominence in Republican politics and Cincinnati's Jewish community. His connections led to being named special counsel by Ohio Attorney General William Saxbe in 1963, the same year he became an assistant Hamilton County prosecutor. In March 1965, Signer was considered to share the ticket with Judge George S. Heitzler and in October was named chairman of Judge William S. Mathews's re-election campaign.

While working as full-time assistant prosecutors,

Roney and Signer became embroiled in a venture that would close their prosecutorial careers.

While a member of Rueger's staff, Signer was investing in Cincinnati and Miami, Florida real estate. In 1961, he cut the ribbon at the self-named Signer Building, owned by Burt and his wife, Arline. The Green Savings and Loan was the first tenant at the corner of Reading and Section Roads in Roselawn, the same address as Ringgold Building and Loan.

In 1962, Signer became president and general counsel of Ringgold. Joining Signer on the Ringgold board were Roney as secretary and managing officer; C. Watson Hover, Hamilton County prosecutor from 1951 to 1963 and presiding judge of the First District Court of Appeals; court investigator Neil Quinn; and Cincinnati *Enquirer* columnist Frank Weikel.

Hints of fraudulent conduct at Ringgold began surfacing in August 1966, ending in the Ohio Deposit Guarantee Fund seizing the building and loan in November 1966.

Rueger was incensed his assistants committed serious financial malfeasance, forcing their resignations. Rueger benevolently extended their termination date to the end of the year, assuring their paychecks as they hurriedly set up a joint private practice.

Roney and Signer's financial misdeeds snowballed over years into indictments for embezzlement and tax fraud. Signer was disbarred in 1972, while Roney escaped disbarment by a technicality. In 1977, Signer was disbarred in Kentucky for nondisclosure of his unethical conduct when he applied for a Kentucky license in 1966.

On March 30, 1972, Signer was found guilty on charges tax evasion and filing a fraudulent tax return and sentenced to a year and a day in federal prison, but was exonerated by his old political sponsor, William Saxbe, then the Attorney General of the United States.

Roney continued plying his hand in finance, setting up Casino Realty, a dummy corporation. Fred Englehardt, Jr., a custodian in the Hamilton County Courthouse, was appointed president. Casino refinanced fourteen real estate loans on properties assumed from Gene Graff, Ringgold's former treasurer, totaling $355,750. Refinancing was handled by Ringgold in amounts appreciably above the mortgages, known as over-loans, with the excess skimmed off the top. Before becoming a courthouse custodian, Englehardt had operated a refrigeration repair service where Roney's wife, Elizabeth, was his secretary and bookkeeper, roles she assumed with Casino. All of Casino's corporate correspondence was routed to the Roney's North College Hill home.

Roney became city manager of Newport, Kentucky in 1968, having regular dealings with the city's seedy underside, infamous for mob-operated gambling and prostitution enterprises until his ouster in 1971.

Don Roney died in 1996 in Frankfort, Kentucky and Burt Signer passed away in Maineville, Ohio in 2011.

Defendant - Posteal Laskey, Jr.

(Cincinnati Police Department)

Posteal Laskey, Jr. was born on June 18, 1937, in Cincinnati to Posteal Laskey, Sr. and Nancy Jean Mullins Laskey. His grandparents, James and Josephine Nichols Laskey, were both born in Bullock County, Alabama in the heart of the Black Belt, and married there in 1915.

In the wake of the First World War, the Great Migration of African-Americans from the South fled the Ku Klux Klan, lynchings, and the Jim Crow social order. Conditions were made worse by floods and boll weevil infestations devastating the agricultural foundation, leaving behind a ruined economy. Many African-Americans fled to Northern industrial centers, like Cincinnati, but the Laskeys looked west in search of a new life. Richard, Josephine and their two sons, Posteal and Jack, left for Oklahoma where the new oil wealth was booming and money was flowing.

They settled in the rural town of Okemah in Creek

County, south of Tulsa, an odd choice given it was a "sundown town" where the movement of people of color was prohibited once the sun went down. There were regular incidents of racial violence in the area, including lynching.

Around the time of the Laskeys's arrival, the Klan was enjoying a revival across the South and spreading west, becoming a force in Oklahoma. Founded in Georgia during Reconstruction after the Civil War, the Klan succumbed to political pressures evolving into public exhaustion over their violent ways, before re-emerging with the post-World War One nativist movements arising from isolationist sentiments.

James and Josephine lived under something of a shield as employees of Hunter Montgomery, a wealthy White farmer who owned the land and house where they lived. Montgomery enhanced his property holdings through land grabs amid the Oil Boom. These schemes became violent to the extreme in Tulsa in 1921 but not exclusive to that year, nor Tulsa.

On February 1, 1920, Bessie Hance Baker, a seventeen-year-old Indian wife of Jim Baker, was freed from eight months of captivity, locked in a room in Okemah where she was found with her deceased two-month-old infant son, Troy. Bessie was forced by her husband, along with Curly Martin and his wife, Katy, to sign over land deeds in the Beggs oil field Bessie inherited. Curly Martin was already wanted by police for the shooting death of a Black man.

Among those taking part in the scam was Hunter

Montgomery.

The so-called "imprisoned rich Indian heiress" was locked in an Okemah shanty, her room secured by a padlock and chain, windows nailed and barred shut. Though they went to trial, the charges against her captors were dismissed.

Bessie Baker died on December 18, 1921, in Nuyaka, Oklahoma at the age of twenty-one.

It was from this environment James and Josephine Laskey fled north to Cincinnati where they settled in 1923.

In Cincinnati, James Laskey was an illiterate laborer and Josephine, who could read and write, worked as a laundress. James died in 1927 leaving Josephine to raise their two sons, Posteal and Jack. Josephine remarried in 1940 to William Spratley, a post office security officer and Bullock County, Alabama native. Josephine passed away in 1968.

Posteal Laskey, Sr. was born in Alabama in 1913, but little remains of his life in his wake. The births of children, including Posteal Junior in 1937, were milestones but not much else. He worked as a porter and laborer with the Works Progress Administration (WPA) building Columbia Parkway on the east side where he and his growing family lived.

Junior's mother, Nancy, was born on October 1, 1913, christened Evely J. Mullins, in Mount Vernon, Kentucky, to Richard Mullins, a coal miner, and Mollie Buford in Rockcastle County, south of Lexington.

The Cincinnati Strangler

Nancy Mullins, a domestic in Cincinnati, married Posteal Laskey in 1934. The couple settled in a crowded wood frame tenement on East Third Street in the East End river flats at the busy Fulton railyard. Grandmother Josephine lived nearby at 337 Ellen Street.

Nancy's first child, Mollie Ann, was born on January 9, 1932 and died in 1957, at the age of twenty-five, from a botched kitchen abortion.

Hilda Jean, was born on July 13, 1935. She remained single until age thirty-six when she married fifty-eight-year-old post office guard, James Caldwell. Hilda was a longtime laundromat manager who passed away in 1996. She is buried beside her mother in the Vine Street Hill Cemetery in Cincinnati.

Nancy's third child, Posteal Junior, was born in 1937. At that time, the Laskeys were living at 404 Butler Street, part of the nineteenth-century African-American neighborhood called Bucktown, now blended into the city's urban center. Three months after the birth of his son, Posteal Senior was arrested for stealing five suits and ten pairs of trousers from a downtown clothing store.

A year and a half later, Nancy gave birth to her fourth child, Larry, whose life carried little note outside of trouble, including a rape charge in the early 1960s netting Larry a sentence of three to twenty years. He was paroled from the Marion Correctional Institution in February 1969 and in the early morning hours of Friday, August 29, 1969, Larry Laskey was found dead in an apartment building hallway at Hausman Alley and Broadway. Patrolman Curtis Herkert was accompanying a man from a traffic stop to retrieve his driver's license in his Broadway apartment. There, Herkert found the body of Laskey lying dead, a .25-caliber handgun wound to his chest.

Eighteen-year-old Carol Ann Estes and her three companions were seen leaving by Herkert, the gun and a knife were in her possession when police caught the foursome nearby. Estes was indicted on a charge of first-degree manslaughter.

The charge was reduced as Estes, along with the other three were indicted for larceny by trick in May 1970. Prosecutors accepted Estes's claim she shot Laskey only after he grabbed her by the throat and started strangling her. There is no sign these cases were ever adjudicated.

David Laskey was born in 1944, and another daughter, Patricia, was born in 1947. David was a talented jazz guitarist who studied at the University of Cincinnati Conservatory of Music, going on to a successful career as a touring and studio artist. Junior followed in his brother into music but never reached similar heights. Patricia and Dave were by their mother's side throughout Posteal's travails.

Posteal Laskey, Sr. died on June 6, 1966, at the family's Freeman Avenue house. He had been separated from Nancy for many years.

Around the time of their separation, Benjamin Johnson moved into Freeman Street as a boarder, David telling the impromptu December 21 grand jury he thought of Johnson as his step-father. Throughout the trial, Johnson would be referenced as "the boarder," but in December 1970, Nancy and Ben Johnson married. Ben passed away in 1986, Nancy in 2001.

Upon Posteal's arrest, police compiled his criminal record, going back as far as 1947 when the ten-year-old was charged with trespassing for stealing apples, plus a pattern of persistent truancy from school, leading to his dropping out after barely finishing eighth grade.

When he was fifteen, Posteal faced a serious charge of assault to rape in the sexual assault of a ten-year-old White girl. Police, responding to a fight among girls at Pearl and Eggleston on the east side of downtown, found Laskey hanging out nearby. He was picked up on a charge of juvenile delinquency but police then questioned him about the sexual assault, bringing in the ten-year-old who identified Posteal as her assailant. Laskey denied it and his mother told police her son was at home at the time of the offense; his parents were noted by police as "uncooperative." Posteal took and failed a lie detector test, police accusing the teen, "guilty of this assault as charged." The case was not referred for prosecution but as evidenced by what came next, Laskey may have been offered a traditional option – join the military or face the court. He chose the Army.

Before joining the ranks, Posteal and brother Larry were arrested in November 1953 for stealing lumber from a highway maintenance yard. Cutting the lumber before taking it led to an added charge of "malicious destruction of property."

Otherwise, Juvenile Court authorities advised police during their 1966 investigation, "there was never any adjudication on Posteal Laskey."

That, along with acknowledged privacy issues, did not deter police from leaking Laskey's juvenile record to *Enquirer* columnist Weikel who encapsulated the young man's rapsheet as a trail of rape, malicious property destruction, and truancy.

On August 20, 1954, Posteal enlisted in the U.S. Army at the age of seventeen with the signed permission of his parents. He was assigned to the Headquarters and Service Company of the 588th Engineer Battalion at Fort Eustis in Newport News, Virginia.

At three a.m. in the morning of May 2, 1955, young Private Laskey was a passenger, on legitimate leave, in a car involved in a collision outside Petersburg, Virginia. The injured soldier was taken to the U.S. Army Hospital at Fort Lee on the outskirts of Petersburg where he was treated over months.

Laskey suffered lacerations to his right leg and right wrist, without severing an artery, but the accident ruptured his right kidney requiring removal of the organ. He remained under medical care into July 1955, while his 588th Engineer Battalion transferred west.

In November 1955, completing a temporary re-assignment to Fort Belvoir, Private Laskey sailed to Europe to join the Petroleum Supply unit in the 526th Quartermaster Company in the Smiley Barracks in Karlsruhe, Germany, arriving December 3, 1955.

At 11:20 p.m., Sunday, February 3, 1957, the private was in the Enlisted Men's Club at Smiley Barracks when suddenly, fueled by too much beer, he struck a female German civilian, Irmgard Haß (Hass), a woman he later claimed was his girlfriend. Laskey struck her across her face with his open hand, drawing MPs who arrested him. Two days later, Laskey was arrested for speeding and reckless driving behind the wheel of a quarter-ton Jeep on the Karlsruhe-Heidelberg Autobahn.

In a February 20, 1957 court martial, Laskey was found not guilty on the driving charge but guilty on the assault charge for which he was sentenced to six months at hard labor.

On March 1, while confined, a hearing was held under the subject, "Elimination of Undesirable Personnel." Citing multiple violations of military rules by Private Laskey, described as a "habitual shirker," Captain David B. Goble told the commission he did not wish for Laskey to be returned to his unit, describing the private as, "not capable of doing anything right either on or off duty."

When he wasn't relaxing with a magazine or simply not present with work to be done, Laskey spent many hours on sick call, often reporting in the morning for minor ailments and complaints, wasting the day in the infirmary rather than on the job. His attitude and influence upon others, compounded by a November 18, 1956 prosecution for being AWOL and sentenced to one month at hard labor, someone the military had no wish to retain.

On March 13, the Assistant Adjutant General, Captain John V. Carolin, ordered Private Laskey separated from service with an Undesirable Discharge Certification and transferred to the Port of Bremerhaven, Germany for transport back to the U.S. on board the USNS *General Robert E. Callan*. The *Callan* arrived at Bremerhaven on March ferrying the nine-hundred members of the 9th Combat Engineer Battalion for duty in post-war Germany, along with their dependents. Laskey was among the passengers on board its return journey.

Laskey was released on March 18, 1957, for transportation to Bremerhaven and his return Stateside.

Arriving at the Brooklyn Navy Yard, Laskey was immediately transferred to Fort Dix for confinement until his discharge on April 4, 1957. "Under Other Than Honorable Conditions," Private Laskey was stripped of rank and provided a one-way train ticket to Cincinnati.

Posteal Laskey, Jr. returned to Cincinnati and trouble quickly followed with his arrest in the brutal assault of fifty-nine-year-old Celia Purvis.

Sometime before noon on Wednesday, November 20, 1957, there was a knock on the door of the caretaker's apartment in the basement at 3437 Shaw Avenue, six steps down from the rear of the building. Celia Purvis, the caretaker, answered the door, finding a young man saying he was a deliveryman from nearby Parke Drug, located on nearby Hyde Park Square. He was looking for someone named "Graham," Purvis telling him no one by that name lived in the building. He then asked if he could use her telephone, Purvis opened the door wide enough to pass him the phone. After completing the call, the man left but soon returned, again asking to use the telephone. This time, Purvis refused, and the man left, but he returned a third time, this time forcing his way into Celia's apartment. He struck Purvis on the head, fracturing her skull and inflicting a serious laceration above her right eye. The blow knocked Purvis to the floor but her scream caused the assailant to flee.

Laskey said he hit Purvis with a broom handle after she viciously responded to his request to use the phone, "Get the hell out – you black son-of-a-bitching nigger." Laskey told police he was reacting to her racist screed.

An earlier psychological examination found Laskey to be a "very impulsive person with a bad temper," seeming to "carry a chip on his shoulder regarding his race," characterizations that would follow, whether true or not, for the remainder of his days.

The 1958 Pre-Parole Personality Evaluation concluded, "In view of his poor impulse control and ethnocentricity he is liable to get in more difficulty." The report described him as, a "psychopathic offender, asocial, with aggressive personality pattern."

The day after the Purvis assault, Detective Lytle Young found Posteal Laskey, Jr. standing at the corner of Richmond and Central Avenues at three o'clock in the afternoon and arrested him. Laskey had been fired as a deliveryman for Parke Drug only five days before the assault.

Posteal was indicted on December 27, 1957, tried in Common Pleas Court before Judge Simon Leis, and found guilty by a jury of Assault with Intent to Kill on February 28, 1958. Upon sentencing twenty-year-old Laskey to an "indeterminate term in the reformatory," Leis vented his frustration, telling Laskey and the courtroom, "Men like you should be put out of society for life. I am sorry that I can only send you to the reformatory."

Laskey was sentenced from one-to-fifteen years arriving at the Ohio State Reformatory in Mansfield on March 12, 1958.

A January 1959 Ohio Parole Commission hearing reviewed Laskey's record – juvenile and adult, noting his reputation for striking women, including the fractured skull and ongoing suffering endured by Celia Purvis in the aftermath of her attack. Judge Leis, who sentenced Laskey to prison in 1958, told the commission, "this boy could have easily been a murderer," recommending they keep Laskey. This paired with the recommendation of parole investigator, Colonel G. Warner Nicholas, that Posteal Laskey, "be given a rather long continuance." Meaning - no parole.

During the parole review, Reverend W.M. Frisby, pastor of the Mt. Sinai Baptists Church, wrote the parole board in support of Posteal Laskey: "I've always thought he was a very fine boy…I'm asking the board please give him another chance, as I've known him from a child."

Nancy Laskey insisted to parole authorities she could not understand how her son had gotten mixed up in the offense as he had not had any prior difficulties.

A 1961 parole evaluation toward release the Lebanon Correctional Institution noted Laskey becoming very guarded and withdrawn when confronted based upon his intense underlying anxiety. The report also cited his good conduct over four years of confinement. Laskey told the board of his self-improvement and that he "acquired better attitudes toward white people."

Laskey was released from the Lebanon Reformatory

on February 21, 1962, and given one year's parole.

After his release, Posteal briefly joined the circus - the Cetlin and Wilson Circus, headquartered in Petersburg, Virginia – the scene of Posteal's 1955 auto accident. The circus tour covered fifteen weeks over the summer of 1962 traveling the Eastern Seaboard and Midwest, but he didn't last the entire tour. It was good experience for an aspiring musician as he backed various acts, like Nat Mercy's All-Star Revue, Red Marcus' Minstrel Revue specializing in twist tunes, and Marcus's Club Trinidad All-Negro Revue, "the best rock 'n' roll show on the road." Club Trinidad was emceed by Pedro Lane, known as the Fat Man with a Cane.

But circus life was tough and soon Posteal was back at his mother's house. With the help of his parole officer, Mike Sherlock, who helped Posteal get a job driving a Yellow Cab in late July 1962, he was earning $50 a week, plus tips. Sherlock requested Laskey's parole supervision be lowered to "minimum."

Posteal drove a Yellow Cab for about six months until refusing to drive the cab he'd been assigned, complaining the heat wasn't working. Refusing to drive was grounds for dismissal and Posteal quickly found himself out of work – and back in trouble.

On Christmas Eve 1963 in Covington, Kentucky, across the Ohio River from Cincinnati, twenty-four-year-old Joyce Hitchcock alighted from a bus at Third and Philadelphia Streets shortly after midnight. Walking south on Philadelphia toward her home, she noticed a car turning around at Elm Street. Thinking nothing more about it, Hitchcock entered her property at 426 Philadelphia and started up the stairs to the second floor when she heard someone following her. She turned around to see a man on the staircase, pausing to ask what he wanted. The man did not reply but reached for her leg; Hitchcock sensing he was reaching beneath her skirt as he scratched the inside of her right leg. She screamed and the man ran away, but not before grabbing her purse. Joyce's husband, Eugene, heard the commotion and gave chase across Philadelphia, west on Fifth Street to Crescent Avenue where he lost sight of the assailant. Returning home, Eugene found his wife's purse lying in the front yard with everything intact.

Hitchcock called Covington Police who learned the assailant drove away in a dark-colored 1955 or 1956 Mercury with Ohio plates.

At 12:44 a.m., police observed a car matching that description at Sixth and Bakewell Streets in Covington with three occupants inside, heading for the bridge to Cincinnati.

When police approached the car, Posteal Laskey was a passenger in the vehicle owned by Orvan Copeland who told police he didn't know Laskey. Copeland said Laskey walked up asking for a ride across the river while Copeland was parked at the Bridge Café. Laskey offered him a dollar for the ride. The dollar bill was lying on the front seat. Police neglected to connect Copeland's address of 2215 Symmes Street in Cincinnati as the same address where the Laskey family had been living.

Brought into custody, Posteal Laskey, Jr. was identified by Joyce and Eugene Hitchcock as the man who attacked Joyce.

An abandoned 1956 Buick with Ohio plates, registered to Laskey, was found at Elm and Philadelphia Streets. Laskey's parole following imprisonment for the Purvis assault expired ten months earlier on February 21, 1963.

Laskey pleaded guilty to the robbery charge and was sentenced to two years in the Kentucky State Reformatory at LaGrange on February 21, 1964. He was released on August 21, 1965, little more than a month before he would be arrested again.

In the late-night hours of October 7, 1965, twenty-six-year-old Judith Buckner was walking to her ground floor apartment at 341 Terrace Avenue in Clifton, taking a path along the western edge of Burnet Woods along Clifton Avenue, near where Mathilda Messer's body would be found months later. Judy sensed she was being followed. Her suspicion was confirmed when a man entered her apartment building right behind her, asking the location of Saint Joe Street, a small side street across Vine from Rose Winstel's house, more than two miles away. Buckner's apartment was close to Good Samaritan Hospital and the Gaslight District.

Without warning, the man suddenly attacked Judy, striking her repeatedly about the head with his fists. Her screams caused the assailant to flee.

Laskey was arrested two days later by Officer William Dehner on an assault and battery warrant at his 1820 Freeman Avenue home. As it was Saturday, Posteal was home from his job at the Adam Wuest warehouse where he worked as a stapler.

Picked out of a lineup, Laskey admitted following Buckner and assaulting her, telling Dehner he didn't know why he struck her. A license plate number provided by Buckner led police to Laskey who told Dehner he'd never make that mistake again.

Posteal entered a plea of No Contest, asking the court to send him to the hospital for psychiatric evaluation, leaving it up to Municipal Court Judge William Mathews to render judgment. On November 30, 1965, Judge Mathews sentenced Laskey to three years' probation.

It was the probation meted out by Judge Mathews that permitted authorities to hold Laskey indefinitely when he was found guilty of assault in the pursuit of Sandra Chapas.

Now, he was facing a trial for the first-degree murder of Barbara Bowman, with the electric chair waiting if found guilty.

Through the ups and downs of his twenty-nine years, Posteal could always count on his mother's love. Too often in the wake of some misdeed, Nancy Laskey insisted there was no way her son could do such a thing; always standing by his side. Throughout multiple hearings and the trial, Nancy Laskey was a stoic fixture in Courthouse hallways and in the courtroom showing support for her son.

Chapter 18
Is a Fair Trial Possible?

The process of assembling a jury for the high-profile trial of Posteal Laskey Jr. began with a "special jury" pool of seventy-five potential candidates, selected from voter registration rolls and drawn from a jury wheel, a large brass drum in the fashion of a ticket tumbler familiar at carnival raffles, made around the same time the courthouse opened in 1915. Capital charges always warranted the large pool of a special jury due to the gravity of the charge—first-degree murder, a capital crime. Selected jurors were summoned to the Hamilton County Courthouse on the opening day of the trial, Monday, March 27, 1967.

As the trial date neared, the defense filed a Notice of Alibi, a common legal step to inform the prosecution of alibi witnesses supporting the defendant's innocence. This move was prompted by the prosecution's request for transparency in the case, aimed at preventing any last-minute surprises. The defense also filed a motion for a change of venue, citing concerns over pre-trial publicity. They referred to the 1966 U.S. Supreme Court decision overturning Dr. Sam Sheppard's 1954 conviction due to excessive pre-trial coverage, which created a "carnival atmosphere." The defense argued that similar conditions now existed in Cincinnati preventing Laskey from receiving a fair trial.

Judge Leis presided over the change of venue hearing.

The prosecution called Dan Young, host of a popular local nighttime radio talk show, Partyline, where listeners called with their thoughts on news and events of the day.

Young nervously cupped his left thumb and index finger to slide his heavy black glasses up the bridge of his nose as he told the court, "In my opinion, it would be difficult to get a fair and impartial jury."

Next up was Dale Schmidt, clerk of the Cincinnati City Council, who was asked about a council resolution containing the phrase, "Whereas the killer has created an atmosphere of fear and apprehension among the population of the City of Cincinnati." Judge Leis intervened to say witnesses could only testify to their personal knowledge about the defendant's ability to receive a fair trial, to which Schmidt said, "I, I, I say it would be difficult in the community."

When the defense questioned Police Chief Schott about his statement—"We think he's the guy"—made at the time of Laskey's arrest, Leis sustained the prosecution's objection, limiting testimony to the issue of whether Laskey could receive a fair trial, rather than revisiting past statements. Ultimately, the defense rested, and Judge Leis held the matter for deliberation.

The trial began under humid, rainy skies on March 27, 1967, the Monday following the Easter weekend. The courtroom holding the trial had been the setting for other sensational trials, such as the 1959 Edythe Klumpp murder trial and the recent trial of Robert Ray Abbott. Interest in the Laskey trial would be different from those other cases involving love triangles and murder. The Bowman murder was simply gruesome while the city was collectively relieved The Strangler had been captured and soon would die in the electric chair. Laskey's trial would not reach an orchestral crescendo; rather, the cymbals clashed upon Laskey's arrest; the music quieting to a diminuendo of foregone conclusions.

When the bailiff unlocked the wooden doors just before nine, the expected throng turned out to be merely a few people, mostly normal courthouse observers mixed with family members of the defendant and some strangler victims.

The tall, solid wood courtroom doors led directly into the spectator area of eight solid oak benches, like church pews, awaiting the curious and committed. A brass rail separated the spectator section from the well of the court. The railing opened at its center to two large tables where the defendant would sit between his two attorneys on the left and the prosecution seated to the right. The judge sat at the center of the scene upon his elevated green marble bench, two steps above the courtroom before him. The judge's bailiff was stationed to his right, one step down. Another brass rail corralled the area in front of the bench containing two smaller desks where the clerk and court reporter sat.

To the left of the bench, beneath the twenty-eight-foot-high vaulted ceiling, the jury would be seated in a two-tiered wooden box, containing twelve oak banker's chairs, upholstered in cushioned leather seats and backs. The bottom six chairs rested on the floor, the top tier on a platform raised one step above, and one step below the judge's bench. Along the entire right side of the courtroom stood tall, steel-framed clear glass windows hinged along their entirety at their midlines to open the full length amid curtains, stopping at the green marble wainscoting wrapping the room's walls. Six light fixtures hung from the high ceiling.

Outside the windows, three stories down, ran Short Court, a compact portion of Court Street where Sandra Chapas walked from her job at Kenner on Sycamore Street to her West Court Street apartment four months earlier.

Laskey was transferred from the Workhouse to the concrete reinforced, thick iron-barred holding cells of the County Jail on the sixth floor, his home for the duration of the trial.

Judge Leis's docket that Monday morning was crowded with arraignment hearings for seven other defendants in nine criminal cases - two auto theft charges, burglary, shooting to kill, assault to rob, incest, second-degree murder, concealed weapon, and a bounced check case. The matter of Posteal Laskey would begin after his hearing in another courtroom requesting postponement of the trial.

A week earlier, the same appeals court rejected the defense request for Judge Leis to be removed from the trial. The defense cited the jurist's remark at the conclusion of Laskey's 1958 trial in the assault of Celia Purvis. The appeals panel concluded Leis showed no signs of bias or prejudice, certainly not through a nineteen-year-old statement.

Again, the appeals panel ruled against the defense and Laskey's trial commenced at 11:40 A.M.

As the court waited for the defendant to appear from the upstairs lockup, Roney fumbled through papers at the defense table, handing a jumble of pages to the judge, telling Leis, "I will have the originals here in a minute."

At that moment, Laskey was led into the courtroom.

"All right, what is before the court," the judge asked?

Roney requested a review on the Motion to Take Depositions, presumably the pages Roney bungled to the bench.

"I have no motion before me to take a deposition," Leis scowled.

"In the shuffling of papers," Roney said as he continued frantically handling papers. "Maybe we left the court out."

Judge Leis exercised patience seldom witnessed in his court.

Roney continued bumbling along, making excuses why they hadn't filed "this deposition – this notice, motion to take a deposition," Leis testily responding no one was denying their taking depositions, reminding Roney he'd been told weeks earlier of the court's willingness to assist in taking depositions. The defense sought to depose key witnesses, but the court noted that those they sought were available in Cincinnati, with the exception Raymond "Bud" Walker, companion of Ruth Ann Bailey the night of Barbara Bowman's murder, who had moved to California, whereabouts unknown.

219

The next motion—request for a continuance—was denied, and the process of jury selection, or voir dire, French for "speak the truth," began. Out of the seventy-five prospective jurors summoned, seventy-one appeared. They were given personal questionnaires to complete, followed by the judge asking if any had medical or personal reasons not to serve. Judge Leis showed little patience for weak excuses but excused those with genuine hardships.

After receiving letters from doctors excusing jurors and pleas from others asking to not serve, Judge Leis then dealt with three prospective jurors who simply did not appear, saying about each: "Send the sheriff."

Once the jury pool was ready, voir dire would begin. Going through a list of standard questions, the prosecution and defense sought to gauge the suitability of each juror to their case. The goal was to identify biases, beliefs, or life experiences that could affect their ability to be impartial. Jurors were reminded of the presumption of innocence and the burden of proof resting on the prosecution.

For attorneys, voir dire is an art form. It requires skill in understanding human behavior and detecting potential biases. The courtroom, with its imposing Latin-based legal jargon, can be intimidating for most jurors. Yet, as each prospective juror faced the court, they began to understand the weight of their responsibility. The task was to fairly and impartially decide a man's fate, possibly sentencing him to death, daunting responsibilities.

Jurors were called one by one from the group waiting

in an empty courtroom across the hall.

The first to face questioning was James E. Long, marking the official start of the trial, State of Ohio v. Posteal Laskey Jr.

No. 88695

Hamilton County Common Pleas

THE STATE OF OHIO

vs.

POSTEAL LASKEY, JR.

Indictment for MURDER 1ST DEGREE

Sec. 2901.01 R.C.

A TRUE BILL

Frank W. Nixon
Foreman of the Grand Jury

Reported and filed this 16 day of *December* A. D. 19 66

ROBERT D. JENNINGS
Clerk of Hamilton County Common Pleas

By *Frank Kispert*
Deputy

MELVIN G. RUEGER
Prosecuting Attorney, Hamilton County, Ohio

Hamilton County Jury Wheel
superimposed over a courthouse detail.

Chapter 19
Voir Dire

Sixty-five-year-old James Long was retired from the construction and real estate trades. He was asked to sit in the witness chair beside the judge's bench.

As was standard practice, the prosecution opened the questioning, with Rueger leading the way. His calm, assured demeanor conveyed professionalism, and his succinct, deliberate words focused directly on the matter at hand. Although not physically imposing—his balding head and average build suggested otherwise—Rueger commanded respect in the courtroom. His extensive knowledge of law and procedure impressed legal professionals and court observers alike. Unlike some prosecutors who might wield their legal acumen as a weapon, Rueger approached his task with restraint, preferring not to intimidate or bully either witnesses or laypeople. Always clad in a crisp white shirt and conservative business attire, Rueger's demeanor was anything but flashy. That flair was left to his assistant, Cal Prem, who wore stylish suits, gold cuff links, and kept his thick hair neatly combed.

Rueger opened the questioning of Long with a perfunctory overview before quickly cutting to the point, asking Long if he opposed capital punishment.

"No," Long responded, "I am not opposed to it."

Satisfied, Rueger informed Judge Leis, "We'll pass for cause," signaling that Long was acceptable to the prosecution.

Next, it was defense counsel Roney's turn to question Long. Roney brought his aggressive questioning style to the defense table. A tall, imposing figure with forward-slouching shoulders, jowls, and prominent nose all packed into a rumpled suit. Roney's appearance and style were as unconventional as his courtroom tactics. In contrast to Rueger's calm professionalism, Roney's demeanor could be abrasive, and his approach erratic.

Roney began by restating Rueger's summary of the Bowman murder, suddenly pivoting to personal questions about Long's wife. "Is she home? Is she ill? Does she work?" Roney's questions meandered, jumping from one topic to another, creating a disjointed and scattershot interrogation. His query about whether Long would believe the testimony of a policeman over that of a civilian drew the first objection from Rueger, an objection that Judge Leis promptly sustained.

Leis reminded Roney that in voir dire it was improper to challenge potential jurors based on hypothetical questions about testimony. Instead, Roney should be asking whether the juror would follow the court's instructions regarding the credibility of witnesses.

In voir dire, it is critical to avoid reprimands from the bench. Judge Leis, known for his irascible nature, had little tolerance for specious or out-of-line questions. He was familiar with both defense attorneys, also knowing this was Roney and Signer's first case since leaving the prosecutor's office. Though the judge occasionally cloaked his corrections in procedural advice, it was clear that his patience with the defense counsel was already wearing thin.

As Roney continued questioning Long, he pivoted to ask about the Bowman murder and media coverage of the case. "Do you recall the name of the woman who was killed?"

"Objection, your Honor," Rueger interrupted. "He's mentioned it a couple of times, and so have I."

Judge Leis sustained the objection, but Roney pressed on, sparking a back-and-forth exchange with the bench. Leis cut him off, telling him he could ask about what the juror had read, but warning that they were not going to go over every published story. Unperturbed, Roney attempted to shift the focus, characterizing his questions as a test of Long's memory, only to be rebuked once more.

"Mr. Roney, this isn't a test of memory," Judge Leis snapped. "This is to test his qualifications to sit as a juror."

Roney tried pushing forward, but Leis quickly steered the questioning back to the basic requirements: Had Long formed an opinion on Laskey's guilt or innocence based on what he'd read?

Long marked the first prospective juror, and it was already clear the defense was struggling. Rueger's objections were consistently sustained, while the defense's questioning yielded little progress. There were seventy more potential jurors to go.

As Roney dug deeper, Judge Leis's patience continued to wear thin. "We are qualifying a juror now," Leis emphasized. "The only question is whether this prospective juror can sit as a fair and impartial juror."

Roney's performance was drawing sharp criticism from the judge with every misstep, while Rueger, watching his former employee stumble, remained calm and composed. Leis soon took over much of the questioning, asking the central question directly: Would Long follow the court's instructions? Yes.

Long was seated.

Next came Harold Mercer, an Allstate Insurance claims adjuster. Roney asked a loaded question: Would Laskey's being Black influence his attitude toward the case?

"No, I don't believe so," Mercer replied. "I have probably had the same experience with the Negro race as everybody else. It's something we all have to face. I would have to say that with the change in social life we are having today, with what we are experiencing, with what is coming about, I probably have about the same feeling that most people do have. I don't think it's any more, and I don't think it's any less."

Mercer's vague response was met without follow-up, and he was seated. Despite the societal upheaval brought by the Civil Rights Movement and rising awareness of racial tensions, the unspoken nuances of racial attitudes went unexamined at a time when the embers Jim Crow had not been extinguished. Cincinnati, with its quieter racial divide compared to cities like New York or Los Angeles, carried a complacency about race relations. People acknowledged racism in the abstract but distanced themselves from its implications in their own lives.

As the clock passed the scheduled one p.m. adjournment, Leis asked if Roney was finished. Hesitating, Roney told the judge, "I think we are, sir, for the moment." With that, Mercer joined Long in the jury box.

Leis dismissed the jurors for the day with his standard instructions: not to speak with anyone about the case, form no opinions, and keep their minds free and open. Court would resume at nine a.m. on Tuesday.

The second day opened with a review of missing and excused jurors. Of the seventy-five originally drawn from the jury wheel, three had doctor's excuses, one called in sick with the flu that morning, and another had a child with measles at home. Sheriffs found that one of the missing jurors had moved to Indiana and another was deceased. One could not be found.

First up this Tuesday morning was Louis C. Henry, a B&O Railroad dining car waiter working the Cincinnati to Washington run for twenty-six years. Henry was the first Black person questioned in voir dire. His name carries a handwritten note on the transcript, "(Colored)"

When asked about what he'd heard about the case: "One trip you hear one way, one trip your hear other things, it's kind of confusing to me. And then, I am trying to serve them, too. A certain amount of courtesy is required there, so – it's just kind of got me confused with all, you know, from the different passengers, of what I have heard."

The prosecution approved Henry to sit on the jury but Roney couldn't shake some unknown misgiving, telling Leis, "I think if there's something in the back of his mind he can tell us."

The judge shot back, "he's indicated his willingness to serve, he's answered your questions."

"Well, there seems to be something bothering this juror in the back of his mind."

Roney concluded, tell Judge Leis, "We'll not pass for cause, because we feel there is something perhaps bothering…"

The judge broke in, "What is the cause? Give me the cause and the court will rule."

Scrambling, Roney concluded, "I am not challenging about his intent, I am going into the man's emotion."

"Have you issued a challenge for cause?" Leis asked.

"Yes, sir."

"All right," Leis quickly responded, "overruled," telling Henry to take his seat in the jury box.

Roney's questioning confounded potential jurors and judge alike, as Leis injected during one line of questioning, "I couldn't understand the question. If you simplify your questions, Mr. Roney."

On top of confusing questions, microphone trouble and outside street noise continued making it difficult to hear the questions and answers.

By the end of the second day, eight jurors had been questioned and all eight were seated in the jury box.

Wednesday opened with Burt Signer returning to the defense table and quickly ran afoul of the judge by following similar lines of questioning that had been rejected the day before.

By the time the proceeding paused for a brief recess, the first twelve jurors, six men and six women, had been seated, something courthouse regulars said was a first; in particular, not one had an objection to capital punishment.

A thirteenth juror was approved after the recess, John Pegg, a twenty-five-year-old warehouse worker, fifteen years younger than the next juror.

Following Pegg's questioning, Leis asked if the state had any peremptory challenge, each side given six challenges to remove jurors.

"The state is satisfied with the jury as presently constituted, your Honor," Rueger responded.

Signer asked the judge for an early adjournment to give the defense team a chance to review transcripts to help decide their peremptory challenges.

Despite more than an hour remaining, Leis acceded to the defense request and adjourned for the day, followed by his daily instructions to close the day.

On Thursday, the entire jury pool was directed to Judge Leis's normal courtroom across the hall as Roney filed a Cincinnati *Post* editorial from the previous day, "Crime…Act Now!" Roney contended the editorial implied Laskey was responsible for The Strangler murders, further evidence the defendant could not receive a fair trial in Hamilton County.

"A year ago, this city was in a state of near-terror because of the stranglings. For reasons unknown, the brutal murders of women have ended," the *Post* editorial posited.

Concluding, the defense also submitted articles about the rarity of the first twelve jurors being accepted, as well as asking the court to withdraw the jury and reset the case for the next term, a request immediately denied by Judge Leis.

Returning the seated jurors to the courtroom, Leis moved on to ask the defense if they had a peremptory challenge.

"If the court please, defense will excuse Juror Number 3," Louis Henry, the Black B&O railcar waiter. Before he was dismissed, Judge Leis asked Henry if he would care to continue his jury service?

"No, I wouldn't," Henry flatly told the judge.

The next morning, sixty-five-year-old Ruth M. Grier, born in South Africa and a Cincinnati resident for more than five decades, sat in the witness chair, enduring questioning with a bad cold. Assistant prosecutor Cal Prem asked her views on the death penalty. Grier, though soft-spoken, made her stance clear: "Well, yes, until we get something better. I'm not opposed to it… It makes me very sad but yes."

Roney was next to question Grier, asking if she'd ever been involved in a criminal case. To the courtroom, Grier humbly recounted an incident from 1914 in Harrison, Ohio where a young girl had been assaulted. Grier hadn't been inside when it happened but testified during the trial of George Trible, who was convicted of the assault.

Rueger objected, but Judge Leis allowed Roney to proceed with questioning her about eyewitness identification. Grier, however, seemed confused, admitting, "I haven't a very good memory."

The back-and-forth meandered from past events to whether Grier distrusted cab drivers—a topic spurred by the case at hand. "A little, yes," she responded when asked if she was hesitant to trust taxi drivers after the murders.

Both sides approved Grier, but following a brief recess, Rueger used one of the prosecution's six peremptory challenges to excuse her.

Next up was Frank Wells, the first to be excused due to his opposition to the death penalty. After Wells stepped down, schoolteacher Alma Frey took a seat, while the defense sought to remove juror #1, James Long.

Ruth Dorger, feeling ill, eliminated herself by admitting she had already formed strong opinions about the case. "It would take hard evidence to change my mind," she explained.

Alabama-born Sallie Mae Hill, a mother of three, became the second Black juror to face questioning. Signer asked her whether she would be able to give Laskey a fair trial, and Hill responded cautiously, "If he is innocent." She admitted to having an opinion based on what she had read, prompting Roney to object when the prosecutor pressed whether testimony could change her views. The judge intervened, telling Hill, "So, don't give us your opinion, OK?" Although Judge Leis continued to ask questions in an attempt to qualify her, Rueger asked that Hill be excused after she said, "I think everyone has an opinion of it."

"That's three for each side, gentlemen," Judge Leis reminded the attorneys about the exceptions they'd already exercised, with three remaining for each.

Hazel Hoffman and Robert C. Gordon were quickly excused due to their opposition to the death penalty. Gordon further complicated things by saying he could only find Laskey guilty if the jury had an option to recommend mercy. Signer objected when the court blocked him from asking Hoffman if her opposition was rooted in religious belief.

"It doesn't matter if it's a religious belief or some other belief," Leis replied.

Signer retorted, "If the court please, I believe this would raise another question here as to the Constitutionality of a juror being deprived of the right to sit on a jury simply because of her religious convictions."

"What has that got to do with Constitutionality?"

Before adjournment, both attorneys approved Albert J. Hammoor, an engineering supervisor.

The final day of the trial's first week, Friday, March 31, 1967, began with the defense excusing juror John Weber, a General Electric photographer.

Roger McBride, an IRS field auditor, was next to be questioned. He admitted knowing assistant prosecutor Mike Mestemaker but assured the court they had never discussed the case. McBride was seated as a juror before Rueger excused Albert Hammoor.

The Cincinnati Strangler

Caesar Wilkins, a sixty-three-year-old Black truck driver from Lincoln Heights, disqualified himself by stating, "I'm a little against capital punishment... I think they should have life, not death." Rueger challenged for cause, and Wilkins was dismissed.

Next up was Charles Woods, a computer programmer whose wife worked at Proctor & Gamble. The defense raised no objection, but moments later, they asked that IRS auditor McBride be excused.

Shirley Edell, a Golf Manor housewife whose husband worked as a General Electric assembler, told Judge Leis on Monday she did not want to serve due to her teenage children at home, a fifteen-year-old daughter and thirteen-year-old son who attended school with Burt Signer's children. Edell was not asked about being a member, with her husband, of the Golf Manor Synagogue where Burt Signer and his wife, Arline, were prominent members, along with Arline's powerful father, Judge Benjamin Schwartz.

Judge Schwartz, a longtime presence in local juvenile law, famously filmed a 1964 speech from his courtroom decrying a recent appearance of The Beatles in Cincinnati.

"Over fourteen-thousand children, mostly girls... and then these girls went into a coma, they ranted, they fainted, their eyes were glassy," his voice rising. "Some pulled their hair out, some tore their dresses, they threw notes of a very undesirable nature..." he continued for four minutes. Judge Schwartz was also reported to have warned Cincinnati's youth that, "if you appear in my court, you better bring a toothbrush."

After Edell was seated, Rueger again said the state was satisfied with the jury, as it stood.

A brief recess followed, during which Signer excused Marie Timmers, who worked with her husband in a family heating and air conditioning business. The next to be seated was Gerald G. Brown, a General Electric inspector and former Parkway cab driver. Following this, Rueger excused Barbara L. Ransler, a Wyoming housewife and substitute teacher.

As questioning of Patricia C. Barnett began, Judge Leis interrupted to ask why Burt Signer was not in the courtroom. Roney explained, "They started an operation on his wife a few moments ago." Roney agreed he'd proceed alone. As questioning continued of Barnett, she revealed to recently moving out of Hamilton County. She was excused.

Janet Tynan, a housewife from Hyde Park married to a Cincinnati firefighter, filled the final seat in the jury of twelve. Six more candidates were questioned for the two alternate spots, with William Nordyke and John Bernheisel selected.

The final jury was all-White—six men, six women—and two male alternates. Of the original twelve jurors initially seated, seven were excused. Thirty-six of the seventy-five in the jury pool had been questioned. Only three African Americans were among them, with one dismissed by the defense and two by the prosecution. Seven jurors were excused due to their opposition to the death penalty, a practice the U.S. Supreme Court would declare

The Cincinnati Strangler

unconstitutional the following year.

The jury was sworn in this same day.

Columnist Frank Weikel noted the stern attendance of Black Muslims at the Laskey trial, spreading word through the Black community of an all-White jury hearing Posteal Laskey's case.

Not only was the jury all-White, it also was predominantly suburban.

The front row of the jury box featured Charles Woods, Harold W. Mercer (the eventual foreman), Charles Cook, Hilda L. Schwartz, Shirley Edell, and Rose K. Hunley. The back row included Janet Tynan, Marvin G. Wasserman, Ola K. Blair, Alma C. Frey, Gerald C. Brown, and John C. Pegg. The two alternates, William Nordyke and John Bernheisel, were sworn in as well.

Immediately following the jury oath, the prosecution asked Judge Leis to overrule a defense motion for a change of venue. Leis wasted no time in denying the request, ensuring the trial would remain in Hamilton County, in his courtroom.

With the jury now seated, Judge Leis issued his instructions, specifically cautioning the attorneys against speaking with the media. Signer objected, but Rueger concurred with the judge's orders. Court adjourned until the following Monday, April 3, 1967.

A stained glass window (in black & white) in Cincinnati City Hall showing Justice seated on her thron holding the scales of fairness in one hand and the sword of authority in the other with books of laws before her. (Connie Roesch, description)

Chapter 20
Presumption of Innocence

Monday's session opened with the dismissal of alternate juror John Bernheisel, who had fallen ill with influenza over the weekend. Judge Leis declared the trial would continue with just one alternate juror.

With the jury gathered in the other courtroom, motions were handled in their absence. A motion for the separation of witnesses was granted, preventing witnesses from communicating with one another—though, by this point, the opportunity for separation had long passed. Another motion for the jurors to view the crime scene was approved.

The jury returned and the court departed for a bus tour of key locations related to the case, including the Lark Café and two intersections in Lower Price Hill: Bowman Avenue and Mistletoe Street, and Grand Avenue and Ring Place. The bus stopped outside the Laskey family home on Freeman Avenue in the West End, while Posteal was escorted on the tour, in a separate vehicle, by bailiff Stanley "Whitey" Heber and Deputy Sheriff Paul Allen.

Back in the courtroom, the trial reconvened with prosecutor Rueger's opening statement. Rueger pulled no punches, telling jurors he would be seeking the death penalty, saying Laskey, "purposely killed Barbara Bowman while perpetrating a robbery." Tying the theft of a handbag to the death of Bowman was critical in charging first-degree murder. A death occurring in the commission of a felony constituted first-degree murder. Without the robbery charge, the death of Barbara Bowman would likely have been charged as manslaughter.

Rueger's case hinged on witness testimony identifying Laskey as the cab driver last seen with Bowman.

"Various witnesses viewed and identified Laskey as the man who picked up Barbara Bowman at the Lark Café, 3001 Vine Street, around 2:30 a.m. the day she died."

He drove home his argument emphasizing Laskey's experience driving a cab in 1962 when he drove taxi #186—the same number associated with the dispatcher calls on the night of the murder.

Rueger also highlighted the assault and robbery charges related to two other women, Virginia Hinners and Delle Ernst, to demonstrate a pattern of behavior. In the end, the cases involving Ernst and Hinners were never tried, but Judge Leis would permit Virginia Hinners to deliver devastating testimony.

Concluding, Rueger appealed to the jury for a verdict of guilty without mercy - death in the electric chair.

Defense attorney Burt Signer offered the jury a more subdued presentation. He maintained that no one knew exactly what transpired on the morning of August 14 but assured the jury the defense would prove that Laskey was not present at the crime scene. Signer laid out Laskey's alibi, that Laskey had been at The Soul Café before going home and falling asleep—contradicting the prosecution's claim that he had been driving a stolen cab and killing his last passenger of the night.

"We simply don't know what took place in the early

morning of August 14. We will establish positive proof that Laskey was not there when the murder did take place and that he was home in bed and asleep."

With opening statements complete, Rueger called the prosecution's first witness, nineteen-year-old Ruth Ann Bailey, a sandwich maker for a catering company. On the night of the murder, she was out with forty-year-old Raymond "Bud" Walker when they happened upon the empty, dark taxi and the woman lying in the street alongside. Ruth Ann, married at fourteen, said her husband had returned from Vietnam just a week before her court appearance. On cross-examination, defense attorney Roney briefly probed into her personal life but quickly abandoned that line of questioning.

Bailey recounted what she had told the police: she and Walker had gone to a drive-in movie, where they watched The Singing Nun, a film about a guitar-strumming, folk-singing nun from Belgium. She couldn't recall the second feature but insisted they watched The Singing Nun twice. Interestingly, no one pointed out that The Singing Nun was not playing in Cincinnati that weekend. Additionally, Bailey said they had gone to the Oakley Drive-In, but Oakley was located on the opposite side of town from Price Hill. A drive-in movie in the pouring rain? Roney failed to ask.

Bailey testified that she and Walker stopped at Skyline Chili on Glenway Avenue around 2:15 a.m. before arriving at Grand and Ring, when they saw the taxi and body alongside. However, inconsistencies in her testimony were apparent. She provided detailed descriptions of the scene, such as the white Chevy driven by another witness, Thomas Tomaseck, and the color of Bowman's clothing, yet she was vague or incorrect about other details.

In response to Roney's question about speaking with police, Ruth Ann repeatedly said she had not; finally admitting a detective visited her home on Sunday, August 14 and later visiting the Homicide Bureau, but Roney did not press on the inconsistencies.

Additionally, the defense wanted Walker to corroborate Bailey's story, but he'd left for California, and no one knew his whereabouts.

While Bailey's testimony may have been inconsistent, she did serve the prosecution in establishing a timeline between seeing the body of Barbara Bowman and reporting an accident to the next witness, Patrolman Frank Sefton.

Sefton was the first officer to arrive at the scene after taking Bailey and Walker's report at the District Three station. Sefton, who grew up in Price Hill, described coming upon Bowman's body with a clear timeline of events. His radio call went out at 2:39 a.m.

The defense, unprepared for the cross-examination, sought an adjournment. Judge Leis, clearly displeased, granted it with an admonishment to Signer, "I'll grant you the delay once, but kindly be prepared with your case to proceed."

When Sefton returned to the stand the next day, the defense covered similar ground as the prosecution, adding questions about the timeline and Tomaseck's behavior. When he arrived, Tomaseck was standing about five feet from Bowman's body, in the rain, doing nothing, "just standing there."

Sefton confirmed that he hadn't seen anyone suspicious, including Laskey, at the scene.

Signer rambled on with circular questions, interrupted by Prem: "Objection, judge. This is repetitious."

"I thought we were through all of this," Leis agreed.

Already, the differences in approach and preparation between the prosecution and defense were becoming clear. The prosecution established the time the body was found with a description of the scene, while the defense was unprepared, throwing questions like spaghetti at the wall. The lack of preparation for cross-examination hints at the prosecution not having been forthcoming in discovery, leaving the defense in the dark at trial.

The prosecution's next witness was Tomaseck, the driver of the white Chevrolet who came upon the scene after Bailey and Walker. A truck driver, Tomaseck was heading home after drinking seven-and-sevens at Ding's Saloon. Despite consuming alcohol, Tomaseck insisted he wasn't drunk.

He recounted arriving at the scene where a small foreign car was parked with a man and woman inside. He spoke with the man before the couple left, saying they would go to the police station. He waited about five minutes without the couple returning, so he too left for the police station, but drove the wrong way. When Tomaseck arrived, he saw the couple at the station, so he returned to Grand and Ring where he stood in the rain until the first officer arrived.

Tomaseck recalled becoming ill when Sefton asked him to assist getting the bleeding woman on the stretcher, telling Sefton, "I don't feel so good, I'm going," to which Sefton said it was OK.

Signer ended his questioning, asking, "Mr. Tomaseck, you don't really know what happened to Barbara Bowman, do you?

"No."

Sergeant Virgil Hall, desk sergeant at District Three, responded to the scene minutes after Sefton. He saw a set of keys and five-dollar bill lying in the gutter, recalling the keychain had a telephone and small silver knife charms, with several keys. He told Prem he thought about moving the cab because it had the intersection blocked, particularly if firetrucks needed to get through.

"I grabbed ahold of the steering wheel and it spun crazily, it was broken. At least, it spun around," recalling the driver-side window was rolled up.

Hall radioed for the Crime and Traffic Bureaus to report an accident, while wondering why the woman was not wearing shoes. "The thing just didn't look right to me." But another call came and he had to leave.

Signer next questioned the validity of the paring knife found in the weeds, asking if there was any way for Hall to verify it was the same knife used to kill Bowman? This was followed by repetitious questions and successful objections.

Focusing the sergeant on the sequence of events, Signer emphasized Hall trying to move the cab, Hall snapping at Signer's characterization. "No, I didn't say that." He recounted grabbing the steering wheel, but without opening the door, just by reaching in; contrary to the original police reports.

"When you looked in," Signer asked, "were the windows up or down?"

"When I looked in, the windows were up," saying he couldn't recall if this was true for all the windows.

Later, Hall repeated his denial that he tried to move the cab, this time saying he grabbed the wheel, Signer asking, "The front window was down?"

"Evidently."

Throughout the morning session, noise from Court Street below made it difficult for the judge to hear questions and testimony; witnesses were often told to speak up or repeat their statements. A microphone was little help in overcoming the din.

After a brief recess, Sergeant Charles Berghausen, a twenty-nine-year veteran of the police force, was called to the stand. Fifty-year-old Berghausen's close-cropped hair crowned a receding hairline with a bulbous nose protruding from his broad face. As the night supervisor of the Crime Bureau that August night, he recalled dispatching Detectives Ken Davis and Tom Gardner to the scene, while he and Detective Paul Ellis went to St. Mary's Hospital. Berghausen coolly provided the gory details of the wounds to Barbara Bowman's body, the stab wounds to the side of her neck severing her jugular and carotid artery, the profuse bleeding, and her badly broken right leg hanging on by flesh and tissue.

Signer tried objecting to the grisly depiction but failed at every turn, and Berghausen continued his descriptions of the deep wounds and the presence of rope burns around the victim's neck.

Proceeding to Grand and Ring, Berghausen had taken charge of the investigation, ordering an all-hands search of the vicinity of the cab for clues. The sergeant also called the fire department to bring their flood lights to illuminate the area. When an item was found, the officer called for assistance and it was photographed before being placed in an evidence bag. While true, some of the evidence, according to police reports, was simply slipped into pockets, as Patrolman Salmon had done with the keys and $5 bill found in the gutter.

Berghausen recounted the paring knife being found in the weeds about twelve to fifteen feet from the spot where the body had laid. Walking along Grand Avenue toward Glenway, he came upon a set of eyeglasses near the righthand sidewalk. Directly across the street was one black suede woman's shoe, the other lying another thirty-five feet toward Glenway.

Prem turned Berghausen's attention to Ring Place where he recalled finding a green, fold-over billfold and then, a bit farther, a faille ribbed cloth black purse. These items were photographed and placed in evidence bags before being locked in the trunk of a Homicide Squad car.

Once the sun was up, Berghausen ordered a door-to-door neighborhood canvass and further examination of the cab before it was taken to the Municipal Garage beneath the District One police station.

Berghausen said Laskey's fingerprints were not found on the knife, but he didn't know about the cab.

Signer then inquired about surgical procedures performed by emergency room physicians, which Berghausen could not answer. It's unclear why the defense didn't call the emergency room doctors who treated Bowman to learn about the original wounds versus incisions made in their lifesaving measures.

On redirect, assistant prosecutor Prem showed Berghausen, for the benefit of the jury, two photographs of the lifeless nude body of Barbara Bowman lying on a morgue rack. Jurors were shocked at the sight of the young, thin woman, eyes fixed into the void, long bony fingers lay lifeless by her side; another view showed her gruesome broken leg. The nude torso was scarred by the Y-shaped autopsy incision running vertically from her lower abdomen to above her breasts, branching to her shoulders. Displaying a close-up photo, Prem emphasized the dark ligature line and stab wounds to her neck.

Amid adamant defense objections, Judge Leis simply interjected, "the photographs speak for themselves."

Berghausen was followed by Sergeant James "Corky" Corcoran, known for his ready smile and sense of humor, as well as exemplary police work. He was a lower-ranked specialist with the Crime Bureau in August 1966 when he responded to the scene with Detective George Fritz around five a.m. Using a handheld microphone to be heard over the noise of the street below, Corcoran stood at a blackboard to describe finding the piece of rope at the southeast corner of Ring and Underwood, a narrow, steep side street running from Ring to Warsaw Avenue. He described the rope as packing twine, about two-and-a-half to three feet long, embedded with several square baubles from a necklace.

On cross examination, defense counsel rapidly bounced from topic to topic – did you see any cars parked in the area? Several. Was it raining? Just stopped. Did you see a Parkway Cab? No. Did you speak with a cab driver? No. What time was sunrise? 5:15-5:30. How many police officers were there when you arrived? Five or six, plus plainclothes. Was the Yellow Cab still there? Yes.

The last question yielded an admission from Corcoran that he looked into the cab through the opened left rear door, saw a newspaper lying on the floor, and square beads strewn about the rear seat.

Detective Robert Bluhm was next to testify. Along with other officers, Bluhm had inspected the Yellow Cab in the Municipal Garage and found no fingerprints matching Laskey's. The defense asked if anything belonging to Laskey had been found in the cab. Bluhm responded, "No, sir."

On redirect, the assistant prosecutor introduced the set of keys belonging to Barbara Bowman found near where her body laid into evidence.

After Corcoran stepped down, Detective Robert Bluhm took the stand. He, along with Detective John Huber and Patrolman Ray Kohler, examined the Yellow Cab in the Municipal Garage. Detective Huber photographed the vehicle while Kohler, a fingerprint specialist from the Identification Bureau, dusted for prints. Finding none, they removed the Sunday *Enquirer* from the rear floor, one white earring, possibly imitation pearl, and a broken string of white beads from the backseat. Additional pieces were found under the seat.

While Bluhm identified the "wrinkled, crumpled front fender" of the Yellow Cab, Signer interrupted to object, preventing Bluhm from explaining how the damage occurred.

Next, Bluhm recounted events of December 9, 1966, when he and Detective Skip Morgan went to the Adam Wuest Company to find Laskey. Signer pressed objections that the events of December 9 had nothing to do with matters at hand, to no avail. The judge permitted Bluhm to say whether the defendant had been taken into custody that day, Bluhm answered, "we arrested him for another matter at that time."

On cross, Signer asked the detective if Laskey's prints were found on the Yellow Cab, to which Bluhm said they had not. He wrapped up by asking if they found anything in the cab belonging to Posteal Laskey?

"No, sir," was his answer and Bluhm was dismissed. As he was stepping down, Prem interrupted by entering a key into evidence, asking the detective to confirm this was the key he found in the ignition. It was.

Detective Ken Davis, the only Black Homicide detective at the time, took the stand. He was responsible for photographing evidence found at the crime scene and transporting it back to the Homicide Bureau. Davis admitted that one of his photos, showing the rope found at Ring and Underwood, didn't turn out. This was not uncommon, given that the police were still using large-format Speed Graphics cameras, the kind favored by press photographers. These cameras took one sheet of film per shot, making it easy to incorrectly expose the black-and-white film, particularly in low light conditions, even using flashbulbs.

Signer asked Davis about the handling of the rope and whether there were any identifying marks to show that the rope found was the same one photographed. Davis explained that once he placed it in the evidence bag, it remained in the sole possession of the Cincinnati Police Department. However, when Signer pointed to a tag attached to the rope that read "FBI," Davis admitted he didn't know when or for how long the rope might have been outside local police custody.

Shifting gears, Signer asked Davis if there was any direct evidence linking Posteal Laskey to the crime scene, directing him to answer only "yes" or "no."

"I don't know," Davis replied, reflecting the ambiguity of the evidence.

As the session neared adjournment, Judge Leis asked the prosecutor if he had a brief witness to call, to which Rueger responded affirmatively, calling Betty Beckman to the stand.

Beckman, along with her date, Larry Goodie, drove Barbara Bowman to the Lark Café that fateful night. She told Rueger how they did not spend the entire evening with Bowman, joining another couple in front of the stage when Barb's friends showed up. The prosecutor asked Beckman if she saw Posteal Laskey in the Lark Café that night? She had not.

Beckman recalled her friend was wearing a two-piece blue dress with pleated skirt, and her purse being a clutch-type bag, identifying the glasses in evidence as Barb's.

With that, the prosecution completed their questioning of Beckman, Signer opting to cross-examine the next morning.

The Tuesday session ended with Judge Leis issuing his repeated daily instructions to the jurors to, "Keep your minds free and open."

The next morning, Wednesday, April 5, Beckman returned for cross-examination by the defense. The questions focused on who was with Bowman at the Lark that night, particularly the two women, Mickey and Bert - Muriel Uchtman and Alberta Walther. Roney's line implied Bowman may have been drunk, but Beckman saw no sign her friend had too much to drink.

When asked if she saw Posteal Laskey in the Lark that night or any time since, "No, sir, I did not," adding she had not seen her friend leave.

Rueger next called Ray Hollstein, who was sitting next to Bowman at the Lark. Hollstein testified that he didn't interact much with Bowman that night, telling the court he liked coming to the Lark to drink bourbon and gingers, and dance. No, he had not asked Bowman to dance. He did, however, recall seeing Bowman dance with some men and turn others down.

After describing the layout of the bar and the lively

scene that night, Hollstein recounted Bowman's departure.

"Well, I saw this cab driver come in. I noticed him when he went by the cigarette machine. It's very bright there, and the reason I noticed him he sort of glided up to the bar. Looked like he wasn't even walking; he just sort of glided... And I said, 'Hey, there must be a cab driver, someone here – there's a cab driver there.' And he turned around and says 'cab,' or something like that. Barbara says, 'Oh, that's my cab,' and she grabbed her - she had a newspaper, and she got her pocketbook and her paper and left with the cab driver."

Rueger pointed to the defendant, asking, "Did you see that man on August 13 or early morning of the 14th, 1966?"

"He was the man come in and says, 'cab.' He was the man that come in to get Barbara," Hollstein said, later describing the man's voice as "muffled."

"Barbara left with him?" Rueger followed.

"She left with him, yes, sir," Hollstein adding without being asked, "He didn't have that hair under his chin when he come up there."

Hollstein's identification of Laskey as the cab driver at the Lark prompted an objection from Signer, who asked for a ruling on the earlier motion to suppress evidence relating to Laskey's being subjected to a December 12 walk past witnesses. With the jury out of the courtroom, Signer argued Laskey was unlawfully removed from the Workhouse without a warrant or legal counsel present and viewed in front of potential witnesses.

Rueger said Hollstein had not viewed Laskey and took issue with Signer's use of the word "view," telling Leis that Hollstein had not viewed a lineup, a technicality Leis was not interested in parsing.

When Signer cited the recent Supreme Court decisions in Escobido and Miranda, Leis quickly retorted those cases dealt strictly with confessions made by a defendant.

"I don't believe the Miranda case or the Escobido case goes that far, counsel," Leis added. "I don't think the Supreme Court of the United States said that a police department in furtherance of their investigation of crime or the prosecuting attorney in furtherance of their investigation of crime would be prohibited from permitting material witnesses in the trial of a case from testifying as to a view they had of the suspect."

Signer insisted Laskey's removal from the Workhouse, his lawful place of residence by court order, without a warrant or counsel present, was a violation of his Constitutional rights.

Leis was not understanding Signer's point and as soon as Rueger withdrew his original question, the issue vaporized.

Rueger got the last word just before Hollstein and the jury returned, reminding Judge Leis he already overruled the defense motion to suppress evidence on March 20. Leis vaguely recalled doing so.

When the jury returned, Rueger asked Hollstein if he saw Laskey after August 14, to which Hollstein started to talk about seeing him at police headquarters, Rueger stopped him short, "I'm not asking you where or when you saw him."

"Yes, I seen him after," and with that, Rueger ended his questioning.

Rather than follow the line of questioning in cross, Roney went off the rails to Hollstein's residence and the car he drove, asking Hollstein what time he arrived at the Lark, calling it a saloon which merited an objection from Rueger and a semantic exchange over what to call the Lark, a spat the judge quashed, "the court will not permit any of this byplay between counsel."

Cross-examination began with Roney veering off course, asking about Hollstein's car and residence. A back-and-forth ensued between the defense and prosecution over whether or not the Lark could be referred to as a "saloon," a spat Judge Leis quickly shut down.

Hollstein said detectives showed him photographs; his recollections focused on little things. "Maybe their eyes or chin or something what I noticed," selecting three pictures that looked similar to the man. Roney pressed Hollstein to describe the pictures but the judge supported the witness's inability to recall in the absence of the actual photos.

One particular recollection for Hollstein was the man's stature. "I, I, I know he was small. I say he was about an inch or so smaller than I was," Hollstein telling the court his height was five-seven.

Hollstein described the man having an average forehead and hairline, without scars or distinctive marks. He "looked dirty, hard-looking."

The witness could not recall what all he told the police. He said he didn't estimate the man's weight, uncertain whether his complexion was light or dark, Hollstein recalled describing the man as dark-complected. The man had neither mustache nor goatee, Hollstein testified.

Describing the man's gait as gliding, Hollstein said, "it was just sort of cat-like."

"That is what caught your eye?" Roney asked.

"Yeah. When he came by the machine, being a colored man, there's hardly any colored persons in there, and I assumed he was a cab driver. He had that little peaked hat on," Hollstein said. "I think there's only been about two in there. And, they come in, they sit, and they leave."

Hollstein was not among those meeting with the FBI sketch artist, saying the outcome did have a resemblance.

Hollstein recounted he'd been at police headquarters several times – in August and another time, about a month later, when they picked up a man, but it wasn't the driver.

The next time he was brought in was "right after they picked this man up and I went down and went over and identified him positively."

Next to testify was Carl Steigleiter, a Lark patron who arrived at the bar around 12:30 a.m. Steigleiter identified Laskey as the cab driver who came into the bar, describing the man as "raunchy looking" and nervous. He said the cab driver seemed "like he was going to rob the place or something."

Steigleiter admitted having been uneasy about the

man's appearance, holding an empty beer bottle under the bar just in case the man tried something. Like Hollstein, Steigleiter was shown mugshots at the police station, initially selecting two—neither Laskey.

Rueger concluded questioning by asking Steigleiter if the defendant was the man he saw. "He's the man."

On cross-examination, he described the night as a "nice evening, not raining or nothing," remembering it being the last day of his vacation,

Steigleiter came to the Lark from a bar in St. Bernard after eating at a chili parlor and visiting another bar, while drinking only one beer. He ordered another at the Lark. Steigleiter was on his third beer when the cab driver walked in. He depicted the cabbie as "raunchy looking," estimating the man weighed one-hundred-fifty pounds the man weighed one-hundred-fifty pounds. "He don't weigh too much, kind of slight," continuing, "in other words, he don't carry any weight to amount to anything."

He said the man was wearing a dungaree jacket, a sort of faded denim, with a short collar, "but I could be mistaken," saying it wasn't the clothing that caught his attention, rather "the looks of his face." Steigleiter said the man, standing about fifteen feet away, was nervous and had shifty eyes.

Signer next asked, "Are you familiar with the characteristics of the Negro race?" Steigleiter said he was.

"As a result of your experience in looking at them and observing them, have you ever noticed that some members of this race have a darker shading in the eyeball, almost tinging to a brown rather than a white?" Steigleiter thought the eyes of the man he saw were dark and shifty.

He said the man had short-cropped hair, a burr haircut. He wasn't clean shaven, but he didn't have a mustache and goatee. His lips were neither thick nor thin, and his ears were rounded at the top and not too close to his head. He didn't notice any scars on the man's face.

Steigleiter told the court he had seen Hollstein at the Lark since that night, and that they "might have made some comment," but he couldn't recall what it was they discussed. Steigleiter did discuss that night with Clyde Vollmer but denied they compared notes; insisting his recollections and descriptions were exclusively his.

He placed the time of Bowman's departure at 2:10 a.m., having noticed the bar clock; more accurately, it would have been 1:55 a.m. as the Lark's clock was fifteen minutes early.

Unlike Hollstein, Steigleiter went to the police the following Tuesday to report being at the Lark on Saturday night.

At police headquarters, he was interviewed by Sergeant Moore and Detective Kersker, telling them the man was wearing an open dungaree jacket that was open; unknown whether it was button or zipper. He recalled telling them about the man acting nervous, like he was going to rob the place.

Visiting the Crime Bureau over two nights, Steigleiter picked out two mugshots from an estimated two-hundred, neither being Posteal Laskey. He was the pair he selected were the wrong people, without explaining why.

Steigleiter denied viewing any lineups, but Rueger's objection truncated further questioning on the topic. He saw the sketch made by the FBI artist and it appeared to include the details he provided, as well as "all the people that were there at the time." Overcoming Rueger's objections, Signer asked Steigleiter if the sketch was true to the man he saw that night? It was similar, particularly the man's height, weight, and burr haircut, saying some of the features were exaggerated.

He denied discussing the case with other patrons at the Lark, maintaining his identification of Laskey was his own.

Lark Café owner, and former Cincinnati Reds player, Clyde Vollmer would close out the day's testimony. Vollmer had owned the Lark for twelve years and was tending the bar the night Barbara Bowman left with the man.

When asked by Rueger if he remembered hearing someone say "cab," Vollmer nodded. It was not a surprise Bowman acknowledged the man's presence as Vollmer knew she'd called for a taxi. The prosecutor then asked Vollmer if the man who picked up Bowman was in the courtroom. As Vollmer pointed at Laskey, Rueger asked, "There's no question in your mind that this man Laskey is the man you saw in your cafe that night?"

"No, sir," was Vollmer's simple response.

Vollmer went on to describe the man entering his bar as being around five-foot-five or five-foot-six, weighing between 140 and 150 pounds, with an oval face. He recalled the man having a burr haircut and thought he was wearing a large plaid shirt. Vollmer, being six-foot-one, plus standing on a platform, emphasized that he had to glance down at the much shorter man.

Vollmer testified that Bowman had four or five Seven-and-Sevens that night, estimating each drink contained about an ounce and a half of Seagram's whiskey.

He did not contact police; they came to him. When detectives laid out mugshots, Vollmer admitted choosing none. Clyde and his wife, Maggie, were called to the Crime Bureau, and shown more mugshots. Again, Clyde selected none, but Maggie came to believe Posteal Laskey was the man who came to the Lark that night.

Clyde recalled the time in September when a group of seven or eight Lark customers gathered for the FBI sketch artist, each providing their version of the man's appearance. Vollmer thought the artist, "had a rough time on it," but agreed the sketch resembled the man he saw, "from the cheeks up." He was quoted upon seeing the finished sketch, "looks like the man to me."

The court session ended with a cacophony of street noise wafting into the courtroom.

Margaret "Maggie" Vollmer, Clyde's wife, opened the trial's ninth day, Thursday, April 6. Vollmer was waiting tables that busy night and noticed a Black man enter the café. Maggie described how the man parted two customers on barstools to push his way to the bar. When he said "cab," Bowman immediately picked up her newspaper and purse, and followed him out.

"Do you see the man who came in the café that night and said 'cab'?" Rueger asked.

"Yes, sir," Vollmer responded, "right there," pointing to Laskey. "The cab driver; Laskey went first, and Barbara followed."

Had she seen Laskey since? "Only in the line-up I saw him." Signer objected to no avail.

There was no question in her mind that it was Posteal Laskey who came into the Lark and left with Barbara Bowman. "That's the man that came in as a cab driver."

She also described him having a burr haircut and sort of big eyes, but she couldn't see "his ears and stuff" because he was facing her and she couldn't see his sides. Vollmer described him as dirty looking, but she did not see a mustache or goatee.

"All I could see was his big eyes and his burr haircut."

Next to testify was Charlotte Barnhart, who was driving around Price Hill with her friend Eileen Aultz in search of an apartment in an unfamiliar neighborhood. Charlotte recounted pulling up next to a Yellow Cab near Warsaw Avenue, where she saw a Black man leaning over the front bench seat from the back. As Eileen was asking him for directions, she saw a White woman rise up in the back seat.

"I saw a man, a colored fellow, leaning over the back seat of the cab," as Eileen was speaking. "Then the colored fellow started sliding over to the driver's side and the lady in the back seat laid back down."

The man started the cab and put his ungloved hand on the steering wheel while swinging his right arm over the seat as he looked back while pulling away in reverse.

The driver had nowhere else to go as Charlotte was alongside and there was a car parked in front, so backwards was the only way out.

She also mentioned Walker's little blue Simca, assuming it was a detective vehicle.

Eileen Aultz followed her friend on the stand, confirming Charlotte's account of the night. She vividly recalled seeing the White woman in the backseat, repeating for the court, "My God, that's a White woman."

She said it wasn't raining hard at that time because she had her window open, as was the cab's.

Eileen noticed the driver was wearing a dark leather jacket and a knit cap. He had a high forehead, dark hands, and medium complexion.

Eileen recalled their return along Grand Avenue.

"We passed Ring Place and I looked and I said, 'Oh my God, Charlotte, there is that cab sitting there, the girl must have got out and the driver probably ran away.' And there was a detective car parked this way."

"Do you see the man in this courtroom, the man that was in that cab that night?"

"Yes, I do," Aultz said, pointing to Laskey.

On cross-examination, Aultz explained that the man was facing her directly the entire time, but she could not clearly make out hair or facial features. The lighting was poor but Eileen insisted she saw his face in the darkness. Later in her testimony, Aultz mentioned one facial characteristic that stood out, the man's pudgy cheekbones.

After a short recess, Sol Thompson, the Parkway Cab driver, was next up. He told the court of coming upon the Yellow Cab at Grand and Ring Place early that morning. Thompson was asked by a police officer to inspect the cab and immediately noticed the absence of a trip sheet. After calling dispatch about a suspicious accident, he left to pick up a fare.

Thompson received a radio call to nearby Queen's Towers where he picked up a woman for a short ride to 1400 Denver Avenue, down the hill from the prominent high-rise.

Thompson's fares that early morning covered multiple streets along the hilltop and hillside, but saw no one along the way. He told defense counsel the stretch along Warsaw to Wilder offered no hiding place beneath the tall retaining walls bounding the sidewalk.

Dropping the fare on Denver, around 3:20 a.m., Thompson turned right on Bowman Street and another right on Mistletoe where he heard someone hail a cab. He waited and when no one appeared, he started to leave. The dome light popped on as the right rear door opened and a man jumped in.

Thompson retraced the drive from Mistletoe to Baymiller and Bank for the court, noting the fare was $1.40, covered by the two soaking wet singles he was handed, the man saying, "This will cover it." He placed them in the glove compartment.

Arriving at Baymiller and Bank, Thompson described slowing his cab at the stop sign but the man jumped out before it was completely stopped, disappearing into nearby alleyways.

After talking with police at Brighton Corner, Thompson was called to St. Mary's Hospital where he told detectives about the man in his taxi. Detective Tom Gardner inspected his cab; taking the seats out, but seeing no mud on the floor, no footprints, but the floor was "pretty wet." Thompson didn't see Gardner dust for prints or check the trunk. His mention of the two one-dollar bills was the only time during the trial.

The man stood out to Thompson, he told the court, when he slid across the seat behind him, making him uneasy he was about to be robbed. "I just had that sixth sense."

Thompson's shift ended when he left St. Mary's around 4:45 A.M.

On cross examination, Thompson described the man being between 100 and 150 pounds, five-six to five-eleven, from twenty-five to thirty years of age. He was unshaven but had no facial hair of note. He wore a zippered black leather jacket and a cap, "just like the dark Navy caps they wore back in World War Two."

Thompson told of going to the Crime Bureau that Sunday night to talk with detectives; returning several more times, possibly six or seven. He also looked at mugshots in the Public Utilities office where they kept ID photos of cab drivers and utility workers, telling the court he'd picked none. Same for the police station where they showed him more.

"Do you see that fellow here today?"

"I do," Thompson replied, pointing to Posteal Laskey.

Leroy Smith was the next witness. He told the court of being with a married woman, Debbie Gray, that Saturday night, when they were picked up by a Yellow Cab on Central Avenue. They'd been at a birthday party at Jim's Bar and took a cab to the Katanga Lounge. Smith said he mentioned the meter not being turned on, the driver replying he'd forgotten, and then had difficulty turning it on. This occurred between 8:30 and 9:00 P.M.

Smith described the driver as, "a colored male, approximately five-seven, -eight, something of this sort, medium built, brown skin, with I would say a goatee, hair on the chin, whatever." He said the driver was wearing a yellow shirt jacket and a cap with a bill on it, like a chauffeur hat, describing his conversation with the driver as "peculiar for a cab driver," but he was not asked to clarify that depiction.

When asked by Roney in cross-examination, "Was it raining that evening," Smith replied, "No, I don't think so."

The prosecutor's next question was, "Do you see this man in the courtroom?"

Smith responded, "I do," pointing to Laskey.

On cross-examination, Roney focused on discrepancies in Smith's timeline and his failure to remember key details, such as the rain falling throughout Saturday evening.

When Smith first met with police, eight months earlier, he told them of hailing a Yellow Cab he thought was driven by his friend, "Smittie," that Saturday night 11:30 p.m. At the time, Smith described the driver as between thirty-eight and thirty-nine years old about five-ten, weighing 155 to 160, wearing a chauffeur's cap, and a yellow shirt jacket.

Smith told the court of speaking with Detective Morgan, Detective Bluhm, and Sergeant Jackson in the Crime Bureau where he viewed dozens of mugshots without picking one. Detectives Davis and Gardner also interviewed Smith about the cab ride when he came to them after seeing a newspaper appeal asking anyone who had ridden in a cab that night to contact police. No such appeal could be found.

Additionally, Smith's testimony in court contradicted some aspects of his earlier statements to detectives. Again, the failure of defense counsel to press such discrepancies points to either the prosecution being less than forthcoming in discovery, or simple malfeasance in defense preparation.

Court was adjourned and Judge Leis permitted Smith to return to Louisville.

Friday, April 7, the last day of the second week of the trial, opened with Arthur Scholl, the Yellow Cab service worker. Scholl was working the overnight shift from 11:30 p.m. to 8:00 a.m., was parking cabs when his supervisor shouted, "Who's that getting out of the cab?"

"I turned to look to see where the man was...I heard a door slam. Then I placed the guy where he was at. So, the man walked around the cab and out into the street into Cortlandt over towards Huber & Huber Trucking

Company. Went after him."

Pointing to Laskey, Rueger asked, "Did you see that man at that lot on August 12, 1966?"

"Yes, I did."

Scholl couldn't catch up as the man walking at a brisk pace, getting no closer than twenty-five to thirty feet. "I hollered at him. He turned around and looked, and just kept on going. 'Come on back,' but he didn't come back," again confirming Laskey was that man.

For a third time, Rueger pointed to Laskey in the courtroom, asking, "Did you see that man on the lot on August 12, 1966?"

Scholl replied, "Yes, I did."

For the defense, Roney asked if taxi bootlegging was "a frequent happening for colored people to go on the lot and remove a cab and take it out and use it as a bootleg cab?"

"Not to my knowledge," Scholl saying this was the first time he'd known of a cab being stolen.

Scholl said the man was wearing dark trousers, and a shirt that was either white with yellow prints or yellow with white prints. He was short and not wearing hat, but Scholl couldn't describe facial features; saying, "The man is Laskey. I mean, how am I going to describe a man's facial features?"

Roney repeated questions about the man's facial characteristics but Scholl could not provide details.

"I don't know how to tell anybody what their facial characters are. I mean, the man I seen is Laskey, and that's all there is to it."

Next on the stand was Harry Burks, Scholl's supervisor. Burks, with Taxicabs of Cincinnati since 1954, recalled being summoned by a radio dispatcher to investigate an accident at Grand and Ring in the early morning of August 14.

Burks also confirmed Scholl's account of hearing a taxidoor slam the night before on the lot and seeing a man walk away. Burks, however, was about eighty feet away and unable to identify the man. Burks did not call police but did file an internal incident report. Contradicting Scholl, Burks said that cab theft was not uncommon.

He told the court cab #870 was a 1963 model Checker but Burks was not familiar with #870 until he saw it blocking Ring Place where he took some pictures and filed a report with personnel manager, Harlan Blazer. Cab 870 was last driven on June 19 having been removed from active duty, not for mechanical reasons, rather due to shortage of drivers, opting to use the newer Plymouth taxis; leaving the 1963 Checkers reserved for emergencies.

The prosecution then called the two dispatchers who had been working at Yellow Cab on the night of Bowman's murder. Vincent Taylor and David Shanklin testified about the radio calls made that night. Shanklin handled telephone calls, including a 2:06 a.m. call for a cab at the Lark Café. Taylor dispatched cab #186 in response to that call at 2:09 a.m., unaware of the driver's identity as they only knew the cab numbers, not the drivers behind them. The Lark call was one of six calls handled by #186 that night.

Taylor said the driver responded to the call by saying "186. Lark Café. Roger."

All calls were tape recorded.

Arlan Blazer, personnel manager at Taxicabs of Cincinnati for fifteen years, knew Posteal Laskey from his six-month stint as a Yellow Cab driver, most notably Laskey's departure.

Blazer said Laskey applied for a job on July 24, 1962, and was assigned to the four-p.m. shift driving cab #162. On September 16, Laskey was moved to days, starting at 6:30 a.m. driving Checker cab #186, an older vehicle that would be replaced in 1963.

Laskey was fired on December 13, 1962, when he refused to drive his cab saying the equipment was defective.

Blazer recalled that cold winter morning when Laskey brought his cab into the garage and got into an argument with the general manager, Edward Schwietering, in the driver's room, drawing Blazer's attention. Laskey barked at him, "I will not drive this equipment!"

According to union agreement, such a statement was grounds for immediate resignation, according to Blazer.

"Everything was a rather high tempo that morning when Mister Laskey left the employment of our company. Nobody was too friendly. The fact of the thing is, if a man walks in and calls one of our cabs a piece of junk and he's not going to drive it and gets on the muscle in this respect, we usually take exception to this pretty strong."

Blazer recalled Laskey visiting his office in early 1966 to ask about a job, "I told him he was wasting his time."

He said Laskey didn't turn in his key, but he did not have an inventory of keys to verify. One key could open and operate any of the fifty Checker cabs, but not the Plymouths. When Blazer was shown the key recovered from the wrecked cab, he told the court the number stamped on the key, #848, indicated it was delivered with one of the newer cabs.

Records indicated #870 had been driven sixty-nine miles on August 13-14, sixteen miles paid. The meter had been tripped twelve times between June 19 and August 14. At the time, fares started with a fifty-cent meter drop and ten cents per one-fifth of a mile, ten cents for each two minutes of waiting.

Blazer said a few taxis had been stolen from the lot, almost all of them by thieves using keys, never hot-wired.

Dr. Frank Cleveland, a pathologist since 1947 and Hamilton County coroner since 1965, was called to testify. Cleveland described the extensive injuries Barbara Bowman sustained, including stab wounds and ligature marks around her neck, along with injuries to her shoulder, back, pelvis, and legs.

His words were illustrated by the morgue photographs of Barbara Bowman's nude, horribly wounded body.

Cleveland could distinguish between medical incisions made during attempts to save Bowman's life and the ragged, violent cuts made by her attacker. The coroner also noted injuries suggesting possible sexual assault and shocked the courtroom with a detailed description of the severe fracture to her ankle.

The most significant testimony of the entire trial came next - Virginia Hinners.

Despite desperate defense objections, Judge Leis permitted Hinners to recount an attack she suffered in September 1966, in which she identified Laskey as her assailant. Laskey was indicted in her assault and robbery, but her case was not part of these proceedings.

Defense counsel argued the state could not enter an unrelated, unproven act to prejudice the jury. Assistant prosecutor Prem countered that Hinners's testimony would prove motive in the charge of assault to rob, the linchpin to the first-degree murder charge.

Judge Leis hearkened back to his experience assisting the 1937 prosecution of Anna Marie Hahn, a female serial killer. Hahn was convicted of murdering several men by arsenic poisoning in a trial highlighted by testimony on poisoning cases not charged against Hahn. On December 7, 1938, Anna Marie Hahn was the first woman in Ohio to die in the electric chair.

Leis also referenced the 1965 Robert Ray Abbott murder trial, alluding to the admission of testimony on Abbott's assault of a girl six years earlier when they were both sixteen, wholly unrelated to the charge of murdering Wanda Cook. Her testimony sealed Abbott's fate.

"The deal in 1960 really killed me. That really done

it," Abbott said as he was led from the courtroom following his March 1965 conviction.

Hinners's testimony would have much the same effect.

The jury was sent across the hall as arguments over Hinners's testifying and they returned to the judge speaking to them about the testimony they would be hearing:

"Ladies and gentlemen of the jury, any evidence that the defendant may have committed other acts has a limited purpose only. It may be considered for the purpose of showing intent or motive, or for the purpose of identity, or the absence of a mistake or accident on the defendant's part, or a scheme, plan or system in doing the act charged. Such evidence may be considered only as it relates to the existence of intent or the absence of mistake or accident if you find that the defendant did commit the act. It must not be considered for any other purpose. The defendant is only on trial for the crime described in the indictment."

"All right, proceed," the judge concluded.

The Clermont custodian entranc with The New Thought Unity Center in the background, across McMillan Avenue.

Virginia Hinners, a forty-six-year-old mother of four, was a "unity teacher and counselor" at The New Thought Unity Center at 1401 East McMillan, directly across the street from Emogene Harrington's Clermont apartment.

The courtroom was hushed as Hinners spoke. Jurors leaned forward in their seats, listening to her every word.

Hinners came to work around 6:30 p.m., her office adjoining the sanctuary stage where a guest speaker would be recorded that night. Virginia was responsible for operating the tape recorder in a small anteroom a few steps above her desk, behind the stage.

She recalled a man stepping from the outside darkness into her lighted office. Hinners dramatically pointed to Laskey, saying,

"This man here came in the office and asked..." Rueger interrupted, "Let the record indicate I'm pointing to the defendant."

"Yes," Hinners said.

Hinners said the man asked about a job, but she suggested he return the next day. Recalling how a former custodian "sub-hired" young men to help on the spot, Hinners directed him to the stairs leading to the basement and the custodian's office. The man turned, went down the metal and concrete staircase, but returned saying there was no answer when he knocked, asking if she could go downstairs with him.

"Well, I'm sorry but I told you that I cannot leave at this time. Why don't you come back in the morning? We're open around 9:30." Hinners wrote the custodian's name on a pamphlet and handed it to him. "Well, why don't you go down with me? I'm a little bit afraid and maybe you could talk to this man? I'm sure this man is your custodian."

Again, Hinners declined and turned away to start the recording. She returned to her desk to type a label for the recording. She was seated with her back toward the door when she sensed someone enter the room. Hinners turned, "and this man was behind me like this (indicating with hands)." There was no description of her hands.

When Virginia jumped up, the man placed his hands on the air conditioner saying, "You know, I used to work on these."

Suddenly, his attitude changed from refined and soft-spoken to bold. She went up the steps to the anteroom, telling him, " 'You better wait outside. Someone will be here to see you shortly, but you better wait outside the office.' And then he came up and grabbed both of my arms and drew me to him and hugged me, and I pushed him back firmly and said, 'Don't do that'."

He began to get rough, bending her arm back, and shoving Hinners across the office toward the exit door, but she managed to close it with her foot so he couldn't push her out. He began speaking very quietly and very fast, saying over and over, "Do you want what the others got? Do you want what the others got? Do you want what the others got? Don't scream. Don't scream. Don't scream. I'll slit your throat. I'll slit your throat. Don't scream."

He tried opening the door leading to a little hallway and landing. Hinners desperately fought to keep the door, angering him further.

"Now, you're going to get it," he said as he punched her in the temple, knocking her against a desk. Before she could recover, he struck again with a hard punch to the chin, sending her to the floor.

"Please don't hurt me, please don't hurt me," Hinners cried as he got behind her.

Hinners said the man was wearing a red and black woolen hunting shirt, visible as he enveloped her neck in the crook of his arm, pressing as he leaned over her. As Virginia was losing consciousness, she spotted the bald head of the custodian, Ernest Ray, coming up the stairs. "Thank God," she recalled thinking. The assailant also saw Ray, tossing Hinners aside to attack the custodian, brutally punching the custodian, knocking him out against the pastor's door. Ray slumped to the floor, unconscious.

Instead of running away, the man returned to the office, Hinners pleaded, "What do you want? If you want money, I'll give you ten dollars." He grabbed her purse from Hinners's purse from her chair, shaking out the contents. "What's in here?" the man asked as he calmly went through her billfold, taking only the bills and throwing everything else aside. He grabbed her again and threw her, face-first, to the floor and left Hinners lying there as he jumped over the stairway railing to the outside door; the same one he entered.

When Ray recovered, he called police.

Rueger quickly asked Hinners, "Mrs. Hinners, is there any question in your mind that this is the man?

"There is none whatsoever," Hinners replied.

The testimony of Virginia Hinners was a dagger through the heart of the defense.

Signer asked Hinners for a physical description of the man and she responded by dramatically pointing to Laskey, "Well, this is the man."

The defense counsel pressed Hinners for a physical description of her assailant.

"Well," Hinners said, "I can say he was a young man, that he was very quick, agile, and slender, and a very fine looking man."

She admitted to having been unable to provide a detailed description of facial characteristics to police, repeating, "he was a very fine looking man, very quiet, that I did not have any idea that he would act the way he did."

On the police report taken about ten minutes after the incident, Hinners described her attacker as being twenty-three, standing five-foot-ten, weighing 180 pounds with short-cropped hair. He was wearing a black plaid woolen shirt, dark trousers, no hat – all around, a neat appearance.

To the court, Hinners testified he did not have a mustache or goatee, and was slightly taller than she at five-five. She described him as "slender but strong," with large hands not covered with gloves.

When asked about the next time she saw Laskey, "I can't answer you honestly because my memory fails me, but I was brought down to Police Court." Prior to the hearing, Hinners identified Laskey through jail bars.

Signer asked about her testimony in Police Court (transcripts have not survived):

"I'll attempt to answer it, but I'm not positive that it will be correct. It was shortly after Mr. Laskey was picked up after he was accused, I think, of assaulting this young girl at the same time that the incident occurred downtown, but I'm uncertain."

Hinners admitted to looking at photo arrays but not picking Laskey.

"If they did, it was a photograph that did not in any way look as he does. I did not find it."

Signer closed with a question about her Police Court appearance, Hinners telling him it was brief and only for the purpose of testifying he had robbed her.

With that, Hinners was excused. Severe damage had been inflicted upon the defense. The best Signer could muster was a motion to strike Hinners's testimony as immaterial.

Overruled.

Nearing time for adjournment, Leis permitted the prosecution to examine their final witness, Detective Bernie Kersker.

Kersker retraced the likely escape route the killer took after the murder. He estimated the distance covered by the killer was little over a mile to the spot where the man jumped into Sol Thompson's cab.

The defense asked if Detective Kersker's testimony could resume on Monday, which Leis permitted. He adjourned the day's session with his admonition not to talk, read, or listen to anything about the case.

"So, keep your minds clear and open during all this long period of recess."

When court resumed on Monday, April 10, the arrival of the jury was delayed as Judge Leis wished to address the courtroom, particularly the defense:

"It has been brought to the Court's attention since the Friday recess a news media interviewed the defendant and transmitted the interview to the public. This was in direct violation of the Court's order that there be no public discussion with the parties concerning the merits of this case on any news media."

On Friday night, WCPO-TV aired a one-minute segment by Jack Fogarty of an interview with Posteal Laskey.

On camera, Laskey wore a blue-grey sport coat and blue patterned tie; remaining calm and soft-spoken, his words carried a distinctive lisp. His mustache was, indeed, nearly indistinct, but his chin hair goatee was clear. In the midst of a trial for his life, Laskey maintained good eye contact and engaged with Fogarty, answering his questions with confidence and without hubris to attest his innocence. "Confident it will come out alright," Laskey told Fogarty.

"All right, bring in the jury," Leis concluded.

With the jury seated, defense attorney Signer resumed his cross-examination of Detective Kersker. On Friday, the detective laid out what he believed was the escape route the killer took after the murder. When asked if he was certain that was the path followed, Kersker had to admit he couldn't be entirely certain. Kersker followed the evidence along Ring Place to the rope at the corner with Underwood; the rest came into place, based upon his assumptions, as the most logical way for someone to quickly flee.

While Signer was able raise questions about Kersker's certainty on the route the killer followed, he failed to ask the detective a crucial question: Why didn't he take the most direct route into the West End along Gest Street, a route Laskey knew very well from working at the Wuest warehouse. Gest begins at the base of Price Hill, close to the place where the fleeing man would have emerged from the Peerless Street Steps. From there, it would have been a quarter-mile to the warehouse, and then under two miles, in a rather straight route to his Freeman Avenue home. The journey would have been considerably shorter, and none less direct, had the assailant parked his car in the vicinity of the Yellow Cab lot. Gest Street would have been enveloped in darkness with very few people passing through, even fewer along the sidewalks.

With the cross-examination of Detective Kersker concluded, the prosecution moved forward to formally enter items into evidence. The defense scored one dubious victory in keeping the Yellow Cab tape recording out of the trial. Judge Leis agreed with Signer's argument that the tapes were irrelevant to the case.

Following entry of the items of evidence, the prosecution declared, "With that, your Honor, the state rests."

Now, it was the turn of the defense.

Chapter 21
Witnesses for the Defense

Before calling their first witness, Burt Signer entered several motions aimed at weakening the prosecution's case. He began by requesting a dismissal the first count of the indictment – first-degree murder, contending there was no evidence of premeditation. This was immediately overruled by Judge Leis.

Signer next moved to dismiss the second count, robbery, arguing that the evidence was insufficient. Judge Leis turned to Rueger, asking what evidence the state had to prove robbery. The prosecutor cited the black handbag and green purse found near the victim. Because these items were not in her possession, Rueger insisted, meant they had been taken from her, constituting robbery.

Signer countered by portraying the prosecution's case as pure conjecture. He emphasized that no one knew exactly where Barbara Bowman exited the cab or if anything had actually been taken from her purse or pocketbook. "This is all an inference based upon an inference," Signer argued.

The judge disagreed, reasoning if the items had been found next to the cab, then the court would have questions about the robbery charge. As they were away from the taxi, it was obvious, given the victim's severely broken ankle, that she could not have carried her purse there.

Leis firmly overruled the motion to dismiss.

Signer then sought have the testimony of Virginia Hinners stricken from the record. To this, the judge asked, "Who was she?" Signer reminded Leis, "she was the lady from the New Thought Unity Temple who testified on Friday."

Without missing a beat, Leis rejected the request.

Signer continued by asking for the testimony of Detective Kersker to be struck, arguing it was based on conjecture. Again, overruled.

Signer's final motion was a request to view two additional locations: the Yellow Cab parking lot, and the intersection of Ring and Grand at night. Leis denied the request, leading Signer to note his exception. With each denial from the bench, defense counsel stated, "Please note our exception." In the end, there were twenty-nine exceptions, all of which would be reviewed after the trial and throughout appeals, though none would succeed.

With the formalities concluded, the defense called their first witness, Samson Perry – Posteal Laskey's barber. Perry testified that Laskey had been his customer for over a year. Roney asked him if Laskey had a "little mustache" and "little goatee," to which, Perry simply confirmed, "Yes." With that, Perry's brief testimony concluded.

The second witness for the defense was Paul Binder, an assistant production manager at the Adam Wuest Company. After describing his job, Roney also had Binder confirm that Laskey had a mustache and goatee. Nothing more.

Rueger took advantage of Binder's employment, not

to ask about facial hair; rather, to ask if the rope found at the scene was the kind used at the Wuest Company? Binder said the rope was similar but not identical to rope they use.

The third defense witness was Michael Chapel, a school custodian who'd known Laskey for three to four years. Chapel was the first alibi witness, testifying he saw Laskey at The Soul Lounge the night of the murder. Chapel said he arrived at the club between 10:30 and 11:00 p.m. and stayed until around two a.m., "just before the joint got ready to close." He was at The Soul Lounge that night to hear Laskey's band, but they weren't playing. Despite his not performing, Laskey was at the club.

Roney asked Chapel how he remembered the exact date? Chapel told of arguing with his wife that night, leading to him spending the night at his mother's house, and making an impression.

On cross, Rueger asked Chapel, "How often do you get in fights with your wife?"

"Fairly – on and off," Chapel replied, "just no more than you would with your wife, if you're married," the courtroom breaking out in laughter, Judge Leis gaveling order.

After subtly undercutting Chapel's character, Rueger turned to his recollection of seeing Laskey at the Soul, "When did you first think about seeing Laskey on August 13th?"

"Well, I thought about it when I – after he, he – they had, you know, arrested him for this, you know. I said, more than likely I was with him, and come to check up on it and to think about it a little more thoroughly, what really made me remember was the next day after it happened, I was speaking of this Barbara Bowman thing – he came by in the afternoon and picked me up at my mother's house, him and his mother and his sister was in the car, they wanted to go to bingo on Vine and Daniels."

When they arrived in the Corryville neighborhood, knowing what happened the night before, Chapel asked, "Where is that place? Where is the Lark Café?" but neither of them knew, Chapel said. (Vine and Daniels was two blocks from the Lark.)

Charles R. Thompson, a Chrysler employee from Detroit, was the next witness. Thompson testified about visiting Laskey's home around 1:30 a.m. on the night of the murder. He came to the Freeman Avenue house to borrow money from Posteal's brother, Dave, but he wasn't home. While waiting for Dave, Thompson sat with Posteal, talking and watching TV. He said by the time Dave arrived, around 3:00 or 3:30 a.m., Posteal was already in bed. Thompson also confirmed that Posteal had a goatee and mustache.

Dave Laskey, Posteal's brother, then took the stand. He saw his brother on the night of August 13 around 8:00 p.m., as Posteal was preparing to go to The Soul Lounge. Dave, a guitarist, was also getting ready for his gig at the Cue Lounge where he was playing with the Jammel A Combo (led by James Jamaal Halbert, an organist). He returned home around three a.m. when his brother was already in bed. He next saw Junior at home on Sunday, between eleven and noon, after Dave awoke. No, his brother did not have scratches on him, there was no mud on his clothing, and his clothes were not wet. Yes, Posteal had a mustache and goatee.

Rueger asked Dave about his testimony before the grand jury, attempting to show his brother was living on Reading Road, not Freeman Avenue, but Signer successfully objected, not on entering grand jury testimony, rather on its context.

Rueger returned to the second grand jury testimony, asking and answering questions for Dave by quoting from the transcript, without objection from the defense. Grand jury testimony is rarely admitted in trial and an objection should have raised, but the defense team remained mute.

Rueger continued, skewing a quote he attributed to Dave before the grand jury saying Posteal moved to Reading Road, "maybe August…could be July, August or September."

Struggling with the timeline, Dave insisted Junior was living at their mother's house in August.

Neither the prosecution nor defense referenced Brenda Jackson's testimony to the grand jury clarifying where Posteal was living at the time of Barbara Bowman's murder. She told the unusual second grand jury that, in February 1966, she and Posteal were living at 730 Oak Street in Walnut Hills, but returned to their respective family homes in August as bills were piling up while income was not.

The next witness was Posteal's mother, Nancy Laskey. She testified that Posteal lived in her house since the death of his father in June 1966. Signer quickly pivoted to the question of Posteal having a mustache and goatee? Yes, she replied.

Nancy testified that Posteal left home on Saturday, August 13 around 8:30 p.m., seeing him again at five next morning in his bed next to her room. To get to the bathroom, she had to cut through Posteal's bedroom. She told the court she saw no scratches, blood, or mud on him in the early morning.

Joseph L. Riley, a post office mechanic with a side job as an entertainment agent, was called to the stand. Riley had been representing Tiny Charles and His Rocking Outlaws around the time of the Bowman murder. He booked the band on weekends at the Club Embassy in Indianapolis, two weekends in June into July, but Riley told Roney he had not seen Posteal since the first part of July when the band's contract expired and their run at Club Embassy ended. He did not see him during August, but Riley heard the band was playing at The Soul Lounge in July. Riley also confirmed Laskey had a goatee and "little mustache."

The prosecutor referred to Riley's testimony before the second grand jury when he said the Club Embassy engagement was late August; Riley corrected the prosecutor, "No sir, I told you that they came in July. After July, after my bookings in there, I lost contact with the band. I didn't have any more to do with the band," since mid-July.

Riley stepped down and Ben Johnson took the stand.

Johnson, the long-time boarder in the Laskey household, followed Nancy on the stand. He also testified to seeing Junior at home before and after going to bingo on the night of the murder. When he returned home around 1:30 a.m., Posteal was lying on the couch watching TV. Johnson, a dedicated bingo player, remembered the night for winning at bingo, the first time that year. After bingo, Johnson visited friends in Walnut Hills, returning home after waiting out the rain. He knew it was 1:30 a.m. by the clock on top of the Frigidaire.

Signer asked for adjournment as his next witness had yet to appear.

"Ladies and gentlemen of the jury; because of the unavailability of witnesses on behalf of the defendant, the defendant has requested a continuance in this matter until tomorrow," Leis told the jurors.

After the jury left the courtroom, Rueger drew the judge's attention to defense witness Charles Thompson who had returned to Detroit. Rueger wanted him back as, "something has developed." Court officers tried returning Thompson to the courtroom but he was gone.

Judge Leis ordered, "Send the sheriff forthwith."

Thompson did not return to the courtroom and the reason why the prosecution wanted him back went unsaid.

Tuesday's session opened with the defense calling George C. Mumford, Jr., the FBI sketch artist whose composites were based upon descriptions from Lark customers and Sol Thompson a week after the murder.

As Roney stumbled through questions about Sol Thompson's description, Rueger succeeded with three objections to Roney's queries; at each turn, Leis grew more stern telling the defense attorney to properly phrase his questions.

Looking at the sketches, Mumford acknowledged Thompson told him the man in his cab did not have a goatee. Likewise, Clyde Vollmer did not mention a goatee or mustache. Roney's question asking Mumford to differences between Margaret Vollmer's testimony and her description to the sketch artist netted another rebuke from the bench, challenging the defense to show any contradiction in the transcript. The defense counsel did not cite any.

Mumford confirmed the sketch was based upon the descriptions provided by the Vollmers, Carl Steigleiter, and Sol Thompson, without mention of employing any mugshots.

On cross, Prem had Mumford describe the process of taking witness descriptions and melding them into a single composite during which Signer suddenly moved for a mistrial for a mention of Virginia Hinners in Prem's line of questioning.

"For what?" the judge asked.

"On the basis of his bringing..." and Leis cut him off.

"Overruled."

Mumford was excused without Signer following up.

The penultimate defense witness was Emmett Baldwin, chief meteorologist for the U.S. Weather Bureau in Cincinnati, but he had not arrived, despite being subpoenaed to appear at nine a.m.

Signer described Baldwin's testimony as significant since he would be the final defense witness before the defendant would testify on his own behalf. Signer asked for a delay, something Leis did not appreciate.

"We can't delay and delay this. I have given you lots of delays in getting witnesses here now. He should be here."

Leis permitted Signer to call Baldwin, returning to say Baldwin was on his way, "I guess in another five minutes he should be here."

"Eight – seven-minute recess. Seven minutes, not ten," Leis ordering Signer to wait in the hallway for Baldwin.

Once on the stand, Baldwin was asked about the weather on the Saturday and Sunday of the murder.

"What was the weather like between noon and 4:00 p.m. on August 13?" Signer inquired.

Rueger objected, but Signer argued the information was relevant to Leroy Smith's testimony about being in Cutter Park with his nephews. Leis ruled the issue immaterial and sustained the prosecutor's objection.

Yes, Baldwin testified it rained over the 13th and 14th, but his readings came from the Abee Observatory in Clifton, opposite Price Hill across the basin, and of little value to the defense.

Thus, the sum total of Baldwin's testimony.

Signer called the final witness before the court, defendant Posteal Laskey, Jr.

Having a defendant testify on their own behalf is a risky move as his words provided a waiver of the his right to remain silent, something Laskey maintained throughout his custody.

Signer wasted no time painting a rosy picture of his client, then asking if he'd ever been convicted of a state or federal offense?

"In 1958 in State of Ohio and in 1964 in the State of Kentucky," Laskey replied.

From his client's criminal record, Signer turned to mundane questions about his family and his home; about working at Wuest and as a musician.

Signer then asked Posteal to detail his activities from Saturday afternoon into Sunday morning.

"As I recall, I believe I was home most of the day up until the evening about 8:30 when I dressed and left the house to go to work at The Soul Lounge. I had – I was under the impression that we were supposed to play that evening…After getting to The Soul Lounge I found there had been a mix-up on dates and there was another band playing there instead."

While at the club, Posteal saw some people he knew and had a few beers before leaving around one o'clock. Arriving home a half-hour later, he stretched out on the couch to watch some TV. He went to bed shortly after two.

Did he know Barbara Bowman? "No, sir, I did not."

Showing him the paring knife, was this your knife? "No, sir."

Was this your rope? "No, sir."

Did you steal an automobile on August 13? "No, sir, I did not."

Now, it was the prosecutor's turn. Signer successfully blocked Rueger's questions about the specifics of Laskey's criminal record beyond acknowledging the 1958 and 1964 convictions. Once the defendant takes the stand, the prosecution may enter prior convictions to impeach his credibility, but previous crimes cannot be used to show a natural tendency to commit wrongdoing.

The prosecutor did couch a question about his record, asking if he'd been convicted of other offenses beyond the two mentioned by Signer.

"No, sir."

Rueger did not take this opportunity to impeach the defendant for failing to mention his court martial and discharge from the army for assault in 1957; the 1965 assault of Judith Buckner garnering probation he violated in his conviction for the assault of Sandra Chapas in December 1966.

The judge shot down Rueger's request to have Laskey don the beret, but did permit the prosecutor to ask if he wore a cap like it.

"It's a beret and it is mine. I do wear it," was his reply.

Rueger's next question tied the proximity of the defendant's Freeman Avenue home to the intersection of Bank and Baymiller – two blocks north and one block east was his answer.

Moving on to Laskey's time as a cabdriver, Rueger asked, "Didn't you use cab number 186 in 1962?"

Laskey responded, "I think, perhaps, I did."

Rueger assumed a combative approach, aggressively peppering Laskey with a series of rapid-fire questions; Laskey denying his inferences at every turn...

No, he did not steal a taxi from the Yellow Cab lot.

No, he did not drive a cab around using the number 186.

No, he had never been to the Lark Café.

No, he was not at the intersection of Grand and Ring on the night of the murder.

He'd only visited the Lark Café during the jury tour.

The judge denied Rueger's request that the defendant walk toward him.

Then, Rueger reached the coup de grâce of his cross, asking Laskey if he made any statement to police about his whereabouts on August 13-14.

Signer objected and the judge agreed, but permitted the question, "Did you tell police you were home and at The Soul Lounge on August 13th and 14th of 1966?"

"No, sir, I did not."

With that, Rueger closed.

The prosecutor was trying to portray the defendant as less than forthcoming with police and the court. Rueger's underlying, unspoken question was; if you weren't the killer, why wouldn't you provide an alibi to police? The implication hung in the air without rebuttal from the defense that Laskey was not required to tell police anything under his Constitutional right to remain silent, a hot topic at the time jurors would have been familiar with the rights of suspects in the Miranda and Escobedo cases.

Given his chance to address the issue on redirect, Signer instead dwelt on questions to Laskey about his weight – between 130 and 135, and whether he had a goatee and mustache in August 1966 - yes.

Rueger returned with his redirect to Posteal's facial hair, asking him to turn his head in multiple directions for the benefit of the jury before Postal stepped down.

"Defense will rest at this time, your Honor."

After additional items were entered into evidence, the prosecution called new witnesses for rebuttal, beginning with Ray Koehler, a police department identification officer, to ask about a lineup photograph taken of Laskey on December 11.

Koehler was followed by Municipal Court Judge William S. Mathews whom Rueger asked about seeing Laskey in his court during October 1965, but Signer succeeded with an objection. Rueger had no further questions and no cross, so the prosecution rested.

Signer made a motion for dismissal due to lack of evidence – overruled. Another asked that the Hinners testimony be struck from the record, also overruled.

It was approaching the time when it would be the jury's case to decide.

Chapter 22
Closing Arguments

Cal Prem stepped before the jury to open the prosecution's closing argument. He emphasized the importance of evidence over lawyerly words, acknowledging each side shaping the facts to fit their narrative. Prem reminded jurors it would be the judge's final instructions to guide them on applying the law. They alone held the responsibility of deciding whether the defendant was guilty or innocent. And, if guilty, whether he should live or die; decisions founded solely in the facts.

Prem reviewed the two charges against Laskey: the murder of Barbara Bowman, which was carried out with "deliberate and premeditated malice," and the robbery, a crime that escalated the case to first-degree murder. Four essential questions would have to be answered:

- Was the location of the crime known?

- Was the victim alive before the act was committed?

- Was the crime committed purposely; meaning, it was not accidental?

- Was the killing performed with deliberate and premeditated malice?

If the evidence proved these elements, then it would be their duty to return a verdict of guilty.

Burt Signer opened the closing statement for the defense highlighting the imbalance trial procedures favoring the prosecution, emphasizing the state having the last word. When the defense closed their case, Signer told the jury, "our lips are sealed forever, as far as you people are concerned."

Signer cited the defense being blocked from attending the grand jury hearing, but Rueger objected. Judge Leis pressed Signer to concede there was nothing unique in Laskey's case; acknowledging only the prosecutor, grand jurors, and witnesses attended such hearings A defendants would be permitted only if he desired to testify. Signer persisted in describing the grand jury process is a one-way hearing over Rueger's continued objections.

"All right, gentlemen, let's go," the judged ordered.

Signer cast doubt on the testimony of Ruth Bailey, the young woman happening upon the scene with forty-year-old Bud Walker. He wondered what Thomas Tomaseck was doing at the scene, suggesting Tomaseck's conduct was suspicious and implying he may have tampered with evidence. Signer scolded police for failing to take contact information at the scene; quickly switching gears to credit police for locating Tomaseck. "Cincinnati is blessed with probably one of the finest police forces in the United States."

The crux of Signer's argument was the absence of direct evidence linking Laskey to the crimes. He emphasized the adsence of fingerprints in the cab.

"You know, a man can be lucky, maybe he doesn't leave a fingerprint in one place. Let us assume for a moment, take the worse, that Laskey was the man in that cab, and he got extremely lucky, to attack Barbara Bowman in the back, had his hands flying all over that cab, touched various items and miraculously never left a fingerprint. Not a one."

Same for Sol Thompson's taxi. "Miraculous," Signer said.

Signer portrayed each of the prosecution witnesses as unreliable, particularly those drinking in the Lark Café the night of the murder, arguing their recollections were clouded by alcohol and the passage of time, as well as natural biases, prejudices, and beliefs influencing their recollections.

When discussing the robbery charge, Signer pointed to the five-dollar bill found near Barbara Bowman's body as evidence no robbery occurred. Nothing was known to be missing from Bowman's purse or billfold, further questioning if the bag found at the scene was even Bowman's. Signer returned to the mysterious "lone man," Tomaseck, who may have tampered with evidence at the scene.

Then, Signer oddly returned to his client's criminal past.

"You know, little has been said about Posteal Laskey. Let me tell you something about him. He's been in trouble before. He's a purse snatcher, petty thief..."

Rueger objected to Signer's depiction as a "misstatement of fact," which the judge upheld.

After casting an aspersion at his client's character, Signer then depicted the neighborhood where the crime occurred, Price Hill, as "not the best of neighborhoods" with residents as "people [who've] been known to steal from one another." Maybe this was the case with

Bowman's purse and wallet? Casting shade on a White working class neighborhood familiar to many jurors was simply insulting.

Signer complained about the prosecution not playing the Yellow Cab dispatch tape recording, Rueger reminded the judge and jury how the prosecution tried entering the tape but was blocked by a defense objection. Signer could only counter that no one testified to hearing Laskey's voice on the tape.

Signer implored the jury to acquit Laskey since there was no tangible evidence proving his guilt. He argued the case was built upon a weak foundation of circumstantial evidence and unreliable testimony.

With this, Leis brought Tuesday's proceedings to a close. Cal Prem made his argument in half an hour, while Signer had taken an hour and would resume the next morning.

Wednesday opened with Signer returning to focus on the thousands of keys that could have operated Yellow Cab #870 and have been used to steal cabs from the Kenner Street lot.

Signer described the six defense witnesses as having simple, truthful stories, highlighting the testimony of Laskey's mother, Nancy, who had no reason to lie.

Defense counsel hailed Laskey's decision to testify when he could have remained silent. Instead, he chose to face the jury and prosecutor to speak his truth. Signer returned to Laskey's criminal record, insisting the defendant's trouble past did not make him a murderer.

The Cincinnati Strangler

He next turned his attention to Cincinnati's Black community, home to both Laskey and the defense witnesses, telling the all-White jury, "That doesn't make their life worth any less than ours... They can still tell the truth the same as we can."

Taking up the entire morning session, Signer made his final plea, casting doubt on the prosecution's ability to prove Laskey's guilt beyond a reasonable doubt founded in the absence of physical evidence, a hair or a fingerprint, but there were none. This meant the state had failed to connect Laskey to the crime in any concrete way.

"No man can be that lucky. No man can be that smart," he concluded.

When court resumed Thursday morning, Donald Roney stood before the jury to deliver the second closing argument on behalf of Posteal Laskey. Roney began by discounting the gruesome morgue photographs, urging jurors, "Don't let the pictures sway you, they are not evidence against the defendant, only to facilitate the testimony of the pathologist…Put them out of your mind." The image of a dead woman laying nude on a morgue rack, the Y-shaped incisions of an autopsy marking her body, while her shattered leg was unnaturally bent. This was not an image one would soon forget.

Roney dismissed prosecution witnesses as barely worthy of comment, particularly Leroy Smith, sarcastically saying, "What are you going to say about his testimony? I don't know. Maybe someday when you are riding through the country and you run upon a road that seems a little strange to you, maybe you will know who built it.

Be that as it may, the next man to come upon the scene is Leroy Jones <sic>. There's a real testifying witness. There isn't much you can say about Leroy."

He likened Smith's reliability to a fleeting popular song, quipping about a record from a few years ago, "Pass the Ball to Leroy," [1] before adding a rambling personal touch that his daughter used to listen to the song when she was a teenager.

Roney characterized the testimony of Posteal's mother and brother as "honest," but his mention of Nancy Laskey seeing Posteal at five a.m., and Dave seeing his brother early in the evening and then not again until the next day, did not support an alibi for the whereabouts of Posteal at the time of the murder.

"Has there been anything that has occurred in this courtroom that would lead you to believe beyond a reasonable doubt that this man is guilty?" Roney asked. The defense attorney pointed to eyewitness accounts failing to describe Laskey's characteristics, particularly his goatee and mustache, as grounds for reasonable doubt.

"If you are close enough to say it's Posteal Laskey, you are close enough to see if he has a twitch in an eye, a scar on the cheek, a mustache on the lip, or a goatee on the chin. If you haven't been that close, you are not close enough to say who it is."

In an emotional appeal to dissuade jurors from imposing the death penalty, Roney launched a well-known

---

[1] No song with this title could be found but the phrase, "Just give the ball to Leroy," was commonly heard across the South as colleges began desegregating. "Give the Ball to Leroy" was turned into a positive at Purdue University honoring football star, Leroy Keyes.

defense tactic known as "the last mile," describing the final minutes of a man's life before execution. He spoke of the prisoner being transported to Death Row where the lights burn 24 hours a day and the condemned man is under constant surveillance. Roney dramatically described the final walk across a narrow courtyard to the death house, where the prisoner would take his last look at the sky.

As Roney was describing the moment when the condemned prisoner's right trouser leg would be slit, Rueger rose to object. "I hate to interrupt. I think it's unfair…" Before Rueger could finish, the judge sustained the objection, shutting down Roney's "last mile" defense.

To close, Roney urged the jury to take a stand with guidance from above. "Now is your chance to stand up for the principles we believe in. May He give you all that is necessary to stand up and say, 'That man is not guilty.' He has not—the state has not met the burden required of them beyond a reasonable doubt. Have the courage to come forward and say it."

The prosecution had the final word and the Hamilton County prosecutor would deliver it. Rueger opened by reflecting on the weight of the case, emphasizing that trying a first-degree murder case is never an "enriching experience." He spoke of the emotional toll of seeking justice in a case where a man's life is at stake, reminding jurors that while it was his duty to press the case, he was not seeking vengeance.

"Laskey's not my sworn enemy," Rueger stated. "I do so without hesitancy. I do so with a firm conviction."

Rueger criticized the defense for relying on innuendo and creating distractions, particularly in their portrayal of Thomas Tomaseck as a "straw man" in an attempt to shift attention away from the facts. He also cited the duplicity of defense counsel toward police, first finding endless fault and then saying they're the best in the country.

The prosecutor reviewed witness testimony discounted by the defense, reading from the transcript, using their own words to deflect the counter-argument. Supporting the testimony of Leroy Smith, Rueger asked, "Is there any question in your mind who was driving that cab?"

Rueger reminded jurors of the items found along Ring, leading to the rope with embedded beads lying at the corner with Underwood. "A fair assumption whoever did this took that route."

Regarding the injuries suffered by Bowman about her pelvis, genitalia, and right thigh, Rueger asked, "What do you think he was trying to do in the back of that cab? Play tiddlywinks? What do you think he was going to do with Mrs. Hinners?"

When Rueger started reading Hinners's testimony, Signer objected, arguing that Rueger was taking her words beyond the court's instructions. Without fully sustaining the objection, the judge reminded the jury that Hinners' testimony was presented for limited purposes, not as evidence of guilt in Bowman's murder.

The prosecutor immediately returned to the Hinners testimony, reading from a paper, "Do you want what the others got?" repeating it with, "Don't scream" and "I'll slit your throat," as Signer repeatedly implored the bench, "If the court please…" without success.

As Rueger closed, he brought up the matter of mercy, reminding jurors that while they should consider mercy, they must also weigh justice for the victim.

"Our law prescribes that guilt provides this type of punishment… Why is this man entitled to mercy? The same mercy that was extended to Barbara Bowman."

With that, the prosecution rested, and Judge Leis gave his final instructions to the jury before sending them to the jury room to begin deliberations. After nearly three weeks, from jury selection to closing arguments, the fate of Posteal Laskey was now entirely in their hands.

The electric chair in the Ohio State Penitentiary (Ohio Memory)

Chapter 23
Life or Death

"Your oath requires you to accept the law as it is given to you by the court and to apply that law in your deliberations," Judge Leis told the jurors.

"The law presumes that the defendant is innocent... until it is overcome by proof beyond a reasonable doubt... Evidence proves beyond a reasonable doubt; once satisfied beyond a reasonable doubt your duty to find the defendant guilty of one or more of the charges."

The judge read the full indictments before outlining the charges for the jury to consider. If the jury did not agree with the charge of first-degree murder in a death resulting from robbery, they could charge second-degree murder or manslaughter, or not guilty.

Juror were presented two forms. The first, the verdict form offered eight possible outcomes:

"We, the Jury; in the issue joined, find the defendant, Posteal Laskey, Jr., guilty of Murder in the First Degree as he stands charged in the First Count of the indictment," accompanied by seven other possible verdicts, including not guilty.

The other form was the recommendation for mercy.

"We, the Jury, in the issue joined, find the defendant, Posteal Laskey, Jr. guilty of Murder in the First Degree as he stands charged in the First Count of the indictment, and we do / do not recommend mercy."

Below were lines for twelve juror signatures.

Jurors were excused for lunch and alternate juror, William Nordyke, was dismissed as he was no longer needed.

At 12:30, the jurors, with their supervising court officers, walked through downtown to Caproni's, a popular Italian restaurant, returning at 2:15 p.m. with two questions:

"Could the court re-read the testimony of the witness from Detroit?

"Could the court re-read testimony of defense witness, Ben Johnson, the boarder?

"Signed Harold W. Mercer, Jury Foreman."

The court reporter read the testimony of Charles R Thompson, the laid-off Detroit autoworker the prosecution wanted returned to the courtroom without success, and that of Johnson who lived in the Laskey home before jurors returned to their deliberations at 4:41 p.m. They emerged at 6:21 p.m. to tell Judge Leis they were unable to reach a verdict.

Dismissed for dinner, the group again walked through downtown, this time to Kluszewski's Restaurant on Sixth Street, owned by Ted Kluszewski, a popular retired first baseman of the Cincinnati Reds.

Returning after two hours, the jurors emerged an hour later from the jury room to say they were still unable to reach a verdict. Leis ordered their sequester for the night, to return the next morning to the jury room.

When Judge Leis adjourned for the day at 9:40 p.m., few people knew what had transpired behind the closed door of the judge's chamber while they were out.

Leis received a phone call from Jewish Hospital informing him of the death of Miriam Kapson, the sister of juror Shirley Edell. The judge was aware of their close relationship from Edell's request during voir dire to be excused from jury duty as it would interfere with her daily visits with her ill sister.

Not wishing to make a public spectacle of private tragedy, Leis called Edell into his chamber where, in the presence of the bailiff, delicately told her of Miriam's death.

"My sister?" Edell asked in disbelief.

"Yes," Leis replied. "I just received information that your sister had died."

Recovering from the initial shock, Edell asked if she could speak with her parents, which Leis permitted in his presence to ensure nothing of the case was discussed.

Following the call, Edell said she would continue with the trial as the funeral would not be until Friday. For this night, she asked the judge if she could receive some kind of sedative.

Jurors were permitted supervised calls home with requests for clothing and toiletries, free of discussion about the trial. Four court officers had been sworn in to accompany jurors on the overnight stay. The group was comprised of Catherine M. Drach, Judge Leis's sister-in-law, and three male bailiffs. They proceeded to the Netherland Plaza Hotel to retire for the night.

Arriving at the hotel, seventy-six-year-old Drach, a

very matronly matron, had specific instructions to keep watch over Edell, putting her to bed, and giving her the tablet of phenobarbital the judge had delivered from the county jail.

Edell arrived in court the next morning with the other jurors, ready to complete their deliberations.

Court resumed at nine a.m., Thursday, April 13 with jurors convening in the jury room. There were hints of the Edell episode and once defense counsel learned details, an exception was filed.

The judge's action could have resulted in a mistrial but the defense did little beyond filing their exception that, "the court administered a phenobarbital - a drug requiring the prescription of a physician. Both state and federal law forbid sale of a phenobarbital pill without a prescription."

Leis described the incident as, "a delicate situation for the Court. The Court thought it was the only decent, sensible way to handle the situation."

Shortly after eleven, the jury sent a note to the judge requesting a reading of the judge's instructions. The note read: "Re read the charge to the jury. Slowly Mercer – Harold W. Mercer, Jury foreman."

Ronald Johnson, the court reporter, read the requested twenty-one page passage to jurors in the courtroom.

Returning to the jury room at 11:36, they emerged less that forty-five minutes later, at 12:15 p.m.

Judge Leis looked to his right at the twelve in the jury box, his white face enveloped in his black robes. His left arm swept beneath his chin, the robe's wide sleeve reaching the desk.

"I understand the jury has reached a verdict in this case?" Leis asked.

Mercer rose in response: "We have, your Honor."

Mercer handed the paper bearing the verdict to the clerk, Robert Rudig, who read the words to the hushed courtroom.

"We, the jury, in the issue joined, find the defendant, Posteal Laskey, Jr., guilty of Murder in the First Degree as he stands charged in the First Count of the indictment."

"We, the jury, in the issue joined, find the defendant Posteal Laskey, Jr. guilty of Murder in the First Degree as he stands charged in the Second Count of the indictment."

Judge Leis ordered a polling of the jury and, without dissent, the jurors were excused at 12:20 p.m..

Unceremoniously, Judge Leis issued his next order, "All right, Mr. Sheriff, you may take the prisoner."

"I expected it," Laskey told bailiff Stanley "Whitey" Heber as he was led from the courtroom to the sixth-floor lockup.

Nancy Laskey screamed, "Oh, my God, why did they do it?" from the front row behind the defense. She was accompanied by her son Dave from the courtroom where they were met by a phalanx of reporters and photographers. Dave rushed at the assembly warning them to stay away from his mother.

That afternoon's Cincinnati *Post* featured a banner headline on its front page, "LASKEY GUILTY, MUST DIE."

Immediately after the verdict, the prosecutor faced questions: Would he pursue charges in the other murders?

"No," Rueger was quoted in the next day's *Post*, "because death is so final."

The assault and robberies against Delle Ernst and Virginia Hinners were never tried as the state had the outcome it desired.

A sentencing hearing was held on May 5, but first Judge Leis dealt with a defense motion for a new trial based upon the twenty-nine exceptions, or objections raised by the defense and denied by the bench. The judge read each of the exceptions for detailed discussion over more than two hours, and would rule on the matters at a later date. The defense was joined by Donald L. Robertson, professor of Law at Ohio Northern University, who would remain with the case through appeals. The twenty-nine exceptions met the same fate throughout - denied.

After hearing the exceptions, it was time to pass sentence on Posteal Laskey.

Laskey was brought into the courtroom. Once in place, the clerk reminded him he'd been found guilty of first-degree murder, followed by Judge Leis asking, "Have you anything to say why the court should not pass sentence upon you?"

Laskey replied, "You will be passing sentence on an

The Cincinnati Strangler

innocent man."

"Very well," the judge replied, "That was a matter for the jury to decide."

"And the jury having found you guilty of the offense, it now becomes the unpleasant duty of the court to pass sentence upon you," Leis said.

"It is the sentence of this court that you be confined to the Ohio Penitentiary and that the Warden of the Ohio Penitentiary shall cause a current of electricity of sufficient intensity to pass through your body until death."

"Date of execution will be set as of September the 15th."

With the final words, "And may God have mercy on your soul," the trial of Posteal Laskey, Jr. reached its conclusion.

(Cincinnati Public Library)

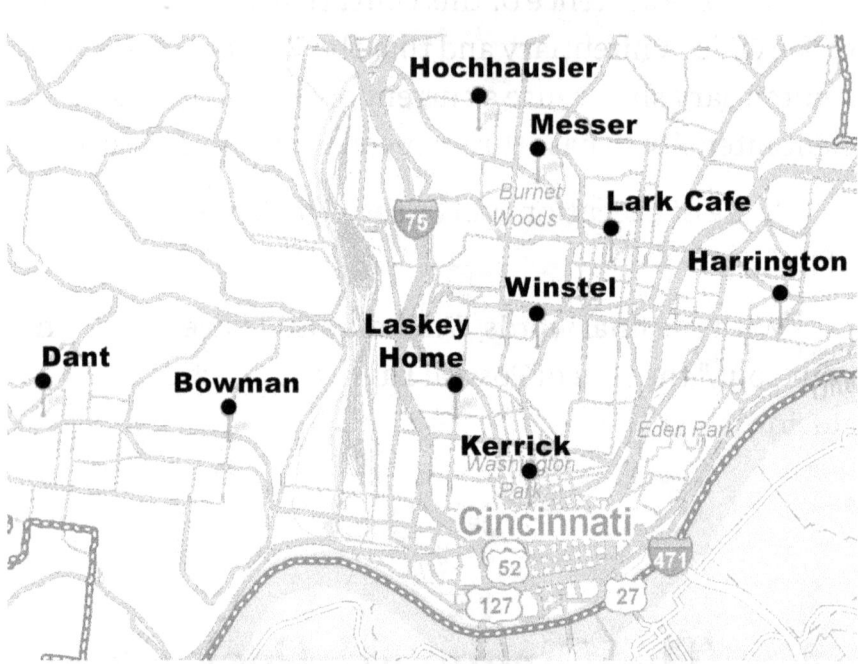

Locations of the murders attributed to the Cincinnati Strangler.
(Base map courtesy of Hamilton County CGIS)

Part IV: Aftermath

The Ohio State Penitentiary in Columbus, Ohio. (Ohio Memory)

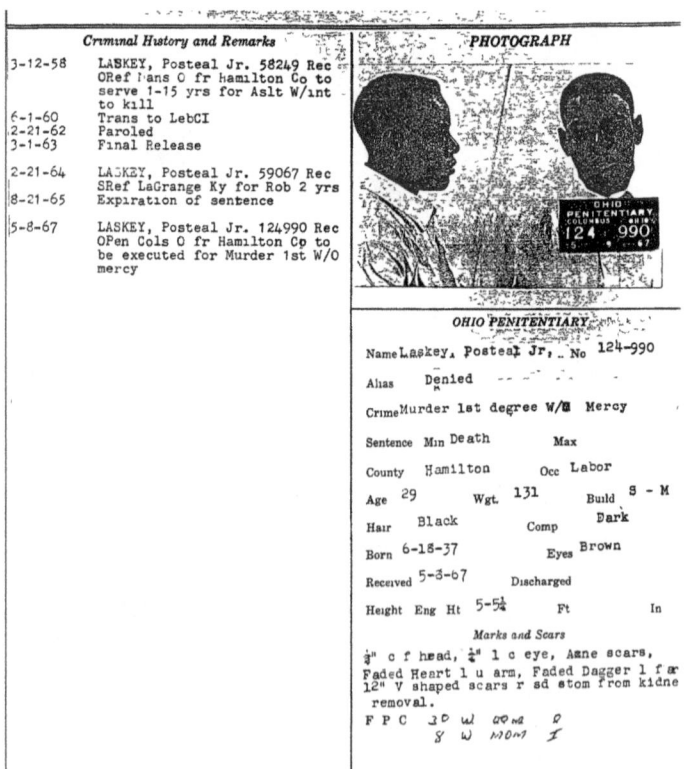

Posteal Laskey's 1967 penitentuary intake form.
(ODRC)

Chapter 24
Welcome to the Big House

"Then Cain went out from the presence of the Lord and dwelt in the land of Nod on the east of Eden." (New King James Bible)

An early spring flowerbed of geraniums and pansies sprayed an array of bright yellows, purples, blues, and reds before the peeling, crumbling façade of the Ohio State Penitentiary. The enormous five-story fortress, a relic of the 19th century, loomed ahead with its concrete cuts, turrets, guard towers, and iron-barred windows. This was the final destination for those condemned to serve their time or die within its impenetrable walls. Situated near the confluence of the Scioto and Olentangy Rivers, the austere prison, opened in 1834, was a short distance from the Ohio Statehouse, the capitol.

Hamilton County Sheriff Dan Tehan personally delivered Posteal Laskey to the Ohio Penitentiary on May 8, 1967. Tehan, a longtime NFL referee, was in his NFL off-season when he made the hundred-mile drive north on the new, only partially-opened, Interstate 71 from Cincinnati to Columbus. Typically, the sheriff would while away the drive talking with his charge about football or baseball, as he was also an umpire, but Laskey was not a sports fan and preferred sitting quietly, reading, enduring the sheriff's AM-radio listening pleasures.

As they approached the grim penitentiary, Laskey sensed a certainty of no return. The aging structure's tall, barred windows loomed above, offering mere slivers of natural light for those inside. Despite the neatly tended flowerbeds, the imposing visage portrayed a place where hopes went to die.

Tehan opened the back door of the vehicle he'd parked in the lot off West Spring Street. Laskey emerged wearing a belly belt, a chain wrapped around his waist with two chains linked to handcuffs. The sheriff placed a firm grip on Laskey's arm while walking his prisoner to the front entrance. Tehan, in full sheriff's dress, was cheerfully greeted by his corrections brethren as they climbed the short set of concrete stairs to the front lobby entrance. Inside, they were directed to an assistant warden's office where Tehan handed over Laskey's paperwork, including the court order for his incarceration and the Death Warrant. Issued by Hamilton County Clerk of Courts Robert Jennings and addressed to Warden E. L. Maxwell, the warrant directed the Maxwell to execute Laskey, "by causing a current of electricity, of sufficient intensity to cause death, to pass through his body, and the application of such current to be continued until he is dead, said punishment to be inflicted within the walls of the Ohio Penitentiary, on the fifteenth day of September, in the year of our Lord, one thousand nine hundred and sixty-seven..."

With that, Tehan's work was done, leaving only the return drive. It was a relief that Posteal Laskey was gone from Cincinnati, forever.

The prisoner was taken to the "bull pen," a large cage-like room with ceiling to floor steel bars, striking a familiar, while much larger, reminder of the processing area of the Cincinnati City Jail.

The Cincinnati Strangler

There, he was presented his special uniform with red stripes down the legs of his blue dungarees along the lapels of his blue denim jacket and on his white shirt; the stripes demoting a Death Row inmate. The prisoner was permitted his own underwear, socks, and shoes, sized seven and a half. He was handed a Bible and a bar of soap for the two showers permitted each week. Shaving was handled by a prison barber on Wednesdays and Fridays.

Inside the bull pen, Posteal Laskey, Jr. became inmate number 124 990, as he would be known for the rest of his life. Laskey was escorted, in handcuffs, into East Hall, L-Block, his new home. Voices followed the new resident, "young meat."

Inside the prison's stark grey walls were stands of grey steel bars, paired with grey steel mesh, all illuminated by harsh bare bulbs. Fear is the near-constant companion of inmates as physical and mental harassment lurks around every corner, but there was no relief in reporting to guards or one would immediately be tagged a "snitch." The sparse interpersonal contact in the solitary existence of Death Row was something of a benefit in avoiding conflict.

Inside the twenty-two-acre property, the prison's intimidating architecture dominated. To the right, L-Block housed Death Row, where those awaiting their final moments were confined. Behind it, an innocuous redbrick building, small and unassuming, concealed its darker purpose. Known simply as the Death House, it was here that condemned men made their final walk. Inside stood the electric chair—Thunderbolt or Old Sparky, as it was known—its mahogany frame polished with crisscrossed straps and snaking cables ready for their deadly assignment. The walls bore the portraits of 312 men and three women who faced their maker from that chair. The last execution had taken place in 1963 when a petty thief named Donald L. Reinbolt was put to death for killing a Columbus grocer in a robbery gone wrong.

The prison's general population lived in oppressive overcrowding; four men crammed into cells built for two. Dormitories were filled with bunks for eighty to one-hundred men sleeping on double-stacked bunks, their belongings kept wherever there was an available makeshift hanger or stowing space.

Laskey's new reality on Death Row quickly set in. Steel doors slammed behind him, one by one, as he was led to his cell—number 8. The seven-by-seven-foot cell, on the second tier of five levels, had only the essentials: a single bunk bed, a wash basin, and a toilet. The musty air carried the echoes of cries and screams, occasionally offset by the sweet chirping of canaries—pets permitted to some inmates.

Cincinnati's Civil War-era Workhouse may have been imposing but it was miniature by comparison. Workhouse residents were largely petit criminals serving thirty-day sentences, with Laskey regarded as legend, the first murder suspect to be housed there. The enormity of the penitentiary was overwhelming to the visitor and crushing to the new resident; worse for those under a death penalty in the knowledge of the only way out was the electric chair.

On his arrival, Laskey was placed on "close watch"

in L-Block to monitor "his reaction, attitude, and overall adjustment." Laskey's prior experience of incarceration helped soften the blow.

Despite Laskey's outward composure, inside, he was shrinking. His relaxed demeanor on the drive belied his twisting stomach. The comparisons to his past incarcerations—the Kentucky State Reformatory, Lebanon Correctional Institution, and even military lock-up—meant nothing now. In the Workhouse, he might have been a legend, but here, he was nobody. Just another prisoner, known for killing old women. The Ohio State Penitentiary was a living hell, and his end was marked for September 15, 1967—130 days away.

By then, days would no longer matter; weeks and months bore no distinction beyond a mark on the wall. L-Block residents endured hearing groups of regular inmates talking as they walked in rows of three along courtyard pathways below. Death Row inmates were not permitted such privileges. Death Row inmates were permitted only an hour each day to step out of their cell to mingle with other prisoners. Posteal would use this time to play chess; more often keeping to himself, reading and listening to music.

Few general inmates saw the men of L-Block who remained locked in their cells all day and night. Guards accompanying Death Row inmates on trips to the hospital or visiting room, as they passed through the general population, would yell, "Dead man coming. Move aside. Dead man coming."

Laskey's admission interview with counselor John

Tabor was brief. Posteal remained mostly silent, telling Tabor he would refrain from speaking due to his pending appeal. The intake paperwork described Laakey as a small man—131 pounds with a medium build and standing just over five feet tall. He bore the marks of past life—scars on his forehead, a faded tattoo of a heart on his upper arm, a dagger on his left forearm, and a long scar on his abdomen from kidney surgery in 1955.

Tabor noted Laskey's history of good behavior at other institutions, including the Ohio State Reformatory, where he'd earned Honor Status working as a boiler fireman. He followed instructions well and had only two minor infractions over four years. In Kentucky, he'd worked in a clothing plant, where his performance was rated as "very good" under minimum security conditions.

As for his personal life, Laskey told the counselor he had a very good relationship with his father, seeing him often, while he had no idea why his parents separated. Nancy Laskey was described in an earlier probation report on Posteal as "literate, of temperate habits."

Laskey admitted to moderate consumption of alcohol without drug use or excessive gambling, telling Tabor he spent most of his time practicing music.

Tabor reviewed Laskey's education: Courter Technical High School to September 1952 and a transfer to Fulton School serving students with behavioral problems when he registered an IQ score of 87.

Old postcard showing the "bull pen" at the Ohio State Penitentiary. (Kent State University)

Statue of Abraham Lincoln doused in whitewash on June 14, 1967, a sign hung around his neck with a paraphrase of Benjamin Franklin: "Better for 100 guilty to go free than for 1 that is innocent to suffer." (Courtesy C. Smith)

Chapter 25
The Long Hot Summer of 1967

As White Cincinnati breathed a collective sigh of relief with the conviction of Posteal Laskey, the Black community felt the unyielding weight of injustice. The lack of access to good-paying jobs, deplorable housing conditions, and the deafness of the political class were endless aggravations, compounded by the heavy-handed sweep of Black men from the streets in the Strangler investigations.

The disparity between Laskey's death penalty sentence and the probation handed to Eugene Fiske for the beating death of Virginia Wolpert in October 1966 added focused rage to the mix. Fiske, the White former editor at The Cincinnati *Enquirer*, was charged with second-degree murder and pleaded guilty to first-degree manslaughter. In sentencing, Judge William R. Matthews, the jurist overseeing Laskey's grand jury proceedings and arraignment, prioritized Fiske's potential for rehabilitation, arguing that prison time would serve no societal benefit. Matthews sentenced him to five years' probation. The Black community was outraged by the discrepancy in justice between the leniency shown to Fiske and the death sentence meted out to Laskey.

Reverend Samuel R. Wright, pastor of Mt. Zion Methodist Church in Walnut Hills, summarized general community sentiment in a letter to the editor of the *Enquirer* addressing justice for Laskey, writing:

"The central issue in the Posteal Laskey, Jr. case is not whether his execution would serve as a deterrent to crime," as a fellow clergyman preached from his pulpit, "not even whether he was guilty, but how was it humanely possible in such a prejudiced and hysterical environment for Laskey, a Negro, to receive a fair trial?"

A delegation of local activists, led by Robert C. Weaver, head of the Evanston Business and Professional Association, along with Laskey's cousin Peter Frakes and William Roper, took their grievances to the state capital. They demanded Ohio Governor James A. Rhodes convene a special grand jury to investigate the civil rights violations suffered by Black and poor White residents in Cincinnati, exemplified by the Laskey case. Instead of meeting with the governor, the group was directed to his legal assistant, Gerald Collins, who informed them that such investigations would not occur until all appeals had been exhausted.

"The very air in Hamilton County was electrified with the desire to convict any Negro," the group's written statement said.

Tensions in Cincinnati were at a breaking point, and the arrest of Peter Frakes tipped the balance. On the night of Sunday, June 11, 1967, Laskey's cousin was arrested for loitering in the Avondale neighborhood. He and a group of some twenty Black individuals had gathered in front of a Jiffy Mart at the corner of Rockdale and Reading Roads carrying signs reading, "Justice for Laskey." Frakes was well-known for his protests, often wearing a sandwich board that proclaimed, "Cincinnati Guilty – Laskey Innocent," around the city.

That night, District 4 Patrolman Dan Patterson approached the group, persuading them disperse. Frakes, however, remained, marching in place, defiantly asserting that he couldn't be arrested because he was technically moving. Patterson drove off in his patrol car, but when he returned to the area, he found Frakes still there. Calling for backup. Patrolman Albert Boston, a Black officer, arrived, and together they arrested Frakes for loitering.

The arrest occurred hours after Reverend Martin Luther King Jr. had addressed an interfaith gathering at Zion Baptist Church in Avondale calling for an end to hatred and violence. "We all have to learn to live together," King implored. "Our cry should not be 'burn, baby, burn,' but 'learn, baby, learn.'"

Frakes was found guilty and fined $50 in Traffic Court, but his arrest, like so many before him, underscored the oppressive nature of the city's loitering ordinance. Between January 1966 and June 1967, 240 people had been arrested under the law—170 of them Black.

Quiet, complacent Cincinnati quickly turned into a powder keg. Years of systemic inequities—Jim Crow-era barriers to employment, redlining in housing, and the city's indifferent leadership—created a growing divide between the Black community and the White establishment. The police dragnet, ostensibly to capture a Black serial killer, made life in Black neighborhoods unbearable. Laskey's conviction was the final insult in a long line of perceived injustices. Frakes's arrest was the straw that broke the city's back.

The next day, temperatures rose to a humid ninety-degrees. That afternoon, one young man counted the number of delivery trucks driving through Avondale, tallying fifty-eight trucks with only one driven by a Black man. Word of this survey spread and young men began interfering with deliveries to neighborhood businesses.

Ben Torf, owner of the Torf Drug Store for twenty-three years, called police about youths interfering with deliveries to his business. Dr. Robert Reid, director of the Opportunities Industrialization Center, had been trying to defuse the free-flowing anger when an unnamed police sergeant arrived asking an officer about the situation, an officer at the scene, according to Reid, told the sergeant, "young nigger punks were disrupting deliveries to his store." [1]

Reid managed to get the kids away from the drugstore, but when he left for a meeting, the young men headed to a junior high school for a meeting protesting the Frakes arrest and the anti-loitering law. Police mobilized but kept their distance from the meeting fearing their presence could incite violence.

"It was the arrest of Peter Frakes by police who don't understand, ever," said one Avondale resident.

Older Black community leaders attempted to calm the situation. The divide between their more conservative approach of community elders and the militancy of the younger generation was becoming clear. At a meeting beneath the statue of Abraham Lincoln at Reading and Rockdale, over one hundred people gathered, carrying "Justice for Laskey" signs, and making appeals for contributions to the Laskey Freedom Fund. The generational

---

[1] National Advisory Commission on Civil Disorders (Kerner Commission), 1968

split was evident when younger attendees booed down speakers who urged restraint, throwing a burning ball of paper at the statue amid their catcalls.

At 9:40 P.M., a fire in the Lo Mark drug store's broken display window drew a crowd to watch the fire department put out the flames. Around 9:45, a group of helmeted police officers bearing shotguns and nightsticks marched toward the onlookers, herding them along Rockdale toward Burnet Avenue. As they went, bottles began rained down on police, accompanied by the sound of rocks pinging off passing cars resulting in multiple injuries to vehicle occupants. Scattered incidents continued through the night. The fuse was lit.

Tuesday morning, Black community leaders presented the Cincinnati City Council with a list of eleven demands, including the repeal of the loitering ordinance. They called for the release of those arrested during the disturbances, and full employment for Black residents. While city leaders expressed willingness to consider some demands, they refused to attend an open-air meeting in Avondale, unwilling to legitimize militants as co-equals to the establishment.

The city's refusal to engage with the city's younger activists only fueled further unrest. By Tuesday evening, tensions exploded as bricks, rocks, and Molotov cocktails were thrown at passing cars and police. Firefighters were also targeted. By 7:15 p.m., Police Chief Schott declared, "All hell broke loose."

The violence claimed two lives: Dr. John Falk, a White motorist struck by a rock that shattered his windshield, and Robert Boyd, a Black man shot while sitting on his porch. Though rumors swirled saying the riots were spilling into White neighborhoods, the violence remained largely confined to Avondale.

Ohio National Guard and Cincinnati police. (Tom Hubbard)

Toward ten p.m., Cincinnati Mayor Walton H. Bachrach appealed to Ohio Governor James A. Rhodes to send the National Guard.

The guard arrived in the early morning hours of Wednesday, their presence helped calm the situation, but the damage had been done. The statue of Abraham Lincoln in Avondale was doused in black paint, with a sign hung around the statue's neck, quoting Benjamin Franklin: "Better for 100 guilty to go free than for 1 that is innocent to suffer."

The Cincinnati Strangler

The city council convened for a regular business session, but Avondale residents demanded to be heard. Their frustrations, long ignored, boiled over in raucous outcries. National Guard troops were called into the council chamber, further infuriating those who had come to voice their grievances. They walked out in protest, effectively ending the session.

Tensions simmered into Wednesday night, erupting again at around nine p.m. with renewed violence in Avondale, leaving one person with a gunshot wound. State Representatives William Bowen and William Mallory, returning from the state capital, were shocked by what they saw in the neighborhoods they represented. Witnessing the heavy-handed response of police and National Guard troops, Bowen told The Cincinnati *Post*, "I'm sure the arrest of Pete Frakes didn't help… I don't think Laskey helped either."

Peter Frakes, right. (Cincinncati Police Department)

Reverend Fred Shuttlesworth, a local civil rights leader and veteran of the Birmingham struggle, also pointed to the arrest of Peter Frakes as a flashpoint. He cited comments made by Laskey's brother, Dave Laskey, earlier in the week as further inciting the unrest. "I think the situation last night came up as a result of many Negroes feeling that there was some miscarriage of justice in the Laskey case," Shuttlesworth observed.

On Thursday, H. Rap Brown, a militant Black activist who had risen to prominence with Stokely Carmichael in the leadership of the Student Nonviolent Coordinating Committee (SNCC), arrived in Cincinnati amid the upheaval. Brown presented a list of twenty demands, including the removal of White businesses from the ghetto and control over which police officers could patrol the area. While Brown's presence had little direct impact on the events, his appearance was widely reported, and Brown presented a well-known boogeyman by Police Chief Jake Schott during testimony before the U.S. Senate Judiciary Committee.

The June riots in Cincinnati, as well as two smaller ones later in the summer, were cited in the 1967 National Advisory Commission on Civil Disorders, also known as the Kerner Commission. The commission pointed to the Laskey prosecution as a foundational cause of the unrest, highlighting the broken lines of communication between city officials and the Black community. It noted that city leaders would invite only a select few representatives to meetings, allowing them just minutes to present their demands, a process that bred frustration and resentment.

Mayor Bachrach, in his later testimony to the Kerner Commission, expressed surprise at the violence, claiming the council had "worked like hell" to address the concerns of the Black community.

Yet the numbers told a different story: Out of 404 arrests, 338 were under the age of twenty-six, and 128 were juveniles. Nearly thirty percent of the arrested adults were unemployed, a clear reflection of the systemic issues at play.

In the aftermath, those arrested were brought before Municipal Court Judge William S. Mathews, the judge who gave Posteal Laskey probation in 1965, made no secret of his intention to hand down maximum sentences for riot-related offenses. While he later admitted this was a violation of judicial ethics, he justified his actions as necessary to protect a city under siege. The disparity in charges was stark: White defendants were mostly charged with misdemeanors like disorderly conduct, while Black defendants, even those attempting to de-escalate the violence, were charged under the Riot Act, facing potential fines of $500 and up to a year in prison.

Christopher Harrison, a seventy-one-year-old barber from Youngstown was in Cincinnati for a VFW convention. While there, he attended a fundraiser for the Laskey Freedom Fund in Avondale. He left the event carrying a Laskey defense poster and went downtown to catch a bus home. At the depot, Harrison was denied entry to the restroom. Using the facility anyway, he was arrested for disorderly conduct, allegedly striking an officer. Police found policy slips, papers associated with illegal numbers gambling, on Harrison, leading to conviction of possessing policy slips, disorderly conduct, and assaulting a police officer, sentenced to six months in the Workhouse and a $125 fine.

The funds raised by the Laskey Freedom Fund ultimately never reached his attorneys to help pay for the ongoing appeals. Much of the money likely went to pay fines and legal costs for individuals arrested during the unrest, but its exact use remains unknown.

As the dust settled, a young police officer named John Rockel, known only by his badge number—584—became a legend in Black Cincinnati. Just twenty-two years old, Rockel made sixty-five arrests during the Avondale riots, gaining a reputation for heavy-handed tactics. State Representative Bowen recalled an incident where Rockel ordered him to leave the area. When Bowen tried to explain who he was, Rockel drew is gun, saying, "I don't give a damn who you are, you get out of here like the rest of them before I bash your head in." Fourteen witnesses testified before a police board about Rockel's conduct but the young officer was cleared of wrongdoing.

Rockel was later accused of intentionally stepping on the foot of John T. Poole, vice chair of the local CORE chapter, three times in August outside the Criminal Court where Judge Mathews found Rockel not guilty of assaulting Poole during the riots. Poole said Rockel came out of the courtroom going directly to him, repeatedly stepping on his foot, calling Poole "boy." Poole grabbed Rockel by the arm, saying, "I'm gonna make you say, 'I'm sorry.' You don't call me 'boy'."

While Judge Mathews exonerated Rockel saying there was no evidence of Rockel's action outside the courtroom was intentional, while giving Poole thirty days in the Workhouse on the disorderly conduct charge filed by Rockel.

In a press conference afterward, CORE chairman, Curtis Freeman, called Judge Mathews, "a racist that no black man should vote for in any election. He is more detrimental than any other judge."

In 1968, Patrolman John Rockel founded a community relations organization he named "584" to address issues of police-community relations. The following year, Rockel denounced his actions during the riots as "dead wrong."

"Many of the arrests I made were questionable. But I felt I was doing what the people of Cincinnati wanted me to do."

Rockel attributed his change of heart to a Black History class he took at the University of Cincinnati. "That was a real eye-opener."

Rockel went on to get his bachelor's degree, followed by night courses at the Chase College of Law, becoming a criminal defense attorney who continued working as a liaison between police and communities for the rest of his life.

In August 1967, Police Chief Jacob Schott testified before the U.S. Senate Judiciary Committee hearings on a proposed Anti-Riot Bill assigning criminal penalties on individuals crossing state lines, including using the U.S. mail, to incite violence. Schott placed much of the blame for Cincinnati's unrest on outsiders like Stokely Carmichael and H. Rap Brown, using their visits as evidence of external influence. He described Carmichael's April speech at the Carmel Presbyterian Church as inflammatory, though contemporary reports painted a different picture, with the *Enquirer* describing the address as "persuasive but not rabble-rousing."

Schott depicted Carmichael fleeing Cincinnati immediately following his address, mistakenly calling him "Brown," i.e., H. Rap Brown, further conflating and exaggerating events taking place over months, including his description of Cincinnati being under siege from June 12 through the 19th. Schott described Brown's speech laying out his twenty demands at the Black Guard Society, saying they "had black guards at the door. They wouldn't allow any white people there," Schott confidently telling the committee Brown described Cincinnati as having declared "war on the Negro and that they would have to fight back."

Outside the church where Carmichael was speaking the previous April 29, Ku Klux Klansmen in white robes and hoods gathered, but were persuaded by police to leave the scene without incident. The chief made no mention of the KKK presence in his testimony, no doubt, some crossing state lines, while exclusively pointing to Black outsiders stoking riotous anger in his city.

Schott also told the Senators of the arrest of several persons with sawed-off shotguns during the unrest, "but these arrests have been of white people who were going out to retaliate."

One example was that of twenty-two-year-old Francis E. Gast, arrested for possessing a sawed-off shotgun during one of the later upheavals. Gast was in a car with two others when they were pulled over in Avondale for driving erratically. Pulling the vehicle over was an all-star cast in the patrol car - Chief of Police Schott, police Lieutenant Colonel Embry Grimes, Safety Director Henry Sandman, and Major General Erwin Hostetler, adjutant general of the Ohio National Guard. Gast was arrested for carrying a loaded sawed-off shotgun. Gast and another White man were in the car with a man they said they'd picked up hitchhiking, a Black female impersonator. Gast said they were "only out for fun," to which U.S. District Judge Timothy S. Hogan advised Gast to meditate during his weekend in lockup on the thought of just how serious this could have been. Gast was facing five years in prison and $10,000 in fines but was sentenced to three days in jail and placed on two years' probation, minus the three days served.

To the Judiciary Committee, Schott whitewashed the situation in Avondale, a neighborhood destroyed in a concerted effort of city officials and their real estate partners through redlining and blockbusting to create an Avondale ghetto.

The stately 19th and early-20th century homes of Avondale had been home to many of Cincinnati's wealthiest Jewish families. Generations passed, families and temples moved, the houses were showing their age. Many of those structures are standing today, some renovated to their former glory.

Avondale fell susceptible to the drive for urban renewal through age and design, accelerated when the community was forced to absorb a large share of the sudden relocation of West End residents into Avondale, specifically designated as an area suitable for non-White residents by literal red lines drawn on maps.

Avondale was a neighborhood intentionally doomed to failure by its own city's hand. Avondale residential real estate had been under assault. To facilitate the relocation, brokers employed blockbusting techniques, hiring Black people to walk along Avondale sidewalks to give the image of a neighborhood in racial transition to accelerate sales, and worse. Developers scooped up the large houses and sliced them into multiple units, resembling the tenements of old. Many were overcrowded without full facilities, while the new owners collected subsidies for housing displaced persons.

The root of the displacement from the West End was Queensgate, a redevelopment plan leveling swaths of the nineteenth-century urban sprawl of the West End where thousands of poor Black residents lived, including the Laskey family. Many were displaced on short order to make way for low-rise, light-industrial development. They needed somewhere to go, so the city rushed to open public housing units, while Avondale handled the overflow.

Avondale has struggled to heal from the damage done in the mid-20th century over the ensuing decades.

Aftermath. (Courtesy C. Smith)

Interior of the Ohio State Penitentiary (Ohio Memory)

Chapter 26
Life and Death in Prison

The daily grind of repetitive routines, drudgery, and boredom ran on a never-ending cycle, one day blending into another. Posteal Laskey's time the state penitentiary was punctuated only by news of his appeals outside the prison walls and ongoing health issues within.

Attorneys Roney and Signer were joined by Donald L. Robertson, a professor of law at Ohio Northern University, to press Laskey's case through appeals. His legal battle first moved to the Hamilton County Court of Appeals, which issued a stay of execution on June 26, 1967, postponing his September 15, 1967, execution date to allow the appeal to be heard.

Since it was a capital punishment case, the next step was the Ohio Supreme Court. On March 25, 1968, the court stayed the execution pending appeal, and on June 20, 1968, an indefinite stay of execution was granted. However, on March 18, 1970, the Ohio Supreme Court, in *State v. Laskey*, upheld Laskey's conviction and set a new execution date for April 13, 1970. A week later, the court issued another postponement, pending appeal to the U.S. Supreme Court.

In February 1972, Posteal wrote a desperate letter to, "The Chief Justice of the State of Ohio," expressing frustration at not hearing from his attorney, Burt Signer: "When I write him, I get no reply. I thought I would write to you, because I don't know what else to do," he explained, noting that Roney had moved to Kentucky. "It has been about eighteen months since I have heard from either of them." Chief Justice C. William O'Neill's office responded, assuring Laskey that his case was before the U.S. Supreme Court and confirming that Roney, though relocated to Kentucky, remained a member of the Ohio Bar. That same year, Burt Signer was disbarred.

On June 29, 1972, the U.S. Supreme Court ruled in *Furman v. Georgia*, invalidating the death penalty as cruel and unusual punishment with disproportionate application to Black and poor individuals. While the decision did not overturn Laskey's sentence, it returned his case to the Ohio courts with a recommendation. On August 1, 1972, the Ohio Supreme Court commuted the death sentences of fifty-four penitentiary inmates, including Laskey, along with eight inmates in other Ohio facilities, converting their sentences to life imprisonment.

In August 1973, Laskey was transferred to the Southern Ohio Correctional Facility (SOCF), commonly known as Lucasville, a maximum-security prison. Lucasville opened in 1972 to replace the aging Ohio Penitentiary, though the old fortress remained in operation for over a decade before its eventual closure. Laskey was moved again on April 1, 1975, to the London Correctional Institution, where he would remain until 1998.

During his decades of incarceration, Laskey accumulated few disciplinary violations. One incident involved eating donuts, and another, in February 1968, resulted in a three-day loss of privileges after a confrontation with fellow Death Row inmate William Banks. Banks had approached Laskey's cell, spat at him, and Laskey spat back, calling a guard to intervene. The guard quoted Laskey saying, "Get this crazy fool from in front of my cell. That crazy son of a bitch belongs in Lima—the crazy motherfucker!" Laskey received a three-day punishment for profanity.

Banks had been convicted in two armed robberies in the late 1950s, and then he was sentenced to death for the 1963 murder of a fifty-two-year-old widow, beating and stabbing her thirty-two times during a burglary. He was sent to the Lima State Hospital the following month as, "not insane but mentally ill." Banks was paroled in 1983.

In October 1986, Posteal faced a potentially serious disciplinary charge when prison guard Patrick Chappel reported chasing inmate Carl Patrick who was, Chappel said, holding six marijuana cigarettes. Chappel claimed Patrick handed them to Laskey, accusing him of disobedience for flushing the joints down the toilet as he was being told to stop. Witnesses contested Chappel's account, but Laskey was found guilty of a rules infraction and given a suspended seven-day sentence in solitary confinement. Patrick escaped punishment. Concerned about the impact of the infraction on his next parole hearing, Laskey appealed, claiming he was sitting on the toilet when Patrick entered his cell, with Chappel following close behind. The appeal failed.

Over the years, prison psychologists and others delved far back into Laskey's life, both his criminal "assaultive" behavior and prior evaluations, sometimes skewing notes to serve circumstances. Evaluators emphasized Laskey's past relying on his military record, a 1957 psychological examination in the assault of Celia

Purvis, tests administered during his time in the Kentucky prison, and a 1965 assessment from Cincinnati's General Hospital following the assault of Judith Buckner. With these, prison officials drew a picture of the man, without regard to his efforts and accomplishment since arriving in 1967. Laskey's past was the albatross hanging from his neck, exemplified by words from a 1957 assessment echoed in decades of evaluations and parole hearings.

"Testing revealed anxiety with women. Anti-social but not a psychopath, violent. Admitted alcohol led to problems."

Typically, a prison entry evaluation provided a good baseline of an incoming inmate's frame of mind, but Posteal refused to speak with counselor John Tabor upon entry in May 1967, leaving Tabor to base his assessment strictly upon Laskey's prior record. From this, Tabor wrote Laskey was, "obviously assaultive and suggestive of the explosive personality." His reticence to speak with the penitentiary counselor due to his pending appeal was recorded as, "Initial interviewer noted him as rather withdrawn and closed."

His health continued to deteriorate over time. Lesions were detected in his lungs in 1972, and he suffered from chronic eczematoid dermatitis. In 1991, at the age of fifty-three, Laskey was hospitalized for a hypertensive crisis and heart failure. His breathing problems worsened, and in 1992, he was diagnosed with idiopathic pulmonary fibrosis. That year, he spent eighteen days in the hospital. His condition required closer monitoring, and later, he underwent double hip replacements and was confined to a wheelchair.

Throughout his time in prison, Laskey pursued educational opportunities. In 1974, he earned his GED and soon began correspondence courses with Urbana College, eventually earning an Associate of Arts degree in 1978 with a 3.63 GPA. He participated in various personal development programs, consistently receiving commendations for his efforts.

Despite his progress, parole remained elusive. In 1979, Adult Parole Authority Investigator Evelyn J. Watson concluded her report by noting that many officials still considered Laskey responsible for a string of murders in Cincinnati, even though he had been convicted of only one. Judges and prosecutors continued to oppose his release, as did law enforcement officers like Detective Tom Gardner who was part of the Bowman murder investigation.

In January 1980, Laskey's parole request was again denied. He was encouraged to continue his positive activities to prepare for "crime-free civilian living." Despite the setback, Laskey persisted in his studies, enrolling in courses at Ohio University.

On a March 1982 pre-parole Personality Evaluation, an unnamed interviewer wrote of Laskey admitting, "while driving a stolen taxi cab and working for fares, he picked up a female passenger. In the process, he made sexual advances toward her. Although she seemed agreeable initially, he reports that he became panicky and killed her. In the process of the struggle between he and the victim, he indicates that he stabbed her several times.

Subsequently, he was arrested on a purse snatching attempt and was charged with the current commitment offense," insisting no one assisted him, and he was not under the influence of drugs or alcohol.

His supervisor in Psychological Services, R.C. Rahn, recommended parole based on Laskey's age, institutional adjustment, and participation in educational programs.

"Positive prognosis for parole," Rahn wrote, based upon his increasing age, satisfactory institutional adjustment, and activities; the only negative being his past assaultive behavior. "Because of the public sensitivity associated with his case, it might be desirable that he be screened psychiatrically prior to his being considered for release."

However, in May 1982, the Parole Board unanimously rejected Laskey's bid for release, citing public opposition as a major factor. Prosecutor Simon Leis, Jr. credited the local letter-writing campaign for blocking Laskey's parole. His next opportunity would come in five years, 1987.

In advance of his 1987 hearing, the board received a letter from Posteal's brother-in-law and his wife in Detroit, offering their home as a place for him to live upon release. Rahn submitted a glowing employment report, recommending Laskey for a job. Over his thirteen years in Psychological Services, Laskey was described as "a loyal, capable, and motivated employee," with highlights including his completion of a bachelor's degree at Ohio University and work as a computer programmer. Rahn concluded by stating, "I am happy to provide this reference."

The 1987 psychiatric evaluation, including Laskey's criminal record, echoed sentiments from a 1965 evaluation, noting, "Again, he was down on himself and 'angry with the world.'"

In June, Posteal turned fifty years old, marking thirty-one years in prison.

Meanwhile, Art Ney, Jr., the new Hamilton County prosecutor, initiated his own letter-writing campaign opposing Laskey's parole.

"There's no way this person can justify to me that he ought to be released," Ney declared.

A notice of Laskey's upcoming parole hearing, addressed to the long-deceased Judge Leis, was returned undelivered. Judge Robert Kraft added a handwritten note at the bottom: "This community will always oppose this defendant's release. His conviction and confinement stopped a reign of terror in Hamilton County. I urge his continued confinement."

In March 1988, his hearing was continued to 1992.

The following month, Posteal Laskey was recognized by the U.S. Chess Trust for his work tabulating results in a computer for the Clockwatchers Chess Club at London Correctional Institute.

In October, Posteal stepped down as editor of The London *Voice* to focus on his work in Psychology Services.

Despite four failed attempts at gaining parole, Laskey continued with programs designed to improve his parole chances, receiving a certificate recognizing his completion of the Interpersonal Counseling Understanding Violence program.

After eighteen years at London CI, Laskey received notice that he was being transferred to a prison in Orient, Ohio. He appealed the transfer, writing, "I am well-placed and happy," and asking for consideration of his psychological well-being. Prison staff expressed concerns that a transfer could trigger a severe adverse reaction given his overall medical condition.

In advance of his 1992 parole hearing, Rahn wrote positively about Laskey, noting that chess, music, and reading remained his favorite pastimes. He highlighted Laskey's fondness for his mother and his respected status among other inmates. Rahn observed that Laskey had evolved over time, learning to control his impulses before they could control him.

Laskey worked in Psychology Services under Reginald Rahn for eighteen and a half years. Records suggest Rahn viewed Laskey as a personal rehabilitation project.

Before Laskey's 1992 parole hearing, a full MMPI (Minnesota Multiphasic Personality Inventory) was administered, revealing that Posteal no longer felt the need to act aggressively. Instead, he sought love, affection, and understanding.

The interviewer wrote of Laskey admitting he'd killed a woman in a stolen cab he was driving. According to the unnamed interviewer, Laskey admitted killing the woman by stabbing her and then accidentally running over her when the tie rod broke. The interviewer noted it as a crime with sexual undertones. Despite the negative tone, the review ended on a positive note.

"From a clinical point of view, Laskey is given an above-average prognosis for completing his furlough or parole," also citing his overall declining health.

Laskey's fears about the impact of the 1986 Rules Infraction on his parole chances came to fruition when he was again denied in 1992. The finding, "Serious nature of offense. Pattern of endangering offenses. 3rd confinement for offense of violence."

The following year, Posteal Laskey scored well above high school level on an education performance test, placing him in the 99th percentile. He credited his learning to extensive reading.

By February 1, 1994, Laskey, in his 27th year of incarceration, recited his complex medical history from memory. He expressed concern about itching, weight gain, a distended stomach, and a puffy face due to medications. He also reported walking with difficulty because of his painful hip and complained about inconsistent medical care due to too many different doctors visiting London CI. He did not, however, want to be transferred.

A health screening in July 1996 revealed signs of head trauma that Laskey said came from a fall at age twelve. Incorrectly diagnosed with Psychomotor Epilepsy in 1965, he denied ever having seizures. He admitted feeling depressed, especially as his upcoming parole hearing in January approached, but was not optimistic about his chances. His worsening medical condition and low-grade depression led to occasional thoughts of suicide, though he had no intention of acting on them.

After thirty years in prison, Laskey was described as pleasant and friendly, though subdued and mildly depressed. He made good eye contact, appeared coherent, alert, and oriented. In December, he was notified of his sister Hilda's death. He declined to attend the private pre-funeral viewing but attempted to reach his family by phone.

A February 1997 progress report noted that doctors were considering antidepressant treatments for prisoner number 124 990, stating, "This man will probably have some difficulties dealing with the fact that he may never leave prison. I'm not sure medications will be helpful to him in dealing with this eventuality." He was prescribed Prozac, with increasing doses over time.

Laskey's February 1997 parole hearing coincided with front page features looking back to the Cincinnati Strangler and Laskey as one in the same. The February 8 front page of The Cincinnati *Post* featured Laskey's photograph beside the headline, "A Reign of Terror," highlighting Posteal's upcoming parole hearing. The article recounted the murders attributed to the Cincinnati Strangler, pointing to Laskey as the killer. The allegation was backed by retired police officers who worked the cases.

On January 21, 1997, an unknown person submitted a handwritten review of the Bowman murder, on the front of Laskey's parole file. The note, written in block letters, neither Laskey's handwriting, nor that of the examining officer, James Taylor, stating: "I killed Barbara

Bowman - running wild – mad at the world. The more she fought the rape the more I fought her. I just didn't stop – Not involved in any way in the death of any other women – not the 'Cinn. Strangler.'"

A handwritten entry above those words, in the same handwriting, designating Laskey with the Delta symbol, "Δ states he is not a danger to anyone anymore – medical problems"

For his part, examiner Taylor submitted an additional form, answering a question about additional behavioral characteristics, writing, "sexual undertones/spontaneous, explosive act which followed Δ's attempt to have sex with the victim."

In advance of Laskey's 1997 parole hearing, London CI Warden M.L. Turner requested the Common Pleas Court classify Laskey as a "sexual predator" under Ohio law. While other boxes on the form were unmarked, the one next to the word "Torture" was checked, "Yes." The court declined to hold a hearing unless it appeared that Laskey would be released.

In the end, Laskey was denied parole for the sixth time, with the Hamilton County prosecutor issuing a statement: "We're glad Cincinnati will be safe for at least 10 more years."

By 1998, Laskey's lung fibrosis had worsened, though he reported his depression was "better." He was transferred to the Orient Correctional Institute, where he was provided with an oxygen tank to help with his breathing.

Despite his declining health, Laskey maintained his

interest in music with a Gibson guitar, mini-amplifier, and headphones to play with a prison band. He continued his education, earning a certificate in sign language in 1999.

In April 1998, Posteal requested "all persons listed as friends" be removed from his visiting list; the reason, "New friends." Turning one's back on supportive family and friends is common among lifers in prison, a resignation to their fate.

In 2001, Posteal's mother, Nancy, passed away on Christmas Eve. Her death seemed to sap what remaining energy Laskey had left.

His next parole hearing was moved up to 2002; the hearing to be held at Orient CI. The board's preliminary report noted that if Laskey was being tried for the same crime in 2002, the charge would be aggravated murder, not first-degree.

Hamilton County Prosecutor Mike Allen carried on the tradition of leading another public campaign opposing Laskey's release. More than four hundred emails, unanimously opposing parole, were submitted, spurred by an *Enquirer* editorial titled, "Never Let Him Out." In it, Allen recalled how his grandmother, terrified by the Cincinnati Strangler, installed multiple locks on her door.

Despite serving more than 419 months—well above the parole eligibility baseline—the board, in a twenty-minute hearing, denied Laskey's parole, stating that releasing him would "demean the seriousness of the offense." Another five years would pass before his next hearing.

The Cincinnati Strangler

Laskey's health continued to decline, and by 2004, he was confined to a wheelchair. He was described as friendly and clean, but physically deteriorating.

As his eighth parole hearing approached in February 2007, Hamilton County Prosecutor Joe Deters, today an Ohio State Supreme Court justice, was adamant in a press release, "asking the community to join him in voicing the strongest opposition to the possible parole of Posteal Laskey, known as the 'Cincinnati Strangler'."

"Posteal Laskey, known as the 'Cincinnati Strangler,' should never be released on parole," Deters wrote to the parole board citing details of Barbara Bowman's brutal murder, and crimes Laskey committed beforehand.

Judge Dennis S. Helmick wrote on behalf of the Common Pleas Court and "all of the citizens of this community" in opposition.

A local attorney remembered, as a child, an elementary school classmate being upset one day, telling us, "The Strangler killed my mommy."

Police officers held no doubts that Posteal Laskey was the Cincinnati Strangler. He deserved to remain in prison to his dying day, sentiments still held through generations.

Sergeant Russell Jackson's son wrote on behalf of his deceased father and other police who worked on the investigations: "Had my father or any of the other folks involved in solving the 'Cincinnati Strangler' cases ever contemplated the incongruity of a death sentence resulting in the possibility of parole, I am sure they would have disregarded the taxpayers' costs involved and prosecuted

Laskey for six other heinous murders."

Retired officer Frank Sefton wrote as a representative of all prosecutors, the coroner, and Homicide detectives from the investigations, "positively convinced by evidence gathered that Posteal Laskey was the 'Cincinnati Strangler'."

"Posteal Laskey is asking to be released from prison…However, no such reduction of sentence is allowed for the family members, or the women murdered by Posteal Laskey."

Memories of the widespread fear returned to the minds of those alive at the time of the Strangler; one recalling the fear gripping his parents and family members as a six-year-old. A woman wrote of being so afraid that she nailed boards over doors and windows, leaving them in place until the killer was caught. Many repeated the mantra of Laskey's arrest bringing closure to the murders. "The Cincinnati Strangler had been brought to justice."

There were fantastical recollections, such as a woman recounting the killer stalking her neighborhood, telling of Laskey exposing himself to her mother before killing Mrs. Hochhausler.

A man recalled his mother, a nurse at Good Sam, encountering Laskey running out of Burnet Woods, implying she saw him as he ran from murdering Mathilda Messer.

Another shared a wild tale of a friend who lived next door to the Hochhauslers of Laskey entering her basement while she was doing laundry. She was saved by the

.38 pistol she carried and, "ran this coward out of her basement."

Fear was the common thread running through most letters, one writing ABSOLUTE TERROR to describe the times. Opposition ran particularly strong on the West Side where the Bowman murder occurred.

Anger with a tinge of revenge was commonplace, "To turn this two legged garbage can loose on society would be every woman's worst nightmare. He would start his 'old habits' such as killing women as soon as possible."

Shared opposition to Laskey's release was displayed in multiple petitions submitted to the board, one reading: "We, the undersigned, oppose the release of Posteal Laskey, Jr. The year of terror ended only upon his arrest and conviction. We will not feel safe is he is released. Let's keep America safe, and keep predators off the streets."

Roman Catholic women from students at Mother of Mercy High School, to students and faculty at Mount St. Joseph College, and Sisters of Charity nuns, contacted the board in significant numbers in opposition.

The most powerful voices reaching out to the Parole Board were those of the victim families. One letter came from, "Family & Friends of Barbara Bowman," and several from the family of Delle Ernst, but it was the Hochhausler family leading a campaign to keep their mother's murderer in prison.

Alice Hochhausler's children were joined by their children writing in opposition. A conference call was held by the board with the four Hochhausler daughters speaking of the trauma they experienced and the trauma being felt by their children upon learning of their grandmother's murder. Alice's son wrote of being in high school at the time, "My life was indelibly marred by this crime." Friends and neighbors of the Hochhauslers joined the chorus against Laskey's release.

A line in the 2007 form about victim impact statements stood out, "V's daughter – Δ should die in prison based upon original death sent' – NUMEROUS letters of protest."

"Special Request by Family: Inmate should die in prison..."

Of the hundreds of letters submitted, only one from Northern Kentucky supported Laskey's release, "He's old, served forty years and I don't think a threat to society. I am a Christian person who believes in forgiveness." One Cincinnati resident took the opportunity to complain of African-Americans not receiving equal justice in the parole process.

The Parole Board met on February 6 and released their decision on the 13th – "continue to 2/1/2017 unanimous."

On May 26, 2007, sixty-nine-year-old Posteal Laskey, Jr., after forty years of continuous incarceration, died at Pickaway Correctional Institution at 11:46 P.M., one month shy of his seventieth birthday.

Posteal suffered a heart attack, followed by multi-organ failure and decreased blood flow to his intestines led to sepsis, the cause of death.

The Cincinnati Strangler

At 1:00 P.M. on June 1, 2007, Posteal Laskey, Jr. was buried in the Foster Cemetery at Pickaway; formerly known as the Orient Feeble Minded Institute Cemetery. His three remaining family members – sister Patricia Jordan, cousin Russell Laskey, and brother Dave Laskey attended the funeral.

His death marked the end of a long and complicated chapter, with The Cincinnati *Enquirer* headline reading, "Strangler Goes to Grave; '60s Saga Concludes."

Posteal Laskey's death may have brought a sense of closure, but the murders of Emogene Harrington, Lois Dant, Mathilda Messer, Alice Hochhausler, Rose Winstel, and Lula Kerrick remain cold cases today.

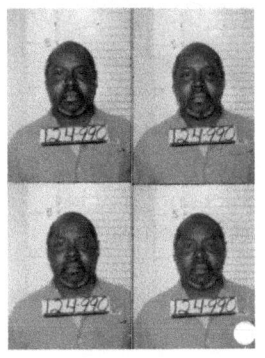

Variety of mugshots over the decades Posteal Laskey served in prison until his release to death (Ohio Department of Rehabilitation and Corrections)

POSTEAL LASKEY

Number A124990
DOB 06/18/1937
Gender Male
Race Black
Admission Date 05/08/1967
Institution
Status RELEASED - Death

Posteal Laskey and the Cincinnati Strangler have sprouted a cottage industry over decades of books and articles, as well as this "fine art" print. (Fine Art Storehouse)

Postscript
Legend of the Cincinnati Strangler

If you've reached this point, it's time to thank you for reading. No, this is not a book where the author hopes the reader "liked" the book, as the stories are quite grim, but hope you learned something new and found the book thought-provoking. In the end, a central question remains: Was Posteal Laskey the Cincinnati Strangler? After years of research in public records, news accounts, police files, court proceedings, personal recollections, and prison records, I, for one, cannot say for certain. An underlying goal has been to let readers draw your own conclusions.

The year of the Strangler, from December 1965 to December 1966, is approaching the passage of sixty years while the renown of Posteal Laskey as the Cincinnati Strangler endures into the present day. People may have forgotten Laskey's name, but he remains synonymous with the Strangler. Ask anyone about the murders and the mantra of police and media at the time remains - the murders stopped when Laskey was arrested. The trouble with that, it is purely circumstantial.

Posteal Laskey was not a saint. No, far from it. His convictions for violent assaults on women were a thread throughout his adult life. His confessions to killing Barbara Bowman recorded during various pre-parole examinations while serving life in prison are not evidence as they were secondhand information, but they are rather compelling.

Regrettably, police at the time of the murders did not

find solid evidence pointing to anyone, let alone Laskey. Some of the evidence remains that possibly could be subjected to DNA testing, but likely degraded over the decades.

Police were under intense public and political pressure to bring a killer to justice driving their haste. Police leadership at the time pressed upon rank-and-file the urgency to find a killer and relieve political pressure brought to bear by the public and politicians.

As the horrific crimes multiplied over the calendar year, police were baffled on the killer's identity as he left no identifying clues. Mixed hair samples and blood types were the only bits evidence criminal labs had to work with. This was nearly twenty years before DNA evidence would be presented in a criminal trial and a time when even if fingerprints had been found, officers would have been faced with boxes of index cards and reports to sift through by hand and then physically compare the prints. There were no computers at the disposal of investigators whose tools of the trade in the 1960s were paper and pavement.

Police work amid the social upheaval of the time was growing more difficult by the day. Heavy-handed tactics and unequal justice were coming home to roost as fewer and fewer people, particularly in the Black community, were willing to cooperate. The citywide sweep of Black men throughout 1966 made their job more difficult. There was no divide between White and Black Cincinnati in the shared desire to find the killer but the manner in which police proceeded was deeply disturbing, reinforcing the sentiment that a Black man could not receive justice.

The Cincinnati Strangler

The book's subtitle, "Murder, Mayhem, and Racial Injustice in the Queen City" encapsulates the time of the murders.

The vernacular of the times was changing and the old offensive racist words were beginning to no longer be tolerated. "Negro" the accepted depiction of Black people in the first half of the 20th century but this was the time when Black Power was on the rise, shouted for all to hear from Stokely Carmichael and H. Rap Brown, two civil rights activists who will appear in these pages.

The worst of Jim Crow was waning but sentiments remained, particularly in a city often described as the "most Southern city in the North," thanks to its proximity to Kentucky. The composition of a nearly all-White police department did little to break from past traditions and prejudices, and the single Black detective was subjected to racism, both subtle and overt.

In mid-1960s conservative, Midwestern Cincinnati, the establishment ruled. Freedom Riders may have been dying in the South and major American cities on fire, while protests against the growing American presence in Vietnam were on the rise, none of these affected Cincinnati. The city seemed immune from such outside influences. But, it was not to be the case.

Laskey's trial was little more than a fait accompli bringing relief to the terrorized city. The harsh light of pre-trial publicity convicted Laskey long before the trial commenced, jeopardizing the ability to find a fair and impartial jury from the Cincinnati area. His defense attorneys were inadequate, to say the least, and the elderly judge was dismissive of the defense counsel foolishness, while desiring to press the trial forward; not dwelling upon procedural and Constitutional issues. That Laskey was convicted by an all-White jury was not the fault of the court, nor the times; rather, it was the defense who rejected potential Black jurors.

Was Posteal Laskey capable of committing murder? Yes, as evidenced by the violent assaults pushing women's lives to the brink. But, Laskey did not strangle or sexually abuse his assault victims, at least those for which he was arrested.

Yes, it appeared Barbara Bowman's killer did attempt to strangle and sexually assault her, but he failed. He then relied on the vehicle as a weapon to silence Barb, finishing his deed through multiple thrusts to his victim's throat with what appeared to be a paring knife.

The women murdered by the Strangler were severely beaten, police often believing the killer used a heavy object - a rock, a two-by-four, or other makeshift weapon; but none was found at any of the scenes. Lula Kerrick was the one exception as she was knocked unconscious but not beaten, and she was not sexually assaulted, but this could have been the result of Charles Minor calling for the elevator from the third floor.

While police sought a heavy object responsible for inflicting, one potential weapon not brought up at trial were Posteal Laskey's hands.

My attention was first drawn to them in the memoir, Courtroom Gladiator, written by former assistant prosecutor, and later judge, Albert "Mike" Mestemaker who assisted with the Laskey trial. The book plays loose with facts but his mention of Laskey's hands was interesting.

The Cincinnati Strangler

"I had been told by Lytle Young that Laskey's hands were way out of proportion to the rest of his body...his hands and fingers those of a much larger man." Young, a retired detective who'd arrested Laskey for the 1965 assault of Judith Buckner, told Mestemaker how Laskey was extremely self-conscious of his hands, keeping them concealed most times.

While, indeed, he may have been self-conscious of his hands, that may have been more a result of his clubbed fingers cited back as far as 1949, as well as rashes and oozing discharge, also cited in various medical records. He commonly clenched his hands into tight fists, but was that due to a medical condition rather than evidence of their use as weapons. Note, that there were no signs of any matter from rashes or oozing detected in the police crime lab and FBI exams.

Appearances sixty years later would not describe Laskey's hands as those of a strangler; rather, more like rocks, clenched and fully capable of assault, common in the injuries inflicted upon the strangulation victims. His assault victims did not receive the disfiguring beatings of the Strangler victims.

Before laying out a quick summary review of the Strangler murders and assaults, it's important to distinguish between serial killers and impulse killers.

The Cincinnati Strangler is often referred to as a "serial killer," which is incorrect.

A serial killer follows a repetitive pattern, a common thread through the murders. Think of Gary Ridgway, the Green River Killer who between 1982 and 1989 confessed to killing 71 women in the Seattle, Washington area who were all known to be sex workers.

An impulse killer acts in the heat of the moment, often triggered by an external factor without planning. A Black man murdering White women added racial anxieties and the rage of the 1960s as more recent preludes to violence.

Psychologists brought in to consult on the Strangler cases commonly pointed to an individual who hated his mother but assigning such motivation to Posteal Laskey was off the mark as he was very close to his mother. His conviction in the murder of a thirty-one-year-old woman also flies in the face of that analysis.

As the killings continued, police sought commonalities among the Strangler cases:

- the victims were women over the age of fifty;

- they were beaten, strangled, and sexually assaulted after they were dead;

- robbery appeared to be a common thread;

- in all but the Hochhausler murder, the attacks occurred during daylight hours;

- four of the attacks occurred on the east side of Cincinnati, with Lois Dant's Price Hill murder the one outlier. Barbara Bowman's murder did not factor into the Strangler investigations but certainly was part of the media coverage.

Here is a quick summary of the assaults and murders:

The Cincinnati Strangler

- October 12, 1965 - Elizabeth Kreco, 65, East Walnut Hills, assaulted, unconscious in apartment garage, knotted clothesline, rape;

- October 25, 1965 - Margie Helton, 39, Walnut Hills, employer parking lot, inside car, rope around neck, laid on horn, assailant ran away;

- December 2, 1965 - Emogene Harrington, 56, East Walnut Hills, midday, apartment building basement, plastic clothesline, "strangler's knot," post-mortem sexual assault;

- April 4, 1966 - Lois Dant, 58, Price Hill, around 10:00 a.m., apartment door forced open by man seeking to use phone, stocking from bathroom, post-mortem sexual assault;

- June 10, 1966 - Mathilda Messer, 55, Clifton, dawn, in open area of a park, frayed necktie, post-mortem sexual assault;

- October 11-12, 1966 - Alice Hochhausler, 51, Clifton, midnight, outside in driveway, bathrobe sash, post-mortem sexual assault;

- August 13-14, 1966 - Barbara Bowman, 31, Price Hill, @ 2:30 a.m., vehicle, stabbing with paring knife, signs of attempted strangulation and sexual assault;

- September 21, 1966 - Virginia Hinners, 46, East Walnut Hills, assaulted and robbed in workplace, across the street from the Harrington murder scene;

- October 19-20, 1966 - Rose Winstel, 81, Clifton Heights, time of death unknown, door broken open, electric massager cord, post mortem sexual assault, possibly foreign object;

- December 9, 1966 - Sandra Chapas, 22, Downtown, midnight, escaped into her downtown apartment, license number recorded leading to Laskey arrest later in morning;

- December 9, 1966 - Lula Kerrick, 81, Downtown, early morning, stocking from leg, in apartment building elevator.

Sixty years have passed since the murderous terror inflicted by the Cincinnati Strangler. The city was traumatized in 1966, finding some comfort the following year with the arrest and conviction of Posteal Laskey, while remnants of those emotions remain part of the city's psyche.

What about those left behind?

Just as with many of the principals in this story, the passage of decades has left few remaining. Five of the six women were older: Emogene Harrington was 56; Lois Dant was 58; Mathilda Messer was 55; Alice Hochhausler was 51; while Rose Winstel and Lula Herrick were both 81. Barbara Bowman was the exception being 31 at the time of her death, the only one who could possibly be alive today.

Efforts to speak with the remaining family members of the victims, as well as Laskey's, were unsuccessful. Rose Winstel, Lula Kerrick, and Barbara Bowman were all single without children. The three Harrington daughters, all born in the 1930s, are deceased. Lois Dant's daughter, Sue Ann, was in the convent on the verge of taking her vows at the time of her mother's death but is now in her

80s, married, and living in California. Mathilda Messer's son and daughter are gone; her other relatives did not wish to revisit Mathilda's murder. Barbara Bowman's parents are gone but at the time of her father's 1971 death, her mother, Edith Bowman, was quoted saying, "He never got over Barbara's murder. Barbara was all we had." Alice Hochhausler, a mother of nine, offered the best chance of gathering recollections from her children but they, too, did not, as daughter Beth Placke told me, wish to reopen old wounds. She did say, with "the utmost confidence, that Mr. Laskey was the perpetrator and we are grateful he's no longer in this world." Sandra Chapas's daughter, Dorothy, wrote of her mopther's encounter, "I am very thankful to God for protecting my mother from this murderer."

While I urge readers, if you so wish, to dive deeper into the cases; to get a sense of where they occurred, to breathe the air; but, please, do not violate privacy and private property of those living at locations today. Also, please do not pester police with inquiries about evidence and materials from the cases as it's all (yes, encapsulated) here. You have a valuable resource for questions and answers at the Cincinnati Police Museum (free admission, 308 Reading Rd, Cincinnati, OH 45202). Likewise, area residents enjoy the tremendous local history facilities at the Cincinnati Museum Center in Union Terminal, and the Genealogy and Local History Department of the Cincinnati & Hamilton County Public Library main branch. All three were leading sources of information for this book. I regret that very few of the principal characters in these stories are alive today. Oh, to have spoken with Detective Bernie Kersker. If I were to fictionalize this story, he would have been my central character. I would have loved to talk with Posteal Laskey's relatives, but those I found would not respond.

So, what I was left to work from were many thousands of pages of police investigation records, court transcripts, prison records, and contemporary accounts.

The arrival of an oddly-marked envelope was a suspicious surprise as it contained a CD with over 5,000 pages of Laskey's prison records was a shock as I filed two unsuccessful public documents cases against the Ohio Department of Rehabilitation and Corrections (ODRC) and never thought I would learn the details of Laskey's life in prison.

Police hold evidence from the cases, meaning there is the possibility of subjecting evidentiary items to modern analysis.

More critical than the mountains of paper compiled in this research is the assistance I received from Cincinnatians who keep the tradition of a living local history alive and well.

Apologies to those I've neglected to acknowledge on the following page as I'm certain too many have been overlooked. I truly appreciate all of your help along the way.

****

Dennis Whitehead is a writer, photographer, and media producer in Northern Virginia. He is a Cincinnati native who graduated from Elder High School and attended the University of Cincinnati before completing college at Ohio University. Immediately following college, Whitehead worked with The Associated Press in the New York and Los Angeles bureaus before leaving to freelance photojournalism in Washington, DC. He is the author of several nonfiction books. *The Cincinnati Strangler* is his first foray into true crime.

Acknowledgments

Perriann Allen
Arabeth Balasko, Cincinnati Museum Center
Darren Blase, Shake It Records
David Bracey
Sgt. Joseph Briede
Randall P. Cain
Jeff Cramerding
Dennis Cusick
Jayne Davis
Dr. Kenneth Davis
Jim Delaney
Judge Patrick Dinklelacker
Jane Friedman
Melissa Gabso
Lisa Gillespie
Melvin Grier
Denny Gulina (Dennis Grant)
Chris Hoffman
Brian Horton
Tricia Huff
Vanity Huffaker, WCPO
Dan Hurley
Tutti Jackson, Ohio Memory
Cliff Kersker
Jim LaBarbara
George Lecky and Chris Lecky
Dr. Annulla Linders, UC
Jack and Epathea Litmer
Elaine Lutz, Esq.
Pat Kelly
Dave Marburger
Alan March, TheHistoryCop
Dustin Marks, CincyMapCollection.com
Colleen McSwiggin, Cincinnati Recycling & Reuse Hub
Dean Meiszer
Bob Newman
Francesca Pitaro, The AP
Dave Pittinger, Hamilton County Office of Recorder
Gene Roberts
Connie Roesch
Shannon Ruark
James Rueger
Ken Segal and Missy Fox, Paradrome Properties
Brad Seitz
Ann Senefeld – Digging Cincinnati History
Amy Sloan
C. Smith
Jim Steiner
Al Stencell
Dorothy Tary
Paul Tenkotte
Cecil Thomas
J.T. Townsend
Annette Utermark
Judge Chris Wagner
Paula Wake-Evans

Alabama Department of Archives and History
Archdiocese of Cincinnati
Cincinnati Police Museum
Equal Justice Initiative
Hamilton County Auditor's Office
Hamilton County Coroner's Office
Hamilton County Law Library, Reference Team
Navajo Austin, Floyd County Historical Society
Price Hill Historical Society
St. Mary Magdealen of Pazzi, Payneville, KY
UCLA Special Collections
UC Archives and Rare Books Library
Utrecht University Library

"THE BOSTON STRANGLER"

Here is the story of the Strangler, yet untold,
The man who claims he murdered 13 women young and old.

The elusive Strangler, there he goes.
Where his wander-lust sends him, no one knows
He struck within the light of day
Leaving not one clue astray.

Young and old, their lips are sealed,
Their secret of death never revealed.
Even though he is sick in mind.
He's much too clever for the police to find.

To reveal his secret, would bring him fame.
But burden his family with unwanted shame.
He hopes to become an object of study, to help psychiatry,
To better society.

Today he sits in a prison cell,
Inside only a secret he can tell.
People everywhere are still in doubt,
The Strangler, in prison or roaming about?

1973 poem written by Albert DeSalvo for sixteen-year-old Vivian Wyatt of San Diego, CA.

www.ingramcontent.com/pod-product-compliance
Lightning Source LLC
Chambersburg PA
CBHW060450030426
42337CB00015B/1536